P9-CKC-240

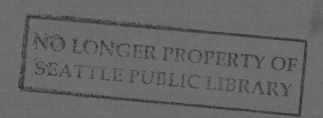

THE
WORLDS
I SEE

THE
WORLDS
I SEE

CURIOSITY, EXPLORATION, AND DISCOVERY AT THE DAWN OF AI

DR. FEI-FEI LI

MOMENT
OF LIFT
BOOKS

FLATIRON
BOOKS
NEW YORK

THE WORLDS I SEE. Copyright © 2023 by Fei-Fei Li. All rights reserved.
Printed in the United States of America. For information,
address Flatiron Books, 120 Broadway, New York, NY 10271.

www.flatironbooks.com

Designed by Steven Seighman

The Library of Congress Cataloging-in-Publication Data is available upon request.

ISBN 978-1-250-89793-0 (hardcover)
ISBN 978-1-250-89794-7 (ebook)

Our books may be purchased in bulk for promotional, educational, or business use. Please
contact your local bookseller or the Macmillan Corporate and Premium Sales Department at
1-800-221-7945, extension 5442, or by email at MacmillanSpecialMarkets@macmillan.com.

First Edition: 2023

10 9 8 7 6 5 4 3 2 1

For my parents, who braved the darkness so I could seek the light.

For the Sabella family, who shined the light of kindness when I was adrift in a world of strangers.

For Silvio, who lights up my life's journey with wisdom, patience, and strength.

For my children, forever the brightest lights in my world.

CONTENTS

1. Pins and Needles in D.C. 1
2. Something to Chase 9
3. A Narrowing Gulf 31
4. Discovering the Mind 69
5. First Light 98
6. The North Star 116
7. A Hypothesis 147
8. Experimentation 180
9. What Lies Beyond Everything? 208
10. Deceptively Simple 241
11. No One's to Control 266
12. The Next North Star 301

Acknowledgments 319

THE
WORLDS
I SEE

1

PINS AND NEEDLES IN D.C.

The hotel lobby was plain and unpretentious, reflecting an itinerary that valued proximity over luxury, and the ambience was gentle: polite conversations between guests and the concierge, the hum of rolling suitcase wheels, the periodic whir of glass doors opening and closing. But I felt anxious, and the hurried clacking of my boots on thin carpet seemed to echo my mood. As a lifelong academic on my way to testify before the House Committee on Science, Space, and Technology on the topic of artificial intelligence, I suppose nerves were to be expected. But they weren't helped by the red-eye flight from the West Coast, the near-total lack of sleep the night before, or the tense rehearsing of my statement—again, and again, and again—that had filled the preceding hours. It was June 26, 2018, and each passing minute brought me closer to a career first: an appearance at, of all things, a congressional hearing.

A pale morning was waiting outside as I stepped onto the sidewalk. The street was densely lined with federal buildings, blunt and monochrome, worlds away from the scenery I was used to in California, where tract housing and trendy office parks abounded, accented by the occasional burst of mission-style architecture. Here, even the masonry felt heavier, and certainly older. The capital is a place that wears its history on its sleeve.

I recalled my first visit here, before AI, before academia, and before Silicon Valley, when the entirety of my identity—as far as the world was concerned, anyway—fit within the confines of a single word: "immigrant." Trips are trying affairs for cash-strapped families with minimal English-speaking skills; most activities fall into two categories—"free" and "prohibitively expensive"—and so much is clouded by a second-language haze that never seems to disperse. Even so, my memories of a visit to the National Air and Space Museum still sparkled. Its life-sized exhibits demonstrated the scale and gallantry of aerospace history, overwhelming my senses and igniting my imagination. I was reminded that even as a teenage girl living well beyond the margins of society, the world I wanted to inhabit most of all was that of science.

Unlikely as it seemed at the time, I found my way to the furthest reaches of that world in the years that followed. Not aerospace, but the science of the mind, and the still-nascent study of intelligent machines. And when a breakthrough technique called "deep learning" began making history barely a decade into my career, AI became a very, very big deal.

Although it had taken more than a half century for the necessary preconditions to align—historic milestones in the evolution of algorithms, large-scale data, and raw computing power, all converging at the dawn of the 2010s—it took less than a half decade for the capabilities they unleashed to change the world. Businesses were transformed, billions of dollars were invested, and everyone from industry analysts to political commentators to philosophers was left scrambling to make sense of a technology that had seemed to explode, overnight, from an academic niche to a force for global change. If nothing else, the sheer speed and scope of AI's emergence, arguably unprecedented in all of history, warranted the attention of legislators like the ones I'd soon face.

Of course, there was more to the story. Within only a few years, the tech industry's exuberance was tempered by the growing concerns of journalists, advocacy groups, and even governments. The mounting harms of biased algorithms, fears of widespread job displacement, and unsettling visions of surveillance became fixtures in the media, souring the public conception of AI to a degree not commonly seen in the world of technology.

I'd tried to summarize these tensions in an op-ed published a few months earlier in *The New York Times*. Although the piece was limited to around eight hundred words, I did my best to balance my excitement about the future of my field with the many legitimate concerns raised by its critics. I wrote that the true impact of AI on the world would be largely determined by the motivation that guided the development of the technology—a disturbing thought in an era of expanding facial recognition and targeted advertising. But if we were to broaden our vision for AI to *explicitly* include a positive impact on humans and communities—if our definition of success could include such things—I was convinced that AI could change the world for the better. I still am.

That belief in the future appeared to have played a role in my invitation to testify. I'd recently cofounded AI4ALL, an educational nonprofit intended to foster greater inclusion in STEM (science, technology, engineering, and mathematics) by opening university labs to girls, people of color, and other underrepresented groups, all at the high school level. In fact, my efforts to diversify the field were cited as a key reason for the panel's interest in my participation. Given the fraught nature of the subject matter, it was encouraging to be associated with something unapologetically hopeful.

My pace quickened. The Capitol Building was now centered on my horizon, every bit as picturesque in person, although I still hadn't quite internalized the fact that it was my destination. I did, however, notice a conspicuous lack of the paper maps that had played such a persistent role during my teenage trip—a reminder of how much smartphones had changed daily life, including tourism, in the intervening years. But smartphones, too, had begun to show their dark side, making 2018 a fraught time for a representative from the world of technology to preach a message of human-centered optimism.

For better or worse, my op-ed came in the thick of the "techlash": a growing consensus that Silicon Valley's ambitions had reached excessive, even predatory extremes. At any other time in my career, such a controversy would have felt light-years away from a little-known academic like me. As it happened, however, I was past the midpoint of a twenty-one-month sabbatical from my professorship at Stanford and was serving as chief scientist of AI at Google Cloud—placing me well within its epicenter. Google was my first nonacademic employer since the dry-cleaning shop I ran with my family, and I was only months away from a full-time return to the university. But there was no changing the optics that afternoon.

Paradoxically, my concerns about being mistaken for some kind of industry insider ran parallel to my now decades-long struggle as an outsider. Like many immigrants, I felt hemmed in by cultural divides that crisscrossed my life, ranging from the invisible to the unmistakable. I spent the majority of each day speaking a second language. And I was a woman in a male-dominated field so consistently symbolized by the now archetypal image of "guys in hoodies" that the phrase had lost any trace of irony. After so many years spent wondering whether I belonged—anywhere, really—Congress seemed like an unlikely place to let down my guard.

If the committee had concerns about the future of this technology, it only reinforced how much we had in common. I did, too. I'd always been an optimist about the power of science, and I remained so, but the tumultuous years leading up to that day had taught me that the fruits of optimism aren't to be taken for granted. While the future might indeed be bright, it wouldn't be so by accident. We'd have to earn it, together, and it wasn't entirely clear how.

Still, something else weighed on my mind as I cut a path across the city. Less than twenty-four hours earlier, I was by my mother's side in a hospital in Palo Alto, as I had been for weeks. She's faced innumerable threats to her health over the decades, both chronic and acute, and we were still reeling from the latest. Much of my written testimony, in fact, was drafted in a cramped chair just outside of her room in the ICU, amidst a blur of blue scrubs and white coats. I'd even attended preparation meetings for the hearing remotely, our conversations compressed into a laptop screen, contending with the bustle of orderlies and the intermittent tones of the hospital paging system.

My being the only child and sole financial support of two parents—not to mention the translator between our caretakers' English and their native Mandarin—there was no escaping the feeling that it was wrong to even consider a trip like this. Disease, however, is no match for the pride of an immigrant mother; the opportunity to see her daughter address the United States Congress, little more than two decades after arriving in this country, was simply too much to pass up. She'd been an unfailing source of support throughout my career, and was, as I should have expected, adamant that I attend.

Her encouragement convinced me to go, but it was hardly enough to assuage my fears. What if she ended up needing me after all? What if I got the call I'd been dreading since I'd boarded the flight that brought me here? What if, for reasons that had nothing to do with technology, or culture, or politics, this was all a terrible mistake?

Then, as if to force my deliberations aside, my first glimpse of the hearing's venue was upon me: the enormous gray exterior of the Rayburn House Office Building. Its styling isn't as iconic as the Capitol Building's rotunda, presiding over the Mall from across the street, but it's every bit as faithful to the city's neoclassical style, a signature that I'd appreciated since my first American civics class. And it's no less imposing to a visitor approaching its facade, with its towering columns and eagle-emblazoned pediment.

Inside, beyond metallic gate-like double doors, I took my place in a slow-moving procession of visitors. Registration, badging, and security checks. The whirlwind that led me here—the hastily booked travel arrangements, the restless preparation, the neurosis of an over-active imagination—appeared to be subsiding, finally; all that remained was to wait for the proceedings to begin. I took a seat and fully exhaled for the first time since waking up, craning my neck toward the vaulted ceilings and the flags that seemed to hang down everywhere I looked. Even the lobby conveyed a sense of national extravagance.

My mother was right to demand I attend. I was certain the future of AI would depend on institutions far beyond science, including education, activism, and, of course, government. As quaint as Washington, D.C., could seem from Silicon Valley, places like this would matter as much as the Stanfords and Googles of the world. The founding ideals of this country, however imperfectly they've been practiced in the centuries since, seemed as wise a foundation as any on which to build the future of technology: the dignity of the individual, the intrinsic value of representation, and the belief that human endeavors are best when guided by the many, rather than the few.

I was energized by the thought of AI being shaped by such a coalition—public and private, technological and philosophical—and it replaced the pins and needles of my walk across the city with a flicker of excitement. In fact, noticing that the entrance to the chamber was open, I couldn't resist the opportunity to look around before the hearing stole my attention. So, glancing slyly in both directions to ensure the coast was clear, I stepped inside.

Through the doors I found an appropriately stately interior, with windows extending from floor to ceiling, wooden shutters, and tassel-clad curtains. Rows of audience seating and room for the press packed the space, with framed portraits lining the surrounding walls. Looming over it all was an ornate dais, its cushioned seats outfitted with microphones and name plates for the committee members who would soon occupy them. At the center of the room was the witness table, waiting for me. I was amused to see my name, DR. LI, printed unceremoniously in Times New Roman on an 8.5-by-11-inch sheet of paper and slid into a reusable name plate of my own. It was charming—even a bit reassuring—to find something so modest in the middle of such an intimidating scene.

The silence hung for a few more seconds before being broken by the murmur of the chamber beginning to fill: representatives and their aides, members of the media, and, finally, my fellow witnesses—Dr. Tim Persons, chief scientist of the Government Accountability Office, and Greg Brockman, cofounder and chief technology officer of a recently founded start-up called OpenAI. This was it.

I took my seat, along with a few deep breaths, and tried to keep cool as I felt the first pulse of adrenaline race through me. This wasn't my classroom, I reminded myself; these weren't students and I wasn't here to deliver a lecture. I had one idea to share today, and I repeated it in my thoughts like a mantra. *It matters what motivates the development of AI, in both science and industry, and I believe that motivation must explicitly center on human benefit.* I tried to put everything else out of my mind—the dark side of AI, the techlash, even, for a few minutes, my mother's condition. Back to that mantra. *It matters what motivates the development—*

"The Committee on Science, Space, and Technology will come to order." They were the first words I heard amplified through the room's PA system, snapping me back into the moment. "Good morning, and welcome to today's hearing, entitled 'Artificial Intelligence—With Great Power Comes Great Responsibility.'"

I pushed the anxieties out of my mind. Whatever awaited me, I was sure of one thing: this technology had the power to transform the world for the better. How exactly we'd reach that future remained an open question, but it was clear, even then, that conversations like the one about to begin were our best chance at answering it. I'd flown across the country and left my ailing mother's bedside to be here, and I couldn't leave without making that clear.

Whatever the committee's agenda for the day might be, I was beginning to understand mine. The room had filled, the cameras were recording, and the microphones were hot. Minutes away from addressing the most important audience of my career, I was resolving, as one moment of slow motion bled into the next, to share it all: my hopes and my fears, my conviction and my uncertainty. Everything. That the power of science was as worthy of our optimism as ever, but that truly harnessing it—safely, fairly, and sustainably—would require much more than science alone.

I believe our civilization stands on the cusp of a technological revolution with the power to reshape life as we know it. To ignore the millennia of human struggle that serves as our society's foundation, however—to merely "disrupt," with the blitheness that has accompanied so much of this century's innovation—would be an intolerable mistake. This revolution must build on that foundation, faithfully. It must respect the collective dignity of a global community. And it must always remember its origins: the restless imagination of an otherwise unremarkable species of hominid, so mystified by its own nature that it now seeks to re-create it in silicon. This revolution must, therefore, be unequivocally human-centered.

More than two decades earlier, a journey had begun that defined the person I'd become. It was an improbable, often inexplicable path that led me across oceans, from the middle class to poverty and back again, to the lecture halls of the Ivy League and the boardrooms of Silicon Valley. Gradually, it shaped everything I'd come to believe about this technology—the inspiring, the challenging, and the frightening—and where I believe it will go next. Most important, it served as a twenty-year lesson on the essential role of humanity in the technological quest that I'm certain will define this century.

2

SOMETHING TO CHASE

A leafy canopy swayed high above us, a frame of pure shadow surrounding a portrait of the night sky. Along with a handful of schoolmates scattered nearby, I craned my neck, transfixed, as our guide pointed out constellations. We were a rapt audience, so quiet that even his near whisper seemed to boom into the canyon below, although a wave of *oohs* would wash over us whenever a shooting star stole our attention.

"Above us is the romance of the cowherd and the weaver," he said. Not quite sure how to respond, we simply continued to stare upward.

"See over there?" he asked while tracing loosely around a glittering handful of stars with an outstretched index finger. "That's Zhī nǚ, a weaver and a goddess. Today, astronomers call her brightest star Vega. And that's Niú láng, a mortal cowherd, a constellation that's home to the star Altair. But their love was forbidden, so they were banished to opposing sides of the heavens."

We were a few days into a hiking trip through the wilderness led by my art teacher. It was a formidable trek, but one that offered surprising luxuries for ten-year-old adventurers like us; rather than camping out, we stayed with families who made their homes right there in the mountains, and the memory of their hospitality has never left me. They provided a warm place to sleep and food truly made from scratch, including generous meals of aromatic rice and a cured prosciutto-like pork called *là ròu*, both of which I miss to this day. Even the streams were a subtle delight, burbling gently with clear runoff from high above, far from industrial contamination, collected by the locals through a network of bamboo pipes. I distinctly recall the water tasting so pure it was almost sweet.

"Now, separating Zhī nǚ and Niú láng is a river of stars. See it running between them?" He gestured at a softly glowing path tracing its way across the sky, like columns of celestial clouds. "That's our galaxy."

In a region where overcast skies were the norm, clear nights like this were very special, igniting my curiosity and stoking my fascination with nature. From my earliest memories, the simple experience of *perceiving* things—anything—preoccupied me in a way I felt deeply but couldn't express. Everywhere I looked, it was as if something new was waiting to arouse another glint of wonder, whether it was the stillness of a plant, the careful steps of an insect, or the hazy depth of far-off peaks. I didn't know much about the world yet, but I could tell it was a place worth exploring.

"Ah, look—here's one of my favorites."

He pointed higher.

"Those seven stars form the base of *běi dǒu qī xīng*—the Big Dipper. Now follow a line upward like this," he said, gesturing up to the right. "You see that bright one? For centuries, it was probably the most important star in the sky. Běi jí xīng. The North Star."

I was born the only child of a family in a state of quiet upheaval. I could feel an air of uncertainty throughout my early years, and sensed from a young age that something—perhaps many somethings—had left my elders reeling. Over time, new layers of their discontent revealed themselves: unrealized dreams, pangs of regret verging on unrest, and a persistent feeling that even the place we called home wasn't truly ours. It was a picture I pieced together gradually, connecting the dots of overheard chats and stray asides as children naturally do.

Although born in Beijing, China, I was raised more than a thousand miles away, in Chengdu, capital of the Sichuan province. It was, nominally, the home of my mother's family, although their arrival was recent. Originally from Hangzhou, near the coastal region of Shanghai, they fled like thousands of others as their towns were ravaged by the Second Sino-Japanese War in the 1930s. They were grateful to have survived, but were left with an inescapable sense of displacement that still reverberated a generation later.

My maternal grandfather was especially given to pained reflections on life before the turmoil; a star student with a promising future, he was left with little choice but to abandon school to support his family, even as they descended into years of poverty. It was an unresolved tension he would carry for decades and pass down to his children. In time, it would come to grip me as well: the dull, wordless feeling that home—indeed, life itself—lay elsewhere.

Though an ancient city of rich heritage, the Chengdu of my childhood was an ode to Soviet-style central planning, built on a series of concentric, ring-shaped roads, serving as a kind of municipal scaffolding extending in every direction toward the countryside. Growth was vertical as well, with buildings of uniform design but ever-rising heights, reaching farther and farther into balmy skies blanketed in near-constant fog and hemmed in by the surrounding basin.

Architecture stretching from horizon to horizon celebrated density in scale but banality in spirit; it was a world built from circles, rectangles, and a disciplined palette of grays and browns—accented with rhythmic predictability by the bold reds of propaganda posters—coarsely woven into a distinct industrial style. The city's roots could still be seen, of course, in narrow streets with low rooflines, pitched and layered in shingles, surrounding open-air courtyards and verdant landscaping. Still, from a bird's-eye view, the trend was clear. It was as if utilitarianism had been elevated to an urban art form, the austerity of its surface masking a relentless ambition still in its early stages.

But even in a nation racing toward a 1980s picture of modernity, in a city built to expand, a child's view of the world is provincial by nature. Its horizons are close and steep, admitting only hints of what lies beyond. For one to see further, to the frontiers that await, there needs to be a special kind of influence.

The highest compliment I can pay my father doubles as the most damning critique: that he's exactly what would result if a child could design their ideal parent in the total absence of adult supervision. Although handsome and clean-cut, with horn-rimmed glasses befitting his training as an electrical engineer and thick, wavy hair that gave him the air of a young actor or a beat poet, his look belied the trait that most defined him: an allergy to seriousness that can only be described as pathological. He was possessed by an unrepentant adolescent spirit and didn't reject the obligations of adulthood so much as he seemed genuinely unable to perceive them, as if lacking some basic sense that comes naturally for everyone else. It made for a mind fanciful enough to imagine toting his daughter through packed streets in a bicycle sidecar, reckless enough to build one from scratch, and shrewd enough to make it work—allowing me to tag along on his frequent trips to the city's parks or the country beyond its limits. There, we'd engage in his favorite pastimes for hours: hunting for butterflies, observing water buffalo lazing in flooded rice fields, or trapping creatures like wild rodents and stick insects to care for as pets back home.

It must have been obvious even from a distance that the traditional hierarchy of parent and child was absent between us, as he carried himself more like a peer than a father, unburdened by paternal neuroses. And although I could tell he was happy to share the experiences of our outings with me, the sheer intensity of his focus—as joyful as it was myopic—made it plain that this was *exactly* how he'd be spending his afternoons whether he had a daughter, a son, or no children at all. But it made his example all the more compelling. Without knowing it, he was showing me curiosity in its purest form.

The trips weren't especially educational—my father was a lover of nature, not an expert on it—but they planted the seeds of a philosophy that would shape my life more than any other: an insatiable urge to search beyond my horizons. They showed me that even in a place like Chengdu, a maze of pavement and concrete, there was always more to discover than what lay before me.

No moment better demonstrates my father's character—equal parts playful and exasperating, thoughtless and clever—than his role in my birth. It was a trying day, as the story was later told to me, more than a thousand miles from Chengdu on the second floor of a hospital in Beijing (not far from the Forbidden City palace), where his family resided. But he arrived late—absurdly so—not because of gridlocked traffic or some unexpected emergency, but because he'd been so absorbed in an impromptu day of bird-watching at a local park that he'd completely lost track of time. Among his many quirks was an affinity for wordplay, however, and the ordeal brought to mind the Mandarin word *fēi*, meaning "to fly." Its whimsical connotations, reinforced by its bird-like rendering in simplified Chinese—飞—made "Fei-Fei" a natural choice for my name. It happened to be unisex, too, reflecting his lack of concern even about an idea as fundamental to the culture as gender, and was uncommon enough among my generation to appeal to his off-kilter sensibilities. But it was also his first contribution as a parent, unpretentious and sweet. And although his own flightiness hadn't exactly won my mother's affections for the day, she conceded she liked the name, too.

If my father was responsible for the magnitude of my curiosity, it was my mother who gave it direction. Like his, her personality sprang from a tension between who she was and who the world expected her to be. But where he was a child lost in the body of an adult, she was an intellectual trapped in a life of imposed mediocrity. Born with a naturally fierce mind into a distinctly intellectual lineage—her own grandmother was among the first generation of women to attend college in the late Qing Dynasty—she was driven from childhood not just to learn but to put that knowledge to principled use. To be a part of the world, to explore its reaches, and to leave a mark on it. It was an energy that propelled her to the top of her class and promised a bright future at any university she liked.

But history had other plans for people like my mother. As the Cultural Revolution roiled, she remained on the wrong side of generations-old divides cutting across politics and society. She came from a family associated with the Kuomintang, the defeated opposition to the now ruling Chinese Communist Party, an affiliation that doomed her prospects well before her own political identity had a chance to mature.

As is so often the case with prejudice, her defeat was the slow, unspoken kind. There was no threat of violence or imprisonment, no conspiracy or scandal, just a status quo that revealed its presence through the passive-aggressive remarks of teachers and administrators, politely but firmly discouraging her, even at her academic peak, from applying to the best schools. Their dismissal, ever-present and stifling, was a malaise that hung over her teenage and young adult years, compounding my grandfather's sense of aggrievement into a now generational burden for her to carry as well. And it coarsened a once spirited youth, contorting her sense of wonder into the mirror image of my father's: every bit as inquisitive but lacking its innocence, sharpened to a formidable edge. Even as she grew into a photogenic woman, with strong cheekbones and

expressive eyes, her prettiness masked a natural renegade, fated to forever bristle at the thought of constraints or the obligations of propriety.

My mother's frustrations grew as the years passed, overshadowing
her erudition with something simpler and more primal: a desire to escape. It burned within her, tightening her posture and leaving her impatient and slow to trust. Whether she imagined an escape from the
circumstances of her work, her country, or even her century, she was
convinced her destiny was waiting elsewhere. In the meantime, she felt
doomed to an inconsolable restlessness, biding her time until a path
toward some unknown horizon revealed itself. She knew it would be a
long wait.

Realizing that her imagination was subject to no such limitations,
she immersed herself in books from an early age. They became her
window to places, lives, and times that exceeded her reach, and she
shared her love for them with me as eagerly as my father shared his
fondness for the natural world. She was happy to put any book in my
hands, but the farther their stories ventured, the more infectious her
enthusiasm became. So although I was familiar with the works of Lu
Xun or Taoist scriptures like the *Tao Te Ching*, I devoured the Chinese
translations of Western classics like *Le Deuxième Sexe*, *A Tale of Two
Cities*, *The Old Man and the Sea*, and *The Count of Monte Cristo*.

I couldn't yet understand what motivated my mother's desire to escape, but the more I read, the more I came to share her love for imagining worlds beyond my own. The stories lingered in my thoughts
long after I read their final words, like alternate realities competing
with the one I lived in. Whether it was the walk to school, a bike ride
to the park, or even a trip to the grocery store, my view of everyday
life was superimposed with a kaleidoscope of faraway imagery: the
cobblestone streets of Dickens's England, the turmoil of Heming-
way's oceans, the romantic adventure of Dumas's European coasts.
Each flash of narrative color made me feel special, like my mother
had pulled back some secret curtain and shown me possibilities I'd
never have imagined otherwise. For an adolescent already prone to

spending more time in her head than among friends, it was an irresistible invitation.

There was no denying my parents were an awkward fit, but there was a dance between their temperaments that kept them balanced, if only precariously. Buried within my father's goofiness was a spark of true ingenuity, and my mother's eagerness to put it to use around the house could be seen as an oblique show of admiration. The chemistry was still volatile, of course, often jostled into combustion by her tendency to scrutinize his handiwork or the inconsistency of his own patience that gave way to sporadic fits of belligerence. But when the dust settled and she was out of earshot, he often confided to me that she was the smartest person he'd ever met.

The true foundation of their marriage, however, was a bond they knew no one else in their lives could understand. In their own ways, they'd both lost faith in the institutions of their world, and that made them partners, even accomplices, in a daily practice of defiance. He may have lacked ambition in all but the most childish pursuits, but she reveled in his antipathy toward the social climbing that preoccupied so many of their peers. And although she could be judgmental, even elitist, he was charmed by her fearlessness as she flouted the norms that surrounded them. As their friends hosted fawning dinner parties for their bosses, purchased them gifts in the hopes of earning favor, and talked endlessly about status in one form or another, my parents sat proudly on the sidelines. Even their jobs—his in the computing department of a chemical plant and hers as a high school teacher turned office worker—seemed more like facades than careers. There were countless pitfalls lurking within my parents' relationship, but there were virtues as well. Rare, maybe, but meaningful.

Unsurprisingly, their parenting was as unorthodox as their marriage. In a community obsessed with inculcating respect in its children—success measured less in terms of grades per se than a reputation for following rules, listening closely, and earning the praise of teachers—my parents were unconcerned, even irreverent. My mother in particular took pride in a subtle twist on the day's parenting norms: I was expected to work hard and pursue the fullness of my potential, of course, but not for the sake of anyone or anything else. She never went quite so far as to state it explicitly, but I could sense she found notions like "model student" and "upstanding member of the community" condescending. My efforts, she taught me, weren't in the service of my teachers, or an ideology, or even some disembodied sense of principle. They were for me.

Cultural fault lines notwithstanding, my parents' love for me was sincere. Both were hardworking providers, even if my mother often took her responsibilities to perfectionist extremes that contrasted awkwardly with my father's nonchalance. And despite their tendency to bicker, I was rarely the target of her temper; she knew how to channel her energy productively, even creatively, when it came to our relationship. She was eager to teach, encourage, and arm me with everything she could to face the world, even turning her burgeoning interest in tailoring into homemade hats, dresses, and pants for me to wear—simple but surprisingly well-made garments for an amateur.

To the outside world, in fact, my parents' philosophy was a nearly invisible distinction. By any measure, we appeared to be exceedingly typical members of China's emerging middle class, not yet swept up in the whirlwind of consumerism to come but largely spared the privation of previous generations. Even still, it would have been a mistake to interpret their tame veneer as capitulation, or even apathy; they knew that one way or another, change was coming—historic change—and they were willing to be patient.

Our family's residence was a fourth-floor apartment in a complex of three identical towers, situated on Chengdu's outermost ring road. It was the leading edge of an expanding world, with industry in one direction and agriculture in the other. Like the city itself, our building's design tended more toward function than form, with fluorescent lighting and cement floors that would have looked especially spartan to modern eyes. Personal touches broke up the monotony to a degree, as more and more homes incorporated painted walls and veneer floors that mimicked the texture of hardwood or colored tiles, but there was no hiding the Soviet influence.

Apart from my mother and father, my maternal grandparents were the most important people in my life. Every Sunday was spent at their apartment, a half-mile walk from our own, where we'd crowd around a circular dining table just big enough for the family and my grandmother's lavish preparations of rice, soy sauce–braised pork belly, tofu mixed with scallions, and an especially elaborate vegetable dish called the "ten treasures." Each visit was the highlight of my week, even as they subtly reinforced our identities as outsiders. My grandparents' cooking was a testament to the style of the coastal region they had left—rich, slightly sweet flavors that stood in striking contrast to the famed spiciness of Chengdu's Sichuan cuisine. To this day, they're the tastes for which I'm most nostalgic, unusual as that is for a Chengdu native.

Strangely, my memories of childhood bear no trace of my paternal grandparents. I knew that my grandfather had died when my father was barely a teenager, and that my grandmother, although still living in Beijing with my aunt, suffered from severe physical and mental illnesses related to her traumatic wartime upbringing. In a way, though, their absence felt appropriate, in keeping with my father's otherworldly nature. It made a kind of poetic sense that a man so incapable of acting like a parent would somehow lack any of his own.

Still, my mother's parents served as extensions of the values she shared with my father when it came to raising me. Although they were warm and doting, I never mistook their sweetness for passivity; they were equally principled in treating me as a person first and a girl second, echoing my family's encouragement of my imagination and eschewing their generation's tendency to prioritize boys. Like my mother, they bought me books in abundance, exploring topics as wide-ranging as marine life, robotics, and Chinese mythology.

Admittedly, my mother and her two sisters were my grandparents' only children—three uniformly headstrong daughters and not a son in sight—so opportunities for chauvinism were limited long before I showed up. But their affection endured with the birth of my cousin—a boy, at last—and I never second-guessed it. It was only as I grew up that I realized the world beyond our doorstep might be a more complicated place.

Every aspect of the schools I attended in Chengdu revolved around students, literally. Each of us sat in a single, fixed seat, from morning till afternoon, and was treated to a rotation of teachers who cycled in to deliver the next lecture. Scholastic talent was recognized from the earliest signs of its emergence and fostered methodically, and, at least at first, it didn't seem to matter whether that talent belonged to a boy or a girl. It was obvious to me, even as a child, that our teachers' interest in our development was sincere. They were consistently hardworking and the first members of the community beyond my parents and grandparents who seemed invested in my well-being.

Our studies were broad and engaging, with math and science complemented richly by the humanities, from geography to ancient poetry to history that reached millennia into the past. I was fascinated to learn that my own city, for instance, was the capital of Shu Han, one of China's legendary three kingdoms. At its best, school felt like an extension of the books my mother shared and the exploration my father encouraged.

It was a time of contentment, but one that ended abruptly—for me, at least—in a single afternoon. On an otherwise unremarkable day near the end of my last year in elementary school, our teacher wrapped up the class with the unusual request that the boys remain seated for a few additional minutes while the girls were dismissed to go home. Instantly curious, I hovered by the door, making sure I remained hidden but within earshot. I've never forgotten what I heard.

"I asked the girls to leave because the time has come to tell you that your performance as a group is unacceptable. As boys, you're biologically smarter than girls. Math and science are fundamental parts of that, and there's just no excuse for your average exam scores to be lower than theirs. I'm deeply disappointed in you all today."

Then, perhaps sensing that a note of encouragement was in order as well, the teacher's tone seemed to soften as the lecture concluded.

"But I don't want you to lose hope. As you become teenagers, you'll find the girls among you naturally grow stupider. Their potential will fade and their scores will drop. Even still, I expect you all to work harder, and live up to your potential as boys. Falling behind the girls is unacceptable. Do you understand?"

It took a moment for the words to trigger any real response in me. Questions abounded in the meantime. Did my teacher really believe that boys were "biologically smarter"? And that we girls would naturally become *stupider*? Was this how all of my teachers saw me? Had they felt this way all along? And what was I to make of the fact that the person saying these things was . . . a woman?

Then, as another moment passed, the questions were shoved aside by a new feeling. It was heavy and jagged, and clawed its way up from a part of me I didn't even know existed. I didn't feel discouraged, or even offended. I was angry. It was an anger I wasn't familiar with—a quiet heat, an indignation like I'd seen in my mother, but unmistakably my own.

As time passed, I began to realize that the incident wasn't the first sign that my family's inclusivity wasn't a given outside the home. Most indications were subtle, if not intangible, like the sneaking suspicion that teachers doled out encouragement more readily to boys when it came to math and science. Others were overt, like the time I volunteered for first-grade soccer—not the "boys' team," but the *school* team—and was told that girls simply weren't allowed to play.

Shocked as I was by my teacher's words, I wasn't dissuaded. They only amplified the mandate of my upbringing: to imagine something bigger than the world around me, no matter what might stand in my way. Now

I didn't just want to see further, but to reach further as well. If fields like math and science were boys' games, so be it. But this wasn't soccer. They couldn't stop me from playing this time, and I was determined to win.

In the years that followed, as I entered a magnet middle school for high-performing students across the city, my impatience with the assumptions that came with being a girl reached beyond my schoolwork. I was already what my generation would call a tomboy, but my teacher's words, still echoing in my memory, elevated what began as a quirk to something more like a personal mission. I cut my hair as short as I could, refused to wear dresses, and flung myself into interests that I knew defied expectations, especially the science of aerospace, the design of hypersonic aircraft, and even paranormal topics like UFOs.

Like any adolescent prone to seeing life as a melodrama, I might have found it easy to convince myself I was alone in my struggle against China's gender norms. Even the handful of friends I'd gravitated toward over the years didn't seem to care the way I did, perhaps because I was already used to hanging out with a mostly male crowd that rode bikes, liked to roughhouse, and chatted about fighter jets rather than schoolyard gossip. Besides, I had compatriots—no matter how jaded I might be, my parents were always on my side, and I knew it.

My father delighted in subtle acts of contrarianism, a tradition that began with the genes we share—thanks to his most conspicuous hereditary gift, I already stood out as the only girl in my class with wavy hair. He was forever on the lookout for opportunities to make a statement, straddling the line between silly and subversive. One such opportunity came during my time in elementary school, when each household was asked to prepare their children for an upcoming school-wide sporting event with a specific style of white button-down shirt. He reviewed the instructions in detail, an impish grin spreading across his face as he ensured he was following them to the letter. When the day arrived, my hair was no longer my only trademark; I was also the only student in a sea of white shirts to sport rainbow-colored buttons.

Unlike my father's support, however, there was nothing playful about my mother's. If he was a prankster, she was a protector, and never hesitated to intervene when she felt her values—*our* values—were in question. It was a lesson one of my middle school teachers learned the hard way during a particularly memorable meeting with her.

"Mrs. Li, there's no question your daughter is a bright girl, but I'm worried she's not taking her future as seriously as she could. It's never too early to start preparing for final exams, for example, so I often ask each student to share the books they're reading with the class. Most cite textbooks, prep manuals, and selections from the school's approved reading list. Fei-Fei's answers this week concerned me, however, and—"

"My daughter has been an avid reader for her entire life," my mother interjected, making no effort to conceal her contempt.

"Well, yes, of course. And uh, she certainly listed more books than anyone in the class—"

"So what's the problem?"

The teacher sighed. It was clear this conversation wasn't playing out as she'd expected.

"It's *what* she's reading. I mean, *The Unbearable Lightness of Being*? The Brontë sisters? And all these magazines she subscribes to. Marine life, fighter jets, something about UFOs . . . the list goes on. She's just not prioritizing literature that reflects the values and ideas of the curriculum."

"Yeah? And?"

I sat beside my mother for the moment of silence that followed, doing my best to keep the glee coursing through my veins from reaching my face. The tension hung in the air for a moment or two longer, before the teacher leaned forward and made one last attempt, a new sternness in her voice.

"I'll be frank, Mrs. Li. Your daughter may be bright, but there are *many* bright students in her class. That's why intellect is only one ingredient in success. Another is the discipline to put aside one's personal interests in favor of the studies that will prove most useful in the years ahead."

I'm not sure if what my mother said next was meant to be a response. She looked down, speaking more softly than before. "Is this what Fei-Fei wants? Is this what I want for her?"

"What was that, Mrs. Li?" The teacher leaned in closer, clearly as confused as I was.

My mother sighed quietly, then looked back at the teacher as a determined expression returned to her face. The look would have to do. She was done throwing jabs. She stood up, thanked the teacher for her time, and gestured to me that we were leaving.

"I might have taught you too well, Fei-Fei," she said with resignation as I tried to keep up with her pace on the walk out. "You don't belong here any more than I did."

Everything changed in 1989.

It began with mandatory time off from school, with breaks that stretched from days into longer and longer lapses, made all the more disorienting by a lack of explanation. When classes finally resumed, the demeanor of our teachers had changed. Overtones of patriotism were woven throughout each of the day's lessons, and not just in literature, history, and civics classes, but even in math and science.

Stranger still was the contrast between life at school and life at home, as a mysterious mood seemed to captivate my parents—a *positive* one, no less. They took to talking cryptically and in hushed tones about something on the horizon, ominous but exciting. My father seemed less scatterbrained than usual, and there was a new hopefulness to my mother's attitude. To whatever extent I understood politics—which, at that age, wasn't much—I knew my parents harbored ideas that weren't entirely congruous with those of other adults. Was this strange new phenomenon related, somehow? Whatever was going on, it defied a twelve-year-old's awareness. But one thing was clear: my world was a much more complicated place than I'd realized.

Then, on an otherwise vibrant summer day, the cheer evaporated as abruptly as it had emerged. The openness of our household—unusually "democratic" by the standards of friends' families—was replaced by uncharacteristic closed-door conversations clearly intended to exclude me. The solemnity that now hung over everything was obvious, but it wasn't enough to keep me from prying. I could make out only so much from my late-night, tiptoed eavesdropping, but it was enough to perk up my ears. "Education" . . . "Opportunity" . . . "Freedom" . . . "A better life for her" . . . and, most frequently, my name. It was a side of them I'd never seen, and I slunk back to bed even more confused.

"Fei-Fei, we need to talk."

The time had come, apparently, for my parents to finally share. We gathered around the table, where so much of our family's democratic spirit had been exercised before.

"Your father is going to be moving for a while. To America."

My thoughts went blank for a moment. Too many questions sprang to mind for me to know where to begin. Rightly interpreting my astonished stare as a demand for elaboration, they went on to explain that the decision was actually only the first step in a larger plan. In the initial phase, which I quickly realized was spearheaded by my mother, my father would find work and secure a place to live. In the second phase, to follow shortly thereafter, we would join him.

My head was spinning. None of it made sense, and I couldn't process how fast it was all happening. Everything in my world was being turned upside down in an instant, and no one seemed to care what I thought about any of it. Within just a few weeks, my father was gone, taking with him a full third of the homelife I'd known since birth. Everything felt different.

It was only in my own adulthood that I could appreciate how much courage my father's journey to the West took. None of it was apparent to my adolescent self. As the world he left behind began to wither, I lacked the perspective, let alone the fortitude, to interpret his absence as anything more than abandonment. At the same time, my mother was slowly enveloped by a gloom that seemed unusual, even for her. She was growing listless, increasingly in need of rest throughout the day, and the rebelliousness of her attitude decayed into something more like hopelessness. Something was very wrong.

I was changing, too. My teenage years were close at hand, and whatever natural moodiness I was destined to foist upon my family was spiked with the confusion of waking up each day to a single-parent household for reasons I still didn't really understand. To my mother's credit, she did her best to fill both parental roles. She knew well the straits of adolescent emotion I was tipping into, and made a point to listen, always, as my need to vent grew more frequent. But it wasn't a substitute for an intact family. I couldn't shake the feeling that my parents had chosen some inexplicable dream over me.

To make matters worse, the supposed second phase of the plan—the one in which my mother and I would join my father in America—was continually delayed by the bureaucratic hurdles imposed by both countries' migration procedures. Although my father lucked into a visa relatively quickly, we fared quite differently. It would be more than three years before either of us saw him again.

In the meantime, I was losing my edge as a student. It was seventh grade, the year of my first physics class, and I was excited by the thought of applying my skills to a new subject. But something was wrong from day one. My intuitions had run aground, robbing me of the fluency I'd displayed in my math classes and confounding every attempt at understanding. I failed to visualize even the simplest concepts—including fundamentals like force and velocity—and after a year of misfires, I limped across the finish line with a bruised ego and cratering test scores.

Was it the emotional toll of my father's move? Was it mounting anxiety over my mother's mysterious exhaustion? Or—and my stomach turned as I considered the thought—was that elementary school teacher right all along? Was this the grim fate that awaits every girl's intellect? The worst part—even worse than my performance in the class—was having no answer.

Another summer was approaching, and while I'd have normally winced at the thought of shying away from a challenge, especially with so much on the line, a year of failure coupled with a faltering support system at home had demoralized me. It was the lowest I'd ever felt, and it made the choice between respite or months of obsessive self-study easy. I chose respite.

It was a welcome period of calm, but I felt more numb than relaxed. There were no flickers of new worlds dancing at the periphery of my vision. I didn't strive to picture some great mandala of realities encircling my own. There was just everyday life: the embrace of family, the chatter of friends, the metallic whir of a fixed-gear bicycle, and the din of a crowded street. The weight of a book in my hand, the sound of my mother down the hall. Mornings, afternoons, nights.

One thing that hadn't changed was how much I missed my father, and the relaxed schedule between school years only made his absence harder to bear. No one in my life seemed to understand the fundamental nature of joy like he did, and without him, it was like my own ability to feel the same way had been attenuated.

Perversely, the more I grieved his absence, the more I realized the things I missed about him were the things physics was trying to teach me. The way he naturally saw the world in terms of light, speed, torque, force, weight, and tension. The way he improvised devices of gears and pulleys to solve problems around the house. The way he harnessed electricity with his multimeter and soldering kit. Physics had always been the hidden foundation of my father's mind, and it was only now, when I missed him most, that I realized it. But the realization itself was something. He may have been a world away, but it was dawning on me that he'd already given me everything I needed.

As quickly as the mental block had appeared, it vanished. I suddenly felt a new dimension to physics, something I can only describe as a *romance* that I didn't recognize before. As if daylight were flooding in, I saw it like my father saw the natural world: a source of pure wonder. The concepts didn't just make sense—they were *beautiful*. When school returned, I revisited physics as if I'd been reborn. I stared down at the textbook, consumed by a hunger to explore its contents I hadn't felt before. Was it really like this last year? How could I have missed this? My heartbeat quickened.

It wasn't just a feeling. I got the highest grade in the class on the first exam. I scored even higher on the second. Then the third, and the fourth, and the fifth. Newtonian mechanics. Optics. Electricity. The streak didn't stop, from the first day of class to the final. Everyone noticed, including the teacher. What had once seemed like a puzzle was now a kind of language, and one I could speak.

But even as this new skill seemed to pour out of me, I was humbled—thrilled, really—by how much more there was to learn. In physics, I didn't see complexity so much as I saw grandeur. It offered the elegance and certainty of mathematics, the tangibility of chemistry, and, most arresting of all, something I never imagined the sciences could offer: a sense of humanity that felt as poetic as the literature I was raised on. Its history read like drama, rich and vibrant, reaching across centuries, and I couldn't get enough of it.

I imagined Archimedes running naked through the streets of Sicily, joyfully mad with the elation of discovery, trailed by bathwater and the furrowed brows of his neighbors. I imagined Newton locked in his bedroom in Woolsthorpe while the plague decimated Europe, gripped with monastic devotion as each frenzied stroke of ink dried on the manuscript that would become the *Principia*. And I imagined Einstein, a lowly clerk in a Swiss patent office until he wielded his intellect with such ferocity that it carried him further into the depths of the cosmos than anyone who had ever lived, unraveling space and time as if he were opening a package, and reaching inside to claim a view of the universe that once belonged only to gods.

My love for literature remained, but physics was now the lens through which I saw the world, everywhere I went. As if in a persistent daydream, I wondered about the changing degrees of acceleration and angular momentum as I rounded a corner on my bike, the gravitational magnitude at work as our cat pounced from the highest cabinet in the kitchen, and the force with which her mass would collide with the floor. I studied the bounce of sunlight through my window, off the walls, and across my pillow. I thought about the heat transferred between every surface in my home, my neighborhood, and the world. And I imagined entropy, relentless and eternal, slowly unweaving everything around me.

By the end of the next school year, a new realization followed: physics had become something more than an adolescent attempt at filling the void my father left in my life. I loved it with a simple purity, the way my parents loved the pursuits they shared with me from my earliest days. They showed me there was something more out there; they gave me the adventures and stories and imagination that had defined my life up until this moment. But these were things to *see*. Physics was the first thing I'd discovered on my own, and it felt different. It was something to *chase*.

Finally, in 1992, not long after I turned fifteen, our visas arrived. Our last months in China were upon us, an emotionally confused period that oscillated between flashes of excitement and anxiety. Sometimes I fantasized about what might await in a country like America, where, for all I knew, I'd discover a life of glamour and opportunity. It's certainly what some of my classmates seemed to think. And who was to say they weren't right? My father had spent years preparing for our arrival, and, like any other student, I'd been given a basic education in English grammar and vocabulary. Maybe this whole ludicrous plan actually made sense. But at other times, the scope of what I stood to lose—my friends, my grandparents, everything I knew—would hit me in a single blow.

Chengdu offered no direct flights to our destination in New York, so our journey began with a trip to Shanghai. Noting the hours of layover time ahead of us, I insisted we walk to the Bund, a waterfront promenade and historical hot spot for tourists. It's the city's most famous district, attracting photographers worldwide for its colonial architecture and scenic views of the Huangpu River, but I was most curious about the lore surrounding the Pujiang Hotel, known to English speakers as the Astor House. Although accounts vary somewhat, Albert Einstein stayed the night there in 1922, either just before or just after he was awarded the Nobel Prize. It was exactly the kind of escapism I needed to keep my spirits up, and his association with the town struck me as a good omen. *Maybe this won't be so bad*, I thought. *Einstein was an immigrant, too, after all.*

I lingered on the note of optimism, keeping close to my mother as our departure approached. No matter how inconceivable our move to America seemed, no matter how absurd I found the idea that we could build a life there—less a destination than some far-off abstraction— and no matter how frightening it was to face the extent of the unknowns that stretched out before us, she knew better than I did. This was the culmination of her lifetime of defiance, an act as drastic as it was inevitable, and I had to admire her resolve.

Sure enough, she seemed poised as ever as we made our way through the winding line toward the gate, her steps determined, her chin up, her gaze unbothered. If nothing else, I had to take some comfort in the fact that the escape she'd spent a lifetime waiting for—sometimes hopefully, sometimes angrily, but always with devotion—was finally here. I didn't necessarily share her excitement, but I was grateful for her confidence.

Then I saw it. Something that transformed the moment. It was only a glance, but it was long enough to notice a detail without precedent in all the years I'd spent trying to follow my mother's example. It was an instantly destabilizing sight, and I wished I could shut my eyes and erase it. Tucked beneath her coat, concealed, but imperfectly so, her hands were trembling.

A crowd of fellow passengers enveloped us as we made our way onto the plane, consumed by the roar of its auxiliary power and the rattling of the jet bridge beneath our feet. We took our final steps over the threshold and into an interior that was smaller than I imagined for a vessel that would take us so far. As the daughter of a family of slow-moving nomads, pushed by fate across China for generations, even a new life on the other side of the planet seemed strangely fitting. At the same time, for a teenager still unsure of her place in the world, it felt impossible.

As I sat down and stared at the back of the seat in front of me, I took stock of all that I had. I had grandparents I loved dearly, though our departure meant losing them, at least for now. I had a father I looked forward to seeing again, even as the wounds of his absence continued to sting. I had a mother I believed in, even if I was no longer sure she believed in herself. I couldn't yet say I had an identity of my own—I was still a teenager, after all—but, for what it was worth, I had physics. The rest, I supposed, would be left to fate.

3

A NARROWING GULF

My life had begun in the East, a hemisphere's diameter from the science I would grow to love. It was a gulf that couldn't have been much wider, in terrestrial terms at least, as the doors of our 747 swung shut, muffling the engines and triggering a slow lurch across the tarmac. Our destination, unbeknownst to either of us, was ground zero of a young field still struggling to establish a fraction of the legitimacy enjoyed by traditional disciplines, but destined, ultimately, to herald a revolution. That moment remained decades in the future, however, and, for me, thousands of miles away. In the meantime, with the first gusts of lift swelling beneath us, the gulf had only begun to narrow.

Two of the greatest changes of the twentieth century took place at the endpoints of my journey. While China endured a painful, century-long transformation of its culture and economy, America was the site of a different kind of revolution: a digital one. As my grandparents were swept up in the chaos of wartime displacement and my mother and father absorbed the shocks of the Cultural Revolution, a loose community of scientists and engineers in the U.S. and U.K.—from Cambridge to Boston to Northern California—were already decades into a scientific quest that would one day rank among the most profound in the history of our species.

Just as Newton had the shrewdness to see the clockwork behind a world of matter and energy, and just as Einstein looked even further to reimagine the relationship between time and space, the computer science visionaries of the mid-twentieth century were true dreamers. Gripped by that same spirit of abandon, they saw a new frontier hiding in plain sight, and took the first steps toward revealing it.

At a time when state-of-the-art technology required entire rooms of hardware to perform arithmetic, pioneering scientists like Alan Turing, the English code breaker famous for helping end the Second World War, were already seeing parallels between machines and the brain. It was a genuine feat of imagination, every bit as audacious as those of the physicists who shaped the scientific revolutions that came before. And like Einstein, Bohr, and Schrödinger, the questions posed by Turing and his contemporaries sparked debates that remain provocative to this day. What *is* intelligence, exactly? Can it be deconstructed in quantitative, mechanistic terms? And, perhaps boldest of all, can we build machines that embody it themselves?

Turing's vision was shared by his fellow computer scientists in America, who codified their curiosity in 1956 with a now famous Dartmouth College research proposal in which the term "artificial intelligence" was coined. Titled "A Proposal for the Dartmouth Summer Research Project on Artificial Intelligence," it called for an informal workshop to explore the programming of computers to perform human-like acts of reasoning, perception, and generalization of knowledge. The project was helmed largely by John McCarthy and Marvin Minsky, mathematicians with long-standing curiosity about the brain, along with Nathaniel Rochester, designer of the IBM 701 computer, and Claude Shannon, progenitor of the field of information theory.

Like Einstein honing his ideas after a long shift in the patent office, these early thinkers took the first steps toward a new world on the margins of busy careers, exploring the early days of AI with a genuine sense of adventure. That connection to physics, in fact, was more than a thematic one; although many of AI's founding contributors would go on to explore an eclectic range of fields, including psychology and cognitive science, their backgrounds were almost exclusively centered on mathematics, electrical engineering, and physics itself. It was a double-edged sword, however; though they were well-equipped to think rigorously and from first principles, they were inclined to treat the pursuit as almost purely theoretical. They saw the human capacity to reason as neatly analogous to a computer program: nothing more than the product of logical rules. Once our understanding of those rules was perfected, it was imagined, any machine that followed them would naturally be capable of recognizing the contents of photographs, understanding human language, exploring abstract ideas, and even solving novel problems in creative ways. It was a valiant effort, especially for its time, and it's hard not to admire their confidence. But it was vastly oversimplified.

The Dartmouth team quickly learned that while *aspects* of our behavior can indeed be described in simple terms, no finite set of rules or criteria—at least not of any practical size—can come close to capturing the depth and versatility of human thought in the real world. Amazingly, the proposal described the endeavor as a "summer project," without any apparent irony, requiring little more than a couple of months' time and a handful of grad students. As the original paper read:

> We propose that a 2-month, 10-man study of artificial intelligence be carried out during the summer of 1956 at Dartmouth College in Hanover, New Hampshire. The study is to proceed on the basis of the conjecture that every aspect of learning or any other feature of intelligence can in principle be so precisely described that a machine can be made to simulate it. An attempt will be made to find how to make machines use

language, form abstractions and concepts, solve kinds of problems now reserved for humans, and improve themselves. We think that a significant advance can be made in one or more of these problems if a carefully selected group of scientists work on it together for a summer.

When it became clear that making a "significant advance" in replicating the depth and scope of humanity's cognitive endowment might take more than eight weeks, however, the feeling of inevitability began to wear off. A more patient posture was assumed, and what started as a kind of academic lark matured into the first steps of a quest—one that would remain far from complete more than a half century later. Nevertheless, something transformative had been born.

Although the challenge of developing artificial intelligence quickly proved far greater than its founders initially expected, its ideas remained compelling and attracted a growing community of contributors. In 1959, McCarthy and Minsky founded the Artificial Intelligence Project at MIT, a loose-knit research initiative that evolved into the MIT Artificial Intelligence Laboratory. In 1963, McCarthy relocated to Stanford, bringing the exploration of AI to the West Coast, and founded the Stanford AI Lab, or SAIL. By the end of the 1960s, both labs were globally recognized centers of activity within the field, each fostering theory, experiments, lively debates, and creative development across hardware, software, and robotics.

Lessons were learned from the outsized ambitions of the field's headstrong early days as well, especially at SAIL. By the 1960s, interest was building around the digital representation of small, abstract virtual worlds, often populated by simple objects like blocks, allowing researchers to focus on the basics of intelligence without being overwhelmed by the details of everyday reality. Among the most famous examples of this approach was a program created at MIT by a doctoral student named Terry Winograd, which allowed the user to manipulate a collection of virtual colored blocks using plain English commands. The following is an excerpt from an especially memorable exchange:

USER: Find a block which is taller than the one you are holding and put it into the box.
COMPUTER: By "it", i assume you mean the block which is taller than the one i am holding.
COMPUTER: OK.
USER: What does the box contain?
COMPUTER: The blue pyramid and the blue block.
USER: What is the pyramid supported by?
COMPUTER: The box.
USER: How many blocks are not in the box?
COMPUTER: Four of them.

Even now, in an era of uncannily human-like AI conversation models, it's hard not to feel as if this is the transcript of a user in dialogue with a fully realized mind. Unsurprisingly, Winograd's program was heralded as a breakthrough achievement, and convinced many observers that an AI revolution was imminent. The more complicated reality was that the program's apparent fluency and flexibility was, ironically, a product of its constraints. Although it could speak eloquently on the topic of blocks, it could do so *only* on that topic. Even slight deviations from a limited set of possible questions and answers ran the risk of breaking the program and generating nonsensical output. Nevertheless, its narrow focus did, indeed, seem to pay off; the program didn't do much, but what it did was strikingly potent.

A deeper exploration of this idea was undertaken in the 1970s by Ed Feigenbaum, another Stanford professor, SAIL researcher, and frequent collaborator of John McCarthy. Rather than attempt to broaden programs like Winograd's, likely falling back into the trap of early AI's attempts at building a general intelligence from scratch, he simply shifted it to another domain. After all, why couldn't the same fluency in language and reasoning be applied to something in the real world, like medical examinations or financial analyses? What if, instead of answering questions about a collection of geometric shapes, a machine could do the same with a database of disease symptoms and patient attributes, or transaction records and quarterly reports?

Feigenbaum's innovation was the dawn of a subfield that came to be known as "knowledge engineering," in which facts about a particular domain—medicine, pharmaceuticals, finance, or just about anything else—were organized into libraries of machine-readable data that could be analyzed just like Winograd's geometric shapes, in the form of naturally written questions and answers that automated the experience of consulting with a human expert.

These programs, dubbed "expert systems," were the strongest evidence in years that AI could perform useful tasks in the real world, and showed that it could be the foundation of a business—even an industry. Their obvious commercial applications, combined with historic reductions in computing costs, inspired the formation of numerous companies throughout the 1970s and 1980s intent on bringing the power of knowledge engineering to the market.

Among the earliest and most well-known expert systems was a program called INTERNIST-I, which operated on a library of five hundred disease descriptions and three thousand manifestations of those diseases. Early trials were encouraging, and saw the program correctly diagnose a patient's condition on the basis of symptom observations provided by the user, a human internist, generating useful output in even complex cases. Other early examples included MOLGEN, which aided molecular geneticists in planning experiments involving DNA; VM, short for "Ventilator Management," advising clinicians overseeing patients relying on ventilators; and SECS, which stood for "Simulation and Evaluation of Chemical Synthesis" and provided an early glimpse into the potential of AI in drug discovery.

Despite a wave of initial excitement, expert system development was frequently bogged down by the logistical hurdles of simply organizing such enormous volumes of information in the first place. With increasing frequency, developers struggled to input the contents of medical textbooks, research papers, pharmaceutical literature, and even interviews with practitioners. Worse, even when such systems appeared to be sufficiently armed with data, they often failed to perform at a level comparable to that of human experts in the real world. Despite reams of information at their disposal and superhuman retrieval and processing speeds, their reasoning remained stilted and shallow, hewing too closely to formally defined rules, lacking in common sense, and routinely confounded by unexpected blind spots.

As commercial interest waned and funding evaporated, many concluded that the idea of intelligent machines was interesting but untenable—yet again. Whatever the future of AI would prove to be—what it would look like, when it would arrive, and how we'd get there—it was increasingly obvious that the road would not be an easy one.

As if to shake me out of a daydream, our plane jostled as its wheels hit the runway at JFK. I'd spent most of the previous fourteen hours reading, a last-ditch effort to escape into the stories that had comforted me for so long. Now, a blunt new reality was here, wresting away my attention no matter how much I resisted. A pleasant but foreign voice over the intercom reminded me that I was no longer in familiar territory. This wasn't a vacation or some kind of adventure; it was the abrupt, inexplicable end to the only life that made sense to me, and the beginning of a new one I couldn't even imagine. Although relieved to be done with the long, cramped trip, I was hardly excited to disembark.

Tensions only rose when we reached baggage claim. Our plan to reunite with my father at the gate, finally, had provided the only happy thought I could muster, but hours passed without his arrival. The sun set, a blur of strangers weaved and sidestepped around us, and confusion gave way to dread. The mind goes to dark places when a loved one is missing for too long, and our thoughts were made all the more harrowing by our circumstances: my mother had exactly twenty U.S. dollars in her pocket, we had no return ticket, and I quickly found that the couple of years I'd spent learning basic English in school were all but useless in practice.

We'd later learn my father's car had broken down—an occurrence that would soon become routine for us, a family of immigrants relying on worn-out, used vehicles—and that his misfortune happened in the middle of a tunnel. It was the kind of bad luck we might have laughed off back home, but not on a day like this. By the time he burst through the doors, frantic and out of breath, we were simply too exhausted for the happy reunion it should have been.

As we drove down an unfamiliar highway, passing sign after sign I struggled to read, the reality of the situation began to dawn on me. I was a permanent inhabitant of this place, as ridiculous as that seemed. No matter how inscrutable our new surroundings, that statement was now, somehow, true. This was it, I acknowledged reluctantly. America.

Our destination was a New Jersey township called Parsippany, chosen by my father for its sizable immigrant community and proximity to nearby highways. It was my first exposure to the American idea of a suburb, and it made an instant impression after a life spent on the other side of the planet. China had an insatiable density that consumed every axis: cars and bicycles packed the streets, people filled the sidewalks, and buildings stretched as high as they could into the haze even as they pushed the space between them to the absolute minimum. It fostered an atmosphere of noise, heat, and hustle that refused to abate, and gave cities their character.

Parsippany, in comparison, felt like pure space: empty sidewalks, leisurely drivers on the roads, and so much room *between* everything. Grassy lots surrounded single-family homes amounting to only one or two stories. Small businesses boasted vast parking lots, with space after space unused. Trees and gardens flourished. It even smelled different, as if the air itself were fresher, lacking the industrial tinge I remembered.

My time to reflect would be short-lived, however; I was forced out of my thoughts the moment we pulled up to our new home, confronted by the litany of tasks we'd face in order to get our American lives off the ground. The first was simply adjusting to dramatically reduced living quarters, as we filed into a cramped one-bedroom unit on the second story of a redbrick apartment building, far removed from the picturesque streets we'd traveled to get there. Realizing the space was too small for a family of three, we had little choice but to improvise clumsily by placing my bed in a narrow gap between the kitchen and the dining area, where it remained as long as we lived there. To furnish what space we did have, we became dedicated spotters of discarded furniture left in driveways and on curbs. The next order of business was waiting for me barely forty-eight hours later: my first day of school.

For a Chinese student raised in the schools of Chengdu, my first days at Parsippany High School were an assault on the senses. The mood was manic and unsteady, and everything around me was brighter, faster, heavier, and noisier than the world I left behind. Nothing quite registered, no matter where I looked, as if the very nature of light and sound were somehow different here.

The colors alone were overwhelming. The clothes worn by students and teachers alike were more vibrant than anything I'd seen before, the palette ranging from earth tones to primaries to fluorescents, solid or broken by stripes and patterns, and adorned with lettering, illustrations, abstract designs, and logos. And they were accentuated with a blur of hats, sunglasses, earrings, purses, and branded backpacks, to say nothing of the makeup the girls wore—something I'd never once seen on teenagers.

The necessity of the backpacks became clear when I was given my new textbooks, which dwarfed their modestly sized paperback equivalents in China. Although most copies were scuffed and ragged along the edges, their quality shocked me; every class was accompanied by a heavily bound volume with vibrant cover art and hundreds upon hundreds of full-color pages. And their sheer weight seemed unreal.

Even more intense was the way everything moved. After a life spent in the ever-stationary seat of a Chinese student, the urgency with which the entire school seemed to spill from room to room was bewildering. My memories of China felt docile in comparison to the ritual that separated classes here, as loud bells unleashed even louder crowds that roared through halls like flash floods of teenage energy.

Finally, there were the people themselves. Rowdiness and irreverence seemed to be the norm among the kids. Even from behind a still-towering language barrier, I knew I'd never seen students talk to teachers the way Americans did. But what astonished me most was how the informalities appeared to cut both ways. Their dynamic was often adversarial, but jocular as well. Even warm. On an otherwise imposing first day, I instantly knew one thing: I would love American teachers.

Life was closer to recognizable back in our apartment—somewhat, anyway—but it was no less draining. My sudden immersion in an English-speaking world meant that even the simplest homework assignments took hours, as nearly every step was saddled with a discouraging appeal to one of two enormous dictionaries, one for translating Chinese to English and the other for the reverse. It appeared as if the fluency with which I approached school in China—much less my budding love affair with physics—would have to be put aside in favor of a humbling return to square one. For the foreseeable future, simply regaining an ability to express myself would be the center of my intellectual life.

Thankfully, my parents were as busy as I was, lending the rhythm of a routine to our days. My father crossed paths with a Taiwanese business owner not long after his arrival and parlayed his knack for engineering into a job repairing cameras in a shop the man owned. The pay was meager and the hours were demanding, but it was just enough for us to survive. My mother found work as well, taking a position as a cashier in a Newark gift shop run by the man's wife. The additional income was welcome, but I found it difficult to witness an aspiring intellectual consigned to a job that ignored the entirety of her talents. Because their shifts ran well into the evening, and because money was far too scarce for takeout, the task of preparing dinner became a rushed affair that my father undertook each night, no matter how exhausted he was.

When moments of downtime did present themselves, I chose to spend them as my father had during the last three years, by writing letters to family and friends. Each handwritten message was a plea to be reminded that the people and things I loved—my grandmother's cooking in particular—still existed in my absence. Each reply, as exciting as it was to see in the mailbox, was a bittersweet confirmation. For the first time in my life, the far-off world I dreamt of wasn't an exotic locale or undiscovered frontier. It was the place I knew better than any other.

I wonder, in hindsight, if my homesickness could have been treated with the realization that I was now closer than ever before to a revolution of modern science, even if only geographically. A home in Parsippany of all places meant that the gulf between my origins and my future hadn't just narrowed, but had closed so dramatically that I would spend the rest of my adolescence less than an hour's drive away from history in the making—mere miles down the Garden State Parkway—without knowing it.

Yann LeCun would one day serve as Facebook's chief scientist of AI, but his career in research was only dawning at Holmdel, New Jersey's

Bell Labs when my family arrived in America. Unassuming but ambitious, he'd been making waves in recent years by demonstrating the startling capabilities of an algorithm called a "neural network" to accurately recognize human handwriting. The technique, still relatively new and far from achieving the mainstream popularity it would one day enjoy, was a radical departure from the decades of AI tradition that preceded it. Rather than attempting to describe handwriting in discrete rules—the straight edge of a "1," the curve of a "2," the symmetrical halves of a "3," and so on—a neural network was designed only to infer patterns in data.

In LeCun's case, that meant showing the network thousands of examples of actual human handwriting, covering a range of styles, textures, and even common mistakes—more than 7,200 scans of handwritten ZIP codes in all, provided by the United States Postal Service—as it *learned* the relevant patterns much like a human does. The result was an internalized set of intuitions that, while difficult to articulate in the form of a traditional computer program, allowed the algorithm to make sense of the messiness of the real world like nothing that came before.

LeCun's work was a spectacular success. Its performance was so accurate, in fact, that within just a few years it would be deployed in ATMs nationwide to read digits written on checks. Decades after the Dartmouth research proposal that introduced the idea of artificial intelligence to the world, the field finally claimed what was, by far, its most practical achievement.

It also prefigured a bold future: after generations of rigid algorithms that attempted to exhaustively describe intelligence in terms of rules, often referred to as "symbolic AI," the end of the 1980s and the early 1990s saw the tide beginning to turn in favor of this more natural approach. Increased attention was being paid to algorithms that solved problems by discovering patterns from examples, rather than being explicitly programmed—in other words, *learning* what to do rather than being told. Researchers gave it a fitting name: "machine learning."

Among the more poetic aspects of the evolution of science is the gestation period of ideas. There's no natural law ensuring that insights emerge only when they can be realized in practice, and history is replete with sparks of inspiration appearing years, decades, or even centuries before their time. What's truly inspiring is the eagerness with which these early thinkers refuse to give up on their discoveries; no matter how impractical the path forward seems, and no matter how unlikely the prospects of experimental success, great scientists are driven by an innate hunger to explore that thrives under even the most obstinate circumstances. For decades, this was the nature of machine learning.

The history of machine learning is arguably the lesser-known half of the history of AI itself, remaining relatively niche, even with one of its first acknowledgments coming from Alan Turing himself. In a 1950 paper entitled "Computing Machinery and Intelligence," Turing succinctly contrasted "rule-based AI," in which a complete agent capable of intelligent behavior is built from scratch, and machine learning, in which such an agent is allowed to develop on its own, asking: "Instead of trying to produce a programme to simulate the adult mind, why not rather try to produce one which simulates the child's?" Indeed, machine learning has drawn at least some measure of inspiration from human cognition since its inception, due in no small part to the contemporaneous evolution of fields like neuroscience.

A dimly functional understanding of the brain existed as early as the nineteenth century, but it wasn't until the twentieth that neuroscience as we know it today began to take shape. Even then, however, the state of our knowledge was primitive. Like the first astronomers struggling to make sense of celestial trajectories mapped across the sky, scientists in those days knew little of the brain beyond what they saw—a torrent of electrical impulses and chemical emissions rippling across layers of wet, mysteriously folded tissue.

If there's a silver lining to periods of such opacity, however, when the world seems all but closed to scientific inquiry, it's that the curious among us are at their most inventive. Hypotheses are conjured from near nothingness. Even minor advances can be transformative. And the snowball effect that follows can be dizzying. As the midpoint of the twentieth century approached, neuroscience was on the verge of identifying its own fundamental precepts—a foundation on which true understanding could be built, one layer at a time. It was an era not unlike the dawn of modern physics, as our first hints of the fundamental nature of the physical world—the particles and forces that would serve as building blocks for all we see—revolutionized our understanding of nature.

A major step forward was taken in 1943, when researchers Warren S. McCulloch and Walter Pitts published a novel exploration of the brain's fundamental unit—the neuron—that simplified the underlying biology to an almost mathematical essence. The key to their insight was abstraction; by stripping away the electrochemical vagaries of a real brain, they reduced the neuron to the comparatively simple exchange of signals. It was a purely transactional analysis—what goes in, what comes out, and how the two relate to each other—and its implications were profound. Unlike any other part of the body, or indeed any other natural structure yet known, the brain appeared to be uniquely suited to the processing of *information*.

In a sense, it was the neuroscientific equivalent of splitting the atom, revealing a fundamental pattern that seemed to repeat with remarkable consistency throughout the brain: by distributing complex behavior across a large network of simple elements, the connections between which can change over time, we can accomplish virtually limitless tasks, all while continually learning new ones, even late in life.

The complexity of the human brain dwarfs that of anything else in the known universe, but it's almost belied by the sheer elegance of its construction. In contrast to what lies beneath the hood of a car or inside a cell phone, the brain isn't an assembly of cleanly distinguished components—at least not in a form any human designer would consider intuitive. Instead, one finds a web of nearly 100 billion neurons—tiny, finely focused units of electrochemical transmission—connecting with one another in vast networks. And although similar concepts govern the behavior of those neurons across the brain—at least at the level of McCulloch and Pitts's model—the arrangement and location of the *networks* they form can contribute to challenges as diverse as seeing, hearing, walking, or even thinking in the abstract. Moreover, the structure of these networks is almost entirely *learned*, or at least refined, long after the brain's initial formation in utero. It's why, although our gray matter may appear anatomically indistinguishable, our personalities, skills, and memories are unique.

With such a clear model in hand, it was only a matter of time before advances in technology would catch up with the curiosity of the research community. One such moment came in 1958, when a psychology researcher at the Cornell Aeronautical Laboratory named Frank Rosenblatt developed a mechanical neuron he called the "perceptron." Although his ideas were simple enough in concept, Rosenblatt pursued them in an era that was still largely predigital. Blending his background in psychology with an understanding of electrical and mechanical engineering, he labored for months to turn a mathematical model into a functional, real-world device.

Even more audacious was the fact that Rosenblatt's work wasn't just an implementation of the ideas of McCulloch and Pitts. It incorporated a complementary hypothesis from Harvard psychologist B. F. Skinner as well, extending the basic model of the neuron with the notion that certain inputs tend to exert greater influence over its behavior than others, analogous to the way readers of the news might develop varying levels of trust and skepticism toward the publications they read. When those influences are allowed to change over time, growing stronger or weaker in response to success or failure in completing a task, a network of neurons can, in essence, learn.

Rosenblatt applied this principle to an array of four hundred light sensors arranged in the form of a 20-by-20-pixel camera. By wiring the output of each sensor into the perceptron, it could learn to identify visual patterns, such as shapes drawn on index cards held before it. Because the initial influence of each sensor was randomly set, the system's attempts at classifying what it saw started out random as well. In response, Rosenblatt, serving as the perceptron's teacher, used a switch to tell it when its behavior was correct or incorrect. This allowed the system to determine how the input of each sensor contributed to its answer and strengthen or weaken its influence accordingly. As the process was repeated, the perceptron incrementally arrived at a reliable ability to tell one shape from another.

Rosenblatt's perceptron was heralded as a significant step toward re-creating the rudiments of cognition in machines, and the research community explored his work eagerly. But the excitement dissipated as the perceptron's limits came into focus, with researchers questioning the scope of problems they could solve, even theoretically, and the technology of the day limiting experimentation to only the simplest implementations.

Interestingly, it was Marvin Minsky, a founding organizer of the Dartmouth summer project, who became one of the perceptron's best-remembered critics with the publication in 1969 of *Perceptrons*, coauthored with fellow computer science pioneer Seymour Papert. While acknowledging the perceptron's elegance, the book was a full-throated critique as well, lamenting the lack of rigorous theory underlying its design and enumerating weaknesses that appeared to preclude its use in all but the narrowest applications. Although few regarded Minsky's arguments as the final word on the matter, and many of his contemporaries offered rebuttals, the damage had been done. Perceptrons in particular, and machine learning in general, would be condemned to the hinterlands of AI for more than a decade to come.

Communication was nearly impossible in the kitchen. The noise was so intense that even shouts weren't guaranteed to register, and, although I'd been hired by a Mandarin-speaking manager, the cooks, largely refugees, spoke only Cantonese, a dialect I could neither speak nor understand. Being new, clumsy, and prone to getting in the way, I tucked myself into a corner and tried to tune out the almost theatrical chaos: blaring fans, sizzling woks, and metal edges of all kinds clunking and scraping against one another. Open flames lit up the entire room with flashes of pure orange while jets of water ricocheted off pots and pans.

With a grunt-like *"Hey!"* and a gesture in my direction, a cook hurriedly placed a completed order in front of me. *Here we go*, I thought. Working as fast as I could, I wrapped the boxes in a to-go bag, threw in napkins, utensils, and the appropriate number of fortune cookies and soy sauce packets, then tied the handles into a knot. Cradling the bag with both arms, I took a breath and slipped out of the kitchen into the dining room. My hurried steps accelerated, gradually at first, until my anxiousness got the best of me and my stride picked up.

"Fei-Fei!" I heard the manager snap under his breath.

I stopped immediately and sighed, realizing what I'd done.

"How many times have I told you? *Do not run in the dining area.* It's your job to get orders to the front desk, not to annoy our customers. Don't make me say it again." *Dammit.* I nodded, stammered through an apology, and walked the bag the rest of the way with measured, deliberate steps.

The most comforting reminder of home came in the form of our monthly calls to my grandparents. I missed them more than anyone or anything else, and hearing their voices instantly pushed my troubles aside. But the long-distance rates were eye-watering and branded each conversation with an urgency I found cruel. It felt obscene to have to count the minutes we spent with people we loved so much, and my heart broke every time I heard the pace of my mother's words picking up as the limit approached. After a few months I'd had enough. There were certain indignities I simply refused to accept. If money was the only way to loosen up our strictures, I resolved to earn some myself.

The classifieds had pointed me in the direction of my first job, at a narrow, dimly lit Chinese restaurant buried in a strip mall. It was an off-the-books position, free from the prying eyes of labor laws and New Jersey's minimum wage, and the terms reflected it: two dollars an hour for twelve hours a day when school wasn't in session, from 11 a.m. to 11 p.m. The surrounding neighborhood—sketchy, the locals warned me—felt intimidating by the time darkness fell. I was strongly advised to get a ride home each night, and did so without exception.

The instability of part-time work encouraged me to seek out other jobs as well, and the classifieds continued to deliver. Throughout my high school career I juggled time spent at the restaurant with weekly rounds as a housekeeper, a job that paid better but offered fewer hours, and a dog walker, which was perhaps my least lucrative but most enjoyable venture—and one my father was particularly excited about.

Securing rides in and out of dangerous parts of town was easy enough as long as I kept a schedule. And while the pay was consistently low, I had no employment history to compare it to, and it was amazing how much difference even a pittance made in our lives. The long hours were tolerable as well; it just meant that much more cash for the family.

What made the work draining was the uncertainty that hangs over the immigrant experience. I was surrounded by disciplined, hard-working people, all of whom had stories like mine, but none who'd escaped the cycle of scarcity and menial labor to which we seemed consigned. We'd come to this country in the hopes of pursuing opportunities that didn't exist elsewhere, but I couldn't see a path leading anywhere near them.

As demoralizing as our circumstances could be, however, the lack of encouragement within our community was often worse. This was especially apparent at work, where the pressure to keep our heads above water conditioned us to view any deviation from the norm with an abrasive skepticism. I learned this firsthand at the restaurant, where I dedicated the lone break in my shift each afternoon to revisiting the Chinese translations of Western classics my mother shared with me. I was still drawn in by the richness of the prose, even then—*especially* then, in fact, as a struggling English speaker desperate to regain confidence expressing herself—and the turning of each page brought me back to a time when my place in the world felt more certain.

Or it did, at least, until my manager insisted rather bluntly that I was wasting time that could be better spent cleaning the bathroom. Looking back, I don't believe it was his intent to condescend—he was a fellow immigrant himself—but it was another discouraging reminder that the imaginations of people like us were superfluous in our new lives.

Still, the effort paid off. We opened a bank account and began a weekly ritual of taking my earnings—always cash, of course—to the teller for a deposit, widening a slim but welcome margin of freedom. For the first time, we could save a little each month. Grocery shopping was slightly less constrained. And most important, my mother enjoyed a measure of restored dignity when calling home. It was a reward I could hear in her voice; her conversations with my grandparents, while still brief, bore traces of the unhurried tone I remembered from their dinner table in Chengdu.

The history of science is often circuitous, ironic, and harsh. Ideas are discovered, lost, and rediscovered. Paradigms treated as bedrock for generations are overturned, sometimes overnight, often by observations of such apparent simplicity that they're overlooked by even a field's most thoughtful luminaries—setting the stage for an outsider to change everything. But it's this lurching rhythm, equally prone to harmony and dissonance, that makes the pursuit such a dramatic one.

Fittingly, the insight that would explain why the perceptron never quite delivered on its hype—and how its successors could—occurred just as Rosenblatt was developing it, but by researchers in a different field. In 1959, neurophysiologists David Hubel and Torsten Wiesel conducted an experiment at Harvard that yielded a seminal glimpse into the mammalian brain—specifically, the visual cortex of a cat. By projecting drawings of basic shapes onto a wall in a dark room, the researchers could control precisely what the cat saw—lines, gaps, and other simple details—and scrutinize the way its neurons fired in response.

Hubel and Wiesel's epiphany was that perception doesn't occur in a single layer of neurons, but across many, organized in a hierarchy that begins with the recognition of superficial details and ends with complex, high-level awareness. For example, the first layers of neurons might notice fine visual features like edges oriented at certain angles, a distinct texture, or a splash of color, with each focused on a narrow region of the overall scene known as a "receptive field." Taken on their own, these glimmers mean very little. But when passed to the next layer, they're integrated into more complex shapes and features, covering ever-broader receptive fields, like puzzle pieces snapping together to reveal larger fragments of a picture.

Eventually, these progressively integrated details are passed to the final layers, at which point we perceive meaningful things like faces, objects, locations, and the like. And because the brain's networked architecture allows these myriad steps to unfold at the same time, in parallel, our experience is one of uninterrupted, vibrant awareness. Hubel and Wiesel's work transformed the way we think about sensory perception, earning the duo a Nobel Prize in 1981.

Although seemingly tailor-made for early AI hopefuls in search of a model to follow, Hubel and Wiesel's discovery took years to reach that world—during which time Rosenblatt's life would be cut short in a boating accident at age forty-three. But its arrival in 1980 was transformative. Kunihiko Fukushima, a Japanese researcher working at NHK Broadcasting Science Research Laboratories in Tokyo, developed an algorithm consisting of multiple perceptrons—now implemented in software—stacked in a connected hierarchy. Because each layer was sensitive to slightly more sophisticated patterns than the one beneath it, the algorithm as a whole could recognize multiple levels of detail, as well as the relationships between them.

The result, which he called the "neocognitron," was especially resilient and tolerant of aberrations in its input, allowing it to achieve breakthrough performance on the accurate interpretation of handwriting—a particularly stubborn problem due to its extreme irregularity and diversity of styles.

As is so often the case in science, however, the success of the neocognitron merely revealed a new obstacle. Although the algorithm was powerful and versatile, its architecture was so complex that it couldn't be practically trained using the methods developed for its simpler predecessors, which lacked the neocognition's densely connected inner layers. Progress once again stalled until, just a few years later, the next piece of the machine learning puzzle fell into place.

In 1986, a small group of researchers led by UC San Diego professor David E. Rumelhart published a letter in the scientific journal *Nature* presenting a technique that made it possible for algorithms like the neocognitron to effectively learn. They called it "backpropagation," named for its defining feature: a cascading effect in which each instance of training—specifically, the degree to which a network's response to a given stimulus is correct or incorrect—ripples from one end to the other, layer by layer.

What truly made backpropagation profound, however, were the changes that would emerge within the network's structure over time.

As the network was exposed to more and more examples, such as a collection of photographs or audio waveforms, the connections between its neurons were reshaped by what it saw, bearing their imprints with increasing detail. Like canyon walls carved by centuries of a flowing river, the network came to *represent* the features it was being trained to recognize. After years of struggling, neural networks were suddenly learning at a scale never before possible, with unprecedented fidelity, heralding a true turning point.

Although Rumelhart was the lead researcher, it was Geoff Hinton, one of his two coauthors, who would become the figure most associated with backpropagation. Hinton, then a professor at Carnegie Mellon University, was captivated from an early age by the enigma of intelligence and had dedicated his career to exploring new methods for reproducing it. He worked tirelessly, exploring an array of novel approaches to machine learning and contributing greatly to a period that would prove to be an early renaissance for the field. It was a time of steadily growing networks, bearing more layers and intricately connected neurons, trained with an increasingly refined set of techniques. Finally, Yann LeCun, one of Hinton's first students, famously applied it all to an impressively practical task: reading handwritten ZIP codes. In less than a decade, machine learning had progressed from a tenuous dream to a triumph in the real world.

My father was studying everything in sight, and I found myself studying him. There was a look of wonderment on his face that must have seemed out of place—a disproportionate show of enthusiasm given our surroundings. It was a look I'd known since our earliest trips to the wilderness together, but even I was surprised to see it in a place like this. It was a Sunday afternoon, and we were hours into a trip dedicated to my father's favorite pastime since coming to this country: garage sales.

Every weekend we'd drive miles and miles in search of a stranger's driveway or front lawn, often hitting more than one in a single trip. The fact that we always arrived at some variation of the same scene never seemed to bother him. Stacks of outdated magazines and decades-old paperbacks, covers faded and creased. Hi-fi speakers with cloth grilles. A child's recently outgrown roller skates. Ancient board games. Action figures. Disused suitcases. Worn but still perfectly usable pots and pans. Camping equipment well past its heyday. Cardboard boxes filled with Atari game cartridges. VCRs and stacks of VHS movies. Exercise equipment. To my father, it was a new kind of wilderness, and it called out to be explored.

Garage sales were also among the few venues where I saw my father put his nearly nonexistent English skills to use, as he was just comfortable enough with the language to carry out a purchase and, on occasion, even haggle a bit. I was glad he had some way of participating, but I knew his struggles with English were much more than a practical setback. Conversation was an art form to him, and he took pride in his skill; he'd loved Chinese wordplay since long before the day he named me, and he often used it as a way to express both humor and affection. Knowing my father's mind for diction, I found it especially hard to see him limited to such basic utterances. But his excitement was contagious, and in the time it took him to move on to another card table display, I'd forgotten about anything other than how pleased he seemed.

A particularly amusing quirk was his obsession with anything of Italian origin, especially leather goods. His English skills made it difficult to distinguish an Italian-sounding brand name from any other, but he'd developed hawk eyes for spotting three tantalizing words: MADE IN ITALY. It added the elements of a treasure hunt to an otherwise aimless pursuit, and it was as baffling as it was endearing to see his eyes light up over secondhand items that often appeared to be worth less than the gas money we'd spent on the drive over simply because of their association with a Mediterranean country he'd never visited. But I had obsessions of my own, and I didn't begrudge him his.

This was my father's true talent—not engineering, or camera repair, or even puns. He had a virtuosity for unearthing the happiness waiting to be discovered in any situation, no matter how mundane. Here we were, spurred by ideology to travel across the world, plunged into poverty, and now faced with a daily struggle to survive. But you wouldn't know any of that to look at him, examining some family's ski goggles or coffee maker with a contentment so pure I could feel it myself, almost forgetting everything else.

I even sensed a kind of latent intellectual journey. Just as he did back home, he sought to build an understanding of his surroundings one detail at a time, relishing each and adding it to an ever-growing database of trivialities he kept in the back of his mind. So while bargains may have been a vital part of our survival as a family, I quickly realized that saving money wasn't all that motivated these outings. It was as if he wanted to *catalog* the world—not by any formal means, and not even for any particular reason, but simply because he found joy in the process.

As an immigrant, it's easy to feel as if all of one's problems are due to incursions from the outside world. But as was the case in China, and as is the case with just about any family anywhere on Earth, our greatest challenges often came from within.

I worried most about my mother, who seemed to be deteriorating before our eyes. Whatever malaise had befallen her during our last years in China was worsening here in America, no doubt exacerbated by the pressures of her new life. As grating as a day spent behind a cash register must have been, she came home in a fog of exhaustion far heavier than her shift could explain.

Then, when it seemed like life couldn't get any more complicated, my father lost his job—although it'd probably be more accurate to say he was fired. I never heard the full story, but I was able to infer that he wound up in a disagreement with the camera shop owner that escalated to a shouting match and, finally, an invitation to leave and never come back. The particulars didn't matter, of course; for a family barely making ends meet to begin with, this was existential.

"What page was that on? The problem you just mentioned."

"Page 134. Next to the yellow box, at the bottom."

"Ah, I see it now. Thank you."

I was studying with three other English-as-a-second-language students—"ESL," as we were generally known—a girl from Taiwan, a boy from Northern China, and a boy from South Korea. It was, to some extent, a relief to sit with a group of peers I could relate to better than I could to anyone else, but it was hard not to feel as if we were a novelty on display for the rest of the students in the library, especially when a sentence or two slipped out in one of our native languages.

The bell rang. We pushed our papers and books into our backpacks, slung them over our shoulders, and made our way out as the crowd compressed itself into the double-door exit. It was a typical crush of hurried students, shoulder to shoulder, elbow to elbow, but some invisible line was crossed that afternoon. One of the ESL boys inadvertently made the slightest bit of physical contact with an American student—stepped on a toe, scraped against a backpack zipper, or did something else so fleeting none of us saw it. But whatever it was, it mattered.

The reaction was merciless and immediate. The ESL boy was dragged through the exit and pushed to the floor of the hallway in a split second of fury, the flow of students instinctively forming a clearing around the commotion. Then, in yet another blur, I noticed the single aggressor had somehow multiplied; two boys were now shouting insults while kicking relentlessly, their target curled up, desperately trying to protect his head as blood poured from his nose and smeared across the floor.

My thoughts came too quickly to categorize them. I was overcome with a feeling of empathy so intense it turned my stomach, but also a helplessness that stopped me dead. I was scared witless, both for the boy on the ground and, for all I knew, myself; maybe the rest of the study group would be next. I wanted to say something, even if it was nothing more than a single-word plea for the violence to stop, but I noticed something strange: in the confusion of the moment, I didn't know which language to use.

My sense of helplessness was shared by my parents upon my return home that evening, and perhaps to an even greater degree. Although their revulsion was as obvious as my own, I could sense that the isolation of their lives here only reinforced the powerlessness we all felt in the face of something as immediate as the threat of violence. Lacking the English skills for even something as perfunctory as a call to the school principal, they had little recourse beyond living with the fear that on top of everything else, the safety of their child couldn't be taken for granted.

We didn't see our friend for weeks after the beating. When he finally returned, after what must have been an especially lonely convalescence recovering from a broken nose and concussion, it was immediately clear that the boy we knew was gone. The cheer and humor that had defined him, apparent even through his broken English, had been replaced by a spirit so withdrawn he might as well have been a different person. As brutal as the assault had been in the moment—the pain, the humiliation, the sheer bodily violation of it all—it was this transformation that felt most dehumanizing: the theft of something innate.

The rest of us were changed as well. Our once loose-knit ESL clique grew tighter, drawn together less by camaraderie than by the nervous air we now breathed. It saturated us. For all my struggles to adapt, the question of physical safety had never crossed my mind. Now, I was afraid to venture to the bathroom or cafeteria alone, to say nothing of the images invoked by the sight of the library's double doors.

And all this just as I was beginning to bond with my new environment. Although I continued to gravitate toward math and physics as a Parsippany student, a third subject was competing unexpectedly for my interest: American history. The more I learned, the more the story of the founding of the country reminded me of what I loved most about physics. Here was another unlikely band of thinkers coming together to contribute a radical idea to the world well before its time. And in the case of Benjamin Franklin, himself a practicing scientist, the comparison was more than merely metaphorical.

Perhaps most important, I began to appreciate how uncannily the spirit of documents like the Bill of Rights echoed the phrases I heard my mother whisper in the months leading up to my father's departure in 1989. These ideals, I began to realize, were why we'd done all this.

I retreated even further into my studies, desperate for some mix of distraction and encouragement to stabilize my thoughts. I was in a hurry to regain even a fraction of the scholastic footing I enjoyed in China, but language was a barrier that obstructed me at every turn. Frustration rose as I trudged through each assignment at an excruciating pace, rarely making it to the end of a sentence without having to appeal to a dictionary. I gradually rebuilt a vocabulary of familiar concepts, as terms like "velocity," "acceleration," "angular," "force," and "potential" revealed themselves to me anew. But none of it came easily. By the time I climbed into bed each night, finally through with the day's assignments, it was the exhaustion of drudgery, not of accomplishment, that weighed on me. To an ESL student, every class is an English class.

An even more frustrating setback was afflicting my math studies in particular, and I had to admit language didn't offer an excuse. Again and again I found myself making purely numeric mistakes— genuinely baffling ones, with no apparent pattern to learn from. Thankfully, I wasn't the only one who noticed, and my teacher asked me to stay after class to discuss the issue. It was obvious that *something* was wrong, but even he found my performance more confusing than concerning.

"Do you mind if I take a look at your calculator?" he asked. I placed it on the desk and watched him prod at its buttons.

"A-*ha*!" he exclaimed. "Tangent! Fei-Fei, it's the *tangent* button! See?"

He set his own calculator next to mine to demonstrate. Sure enough, despite entering the same input on both, my TAN button produced a wildly different output.

"You've been working with a broken calculator all this time! That's gotta be a relief to hear, huh? Hey, do you mind if I ask where this thing came from?"

Suddenly, it all made sense. As soon as he asked the question, I knew why the answer mattered.

"Um, garage sale," I murmured, a bit self-consciously and struggling to remember the exact English term.

"Huh," he replied. I got the impression it wasn't the answer he was expecting. "Well, we'll see about getting you set up with a loaner, okay?"

With some measure of self-assurance gradually reemerging, life as a whole became easier to navigate. My parents and I continued to spend most of our free moments together, for better or worse, running errands, cleaning, and occasionally gathering on the couch to watch a rented cassette of something vaguely recognizable, like a Taiwanese sitcom. Things were far from perfect, and my mother remained in the grips of a subtle but worsening affliction we still didn't understand, but stability appeared to be within reach for the first time.

As the months stretched on, we began to make room for a new tradition as well, dedicating some of our weekend time to exploring the state, a routine that once brought us to the campus of Princeton University, located a bit more than an hour south. Without any awareness of its history or pedigree, I was impressed by its landscaping and architecture but found little else of interest. That is, until I came across a bronze bust with a familiar face. I stopped immediately. The world seemed to disappear around me as I recognized whom I was looking at. My breath suddenly shallow, I read the inscription running down the face of its tall marble pedestal:

Born in Ulm, Germany, on March 14, 1879, Albert Einstein became a resident of Princeton in 1933, residing on Mercer Street until his death in 1955.

Before becoming a Professor at the Institute for Advanced Study, Einstein had already become famous for his Special Theory of Relativity in 1905 and General Theory of Relativity in 1915–1916, both of which explained fundamental laws of the universe. His name became synonymous with genius.

A Nobel Laureate in physics, a philosopher, a humanitarian, an educator, and an immigrant, Albert Einstein left an indelible mark on the world and expressed tremendous appreciation for Princeton.

I practically shivered with each word, as if a fever were breaking. I reread the inscription, then reread it again. It was a sudden reminder of something I'd forgotten after spending so much of my waking life fixated on survival: physics. My passion for the subject had been drained of its color, even as I studied it in school, reduced to one of countless boxes to be checked in the service of enduring each new day. But face-to-face with a monument to my greatest hero, I could feel it returning.

I thought about the Astor House in Shanghai, and that flicker of optimism I'd felt before boarding the plane that put thousands of miles between me and most everything I cared about. Maybe I was right. Maybe it *had* been a good omen all along, just delayed. The curiosity I'd felt since childhood may have been fazed by its new surroundings, but it wasn't gone.

I had something to chase again.

"You know, there are a lot of smart kids in this class."

Mr. Sabella had a reputation for sternness, made instantly manifest by his towering height and curt tone, but it wasn't the reaction I expected as I stood at the edge of his desk. My command of English still left something to be desired, but I could tell I was being written off, and rather rudely, it seemed.

My junior year in high school was also my second year in America, and its arrival was accompanied by a renewed energy to prove myself in math and physics. It was a natural instinct; grades are a well-established target for immigrants desperate to secure some hope of a future worth wanting. But for me, what had begun as a way to rehabilitate my self-esteem was fast becoming an overcorrection. The instability that undergirded my life outside school was turning the simple goal of scholastic success into a fixation.

I'd just taken my first math test of the year, and although I retained some confidence in my ability to solve the purely numeric portion, there were word problems as well, and I wasn't as sure of my interpretation of the text. I could feel the blood pumping in my ears as the papers were passed back. I held my breath as I turned mine over, hoping I'd at least stayed within the 90 percent range of an A-minus. I stared momentarily at the score before sinking into my seat. 89.4.

Frustrated, I took my place among a clutch of students hovering around Mr. Sabella's desk after class. I wasn't looking for favors—even then I knew that rounding up a score for my ego's sake wouldn't change anything—but I'd hoped some opportunity for extra credit might exist. The threshold between As and all other grades had taken on religious gravity for me, and I just wanted a chance to push myself above it. Unfortunately for me, Mr. Sabella was in no mood to offer indulgences that day.

I left the room dissatisfied, but my interpretation softened as I replayed his words in my head over the course of the afternoon. Whereas teachers in Chengdu seemed to want little more than for me to blend in, I began to sense Mr. Sabella was challenging me in a different way. He wanted me to stand out. *No one owes you anything*, he seemed to be saying. *If you want an A so badly, you can work harder for it next time.* I can't pretend I was ready to receive that kind of wisdom, but I had to acknowledge, reluctantly, that there was probably something to it.

Mr. Sabella was no ordinary teacher. He held the most advanced degrees in the department, earning him a dedicated office and the title of head math instructor. And he was a true connoisseur of the discipline, with a sprawling collection of textbooks and reference volumes that created a rainbow of colored spines facing outward from every wall. Like many of his students, I began visiting his office after school, asking questions and getting a head start on homework. It soon became a daily habit.

Unofficially christened "the Math Lab," the office became a refuge. As days became weeks and weeks became months, his tutoring helped compensate for the obstacle of having to juggle math while decrypting a new language at the same time. And with the library assault still replaying in my head on occasion, it was a place in which I truly felt safe. It was also a chance to rediscover the simple joy of conversation, a luxury in short supply as a nerdy immigrant teenager.

Ironically, being an ESL student made it easy for me to speak up. I continued to need so many words and English-language concepts explained that isolated questions became an ongoing dialogue. The more we spoke, the more I realized that he wasn't anything like the teacher I'd overheard dismissing the intellectual capabilities of girls back in China, or the discouraging restaurant boss who'd all but mocked my love for reading. He could be terse and abrasive, but he never wrote me off the way others had. He was challenging me, and it was working.

We also had much more in common than a love for numbers. On the way out of his class one day, I asked what I thought was a simple question:

"Mr. Sabella, can you recommend some books for me?"

"You mean math books?"

"No, any kind. Reading helps my English."

I could tell he was pleased by the request. Mr. Sabella was the kind of guy who had a lot to say when given the green light. He thought for a moment, then smiled.

"Do you know who Arthur C. Clarke is? He's one of my favorite science fiction authors. I think you might like him, too."

"Ah, science fiction! Yes! I also love . . . uh . . ."

I attempted to pronounce the name of an author I'd admired. I knew the resulting mishmash of Anglo-Saxon syllables—something like *"Roov Vannah"*—wasn't conveying what I meant.

"Um, 'Roov,' uh . . . ?" he asked, cocking his head and furrowing his brow but politely trying to work out what I was getting at.

"You know, uh, the book about thousands of, um, kilometers? Um, under the ocean."

Mr. Sabella's mulling continued for a moment, then seemed to stop as a realization struck.

"Fei-Fei, do you mean *Jules Verne*?"

"Yes! Yes! *Juh-les* . . . uh . . . *Vern-ah*," I repeated, clumsily, with a laugh. "I cannot pronounce his name, but I love his books!"

His eyes lit up. As I'd later learn, Mr. Sabella was a lifelong sci-fi buff, and a Jules Verne fan in particular.

"Do you know any other Western authors?"

"Yes, many! I love Mark . . . uh, Tah-wain, Jack-ah London, oh, and Heming-away, and Dickens, and . . ." For some reason I fared better pronouncing these names.

"Wait, wait, wait—you're telling me you've already read all these?"

"Not in English. Chinese translations. My mother shared these books with me in China."

He seemed caught off guard, then fell back into his chair, chuckling in pure, stunned delight. I believe it was the first moment an American had ever seen me as more than a Chinese-speaking immigrant. Our conversations grew more and more expansive, and less formal. He looked past my nationality, my struggles with language, and even my potential as a student, to see a kid, lonely and struggling to fit in, but eager to express herself. Over time, I looked past his status as a teacher and saw an unexpected friend.

In the months that followed, my visits to Mr. Sabella's office became the focal point of my day. He always had something thought-provoking ready to discuss, continued to share book suggestions—I took him up on exploring Clarke, although I still found the language difficult—and even began asking me for titles of my own. As my reading expanded, so did his; on my recommendation, he read through Chinese classics like *Dream of the Red Chamber*, *Romance of the Three Kingdoms*, and *Journey to the West*. But none of it was a distraction from my studies. If anything, by helping me to think more holistically, he reminded me that there's joy to be found in learning. He put me back on the path toward being a complete student. Along the way, my grades took care of themselves.

I wasn't the only student who visited the Math Lab for help after class, but I soon became its most frequent visitor, and Mr. Sabella seemed to respect my appetite for learning. Likewise, I appreciated his patience; earning an immigrant's trust can be a delicate task, but his dedication won me over. Week after week, the lectures became more abstract and problem sets more challenging—tangent vectors, arc length, partial derivatives, the chain rule—but I felt a freedom to confide in him as well, in ways I'd never thought possible with an American. He was the first person I opened up to about my family's financial struggles or my teenage annoyances with my parents. Over time, he seemed to grow naturally into a role that combined teacher, guidance counselor, and friend. It was an outlet I'd lived without for too long.

In many ways, he provided what felt like a missing piece in my relationships with both of my parents. My mother had always inspired me, but she didn't actually share my interests when it came to math and physics, and the challenges of her declining health complicated our bond as the years went by. And while my father's influence was nearest to my heart—he was the first to encourage my curiosity about the natural world, and my introduction to physics—I had to acknowledge I'd long since outgrown his example. Mr. Sabella saw something in me that no one else did—a potential I didn't quite realize myself—and had the expertise to help me foster it.

Interestingly, my presence seemed to have a similarly disarming effect, and I began to learn more about him, too. I was surprised to discover that for someone who seemed so comfortable in his own skin, and so well-established in the American order of things, Mr. Sabella had grown up without something that I'd always taken for granted: the support of his family. The child of Italian immigrants who mocked his bookish disposition and love for science fiction, he felt like an outcast even among his own siblings. Over time, it pushed him to seek a kind of refuge in his thoughts, retreating further and further into the solitary world of his intellect. We were alike, if more in spirit than in detail.

Like the rest of my peers, I spent my senior year consumed with thoughts of graduation, although my sights were set more on state schools and community college than on anything close to the Ivy League. But there was one top-tier school I couldn't stop thinking about: Princeton. Fate had brought me to New Jersey, an hour's drive from a place Einstein called home, and my day trip to the campus still replayed often in my mind. As silly as it was to imagine the same family that scraped by with garage sale supplies and broken calculators suddenly managing an Ivy League tuition, I couldn't resist applying, symbolic as the gesture was. Even that felt special.

When the response arrived on a particularly chilly December afternoon, however, it didn't appear that money would be my obstacle in attending. I'd stopped to pick up the mail after school, digging through a mound of dirty snow that had all but buried the mailbox, when I stopped short and drew a sharp breath. Peering inside, I instantly recognized the insignia on the envelope at the very top of the pile. An orange and black shield. *Princeton.* I knew what to expect; college acceptance letters were mailed in thick, heavy packages full of orientation material and follow-up instructions for incoming students. It was clear that the envelope in my mailbox was the other kind.

I didn't have to read it to know what their decision was, but I figured I'd close the chapter once and for all. Unceremoniously, I tore open the envelope. The first word that caught my eye, confusingly, was "Yes!"—printed on its own in bold type. It took a bit more scanning to make sense of what I was reading; it appeared my application was included in the early admissions cycle, during which *all* replies are sent in thin envelopes. If I was reading it right—and I was far from sure I was—I'd gotten in.

The surprises didn't end there. Also included was a document entitled "Financial Aid," written with a level of legal detail for which my ESL reading skills weren't quite ready. I took the letter with me to school the next day, and showed it to Mr. Sabella . . . who didn't seem to understand it, either. He paused, squinting and looking closer at the page. I watched the expression on his face change as he read further, until he finally looked up, took a breath, and asked if he could hold on to it for a bit.

"I *think* I know what this means," he said, "but I want to be sure."

I was taken aback. How could it be that *he* was as confused as I was?

Mr. Sabella suggested we take it to the principal for a third opinion. Right on cue, the letter seemed to have the same effect on him, at least at first. He reacted with a similarly quizzical look, followed by a faraway stare aimed at neither of us as he sank into his seat. Then, after a moment of silence, he explained that I'd indeed been accepted, but that there was more. Apparently, my admission included something extra: a nearly full scholarship.

It would take years for the gravity of this moment to fully register with me, and even with my parents. But despite my mother's steely demeanor upon hearing the news, I could tell how much it meant to her. Every milestone of her life had been a reminder that she was on the wrong side of divides she had no hope of bridging, conditioning her over decades to feign a confidence I knew she never truly felt. Now, for the first time, maybe ever, she had reason to believe there might be more to the story. For her, after everything she'd gambled, it was a relief I don't think I'll ever fully appreciate.

The final months of my senior year were probably the first time I'd felt anything resembling self-confidence since I'd arrived in America. Mr. Sabella's mentorship helped me rediscover a sense of dignity and reminded me that friendship—trust—was possible for outsiders, too. I even got to know his wife, Jean. They were both strikingly tall and taught high school math, but where he was guarded and pensive, she was outgoing and joyously talkative. He'd apparently taken to bringing up our after-school conversations at home, regularly, prompting her to invite me to join them for dinner as the year came to a close. It was my first glimpse of family life in suburban America.

Intellectually, I remained as committed to math and physics as ever—they were passions first and college prerequisites second, after all—but after three years of working around the clock on school, work, and a struggle with English I was only just beginning to overcome, slowing down felt right for the first time, maybe in my entire life. It was a bittersweet peace, a moment of welcome calm, but with it came the unsettling realization that I couldn't be Mr. Sabella's protégé forever. I wondered if I'd ever see him again once I graduated.

As if he knew the thought had crossed my mind, he approached me one day, uncharacteristically timid. It was a side of him I rarely saw: not outwardly nervous per se, but unusually long-winded, as if he knew what he wanted to say but couldn't quite bring himself to get the words out. He was just curious—you know, if it wasn't too big a deal or anything—did I maybe want to stay in touch with him and his family after the school year ended?

I couldn't help but laugh. It was a hard thing to answer casually. What he clearly hadn't realized is that he'd become my closest, deepest, and, I suppose, *only* American friend—and that the Sabellas already felt like my American family. The question wasn't whether I wanted to stay in touch. It was how I'd possibly survive in this country without him in my life.

Streams of wind hissed between branches, drawing whispered consonants from brittle leaves. Pale cement paths sliced green lawns into polygonal fragments. Walls of brown brick kept a silent watch, their surfaces pockmarked by centuries of history. And above it all, the sky was so clear I still found it hard to believe it was real at times. There were moments on autumn afternoons like this that Princeton seemed like something I'd dreamt. I had to remind myself—sometimes repeatedly—that I wasn't merely a visitor in this place.

I'd spent an idyllic childhood in China's middle class, an adolescence in American poverty, learned a second language—more or less, anyway—and, with my recent acquisition of a green card, taken a step toward citizenship. At the same time, I'd lived in an immigrant community full of bright, hardworking people who'd never climbed a rung on the ladder of economic fortune. And I'd had to watch, helplessly, as a fellow student was beaten senseless for little more than the crime of not fitting in—a sight I've never been able to unsee.

These were dark moments, but they made me all the more appreciative for the wealth of humanity I discovered along the way. A community that offered a place, however modest, for an immigrant family to build a life. Teachers who encouraged a student who barely spoke

English, one of whom made her struggles his personal priority. An Ivy League school that offered her an education. And a country that, alien as it seemed, was beginning to feel knowable. Even my language skills, though still a work in progress, had turned a corner. I had a voice again. It was rough around the edges, but it was mine. If I were to dedicate my life to science, whatever form that might take, it would be by the grace of the people I'd met during my lowest and most confusing days. More and more, I was feeling something I hadn't in a long time: I was grateful.

Whatever my family's story would be in the end, it was not yet written. We were still poor, we were still outsiders, and nothing about our future felt certain. But we were no longer alone.

4

DISCOVERING THE MIND

The lab was entirely dark, drawing all eyes to the glow of a looping sixteen-second black-and-white video clip projected on the wall. Most of those eyes were human, but two of them—the two most important—belonged to an anesthetized cat on the table before us, an array of electrodes delicately probing its brain. Completing the scene was a web of wires, a dimly lit tangle of metallic streaks connecting the electrodes to an amplifier that translated spikes of activity in the cat's visual cortex—the part of its brain dedicated to its sense of sight—into an audio signal. As the video continued to play, over and over for its feline audience of one, crackling noises erupted from a pair of loudspeakers, filling the room with an erratic, aural texture.

What the cat saw, we *heard*.

The year was 1997, and although I'd entered that lab as a physics undergrad—a lowly sophomore, to be precise—I could feel something changing within me as the experiment unfolded. I was face-to-face with a mystery that somehow seemed bigger than the cosmos itself, yet infinitely more delicate. In just a few short years, it would swallow me whole.

* * *

"Well? How's life as a college student?"

It was my first call to Mr. Sabella since starting Princeton.

"Where do I even begin? The campus is like something out of a dream, there are more meal options in the cafeteria than I think I've ever seen in my life, and—oh! *oh!*—I have a *roommate*! But really, you wouldn't believe what they served for lunch today."

"So your first impressions are pretty much all . . . food-related?" He laughed. "What about the dorm?"

"It's funny—I heard so many people complaining about how small the freshman quarters are. Honestly, my room might be a couple of square feet bigger than our place in Parsippany."

I'd arrived in a world that barely seemed real. For what must have been twenty minutes, Mr. Sabella listened patiently as I prattled on about the many marvels of the Ivy League experience—at least, those I'd been exposed to over the course of my first five days—from genuine luxuries like the campus's extensive art collection to conveniences more likely to impress those of us attending on the graces of financial aid, like the fact that our dorms were assigned individual phones and mailboxes.

There was also the sheer scientific magic of the place. On the walk to my very first biology seminar, I passed the door to a laboratory with a glass pane I could have mistaken for a window into my daydreams: researchers scurrying about in goggles and white lab coats, assistants ferrying samples to and from equipment so sophisticated it looked like something out of a movie, and walls covered in posters summarizing results and findings.

There was so much to take in, but it was the campus's many libraries that truly captured my heart. The flagship Firestone Library towered above them all, both in stature and in spirit, bearing a scale and beauty that simply beggared belief. But it was the basement-level math and physics library that drew me back most often. What it lacked in architectural grandeur it more than made up for in scholarly wonder.

From the students studying around the clock to its impressive collection of texts, I knew I was in the presence of something transcendent. It was home, instantly.

Princeton felt like my first breath of truly fresh air since I'd arrived in America, though one I drew in gradually. As an immigrant, I couldn't shake the feeling that I was expected—obligated, even—to treat my scholarship as an economic lifeline: an entrée into a lucrative field like medicine, finance, or engineering, and thus an escape from life at society's margins. There was no arguing with the logic. The possibility of providing for my parents without compromise was hard to dismiss.

Countering that chorus of pragmatism was a voice inside me, no louder than a whisper but indefatigable, pleading with me to chase the spark of curiosity I'd felt since childhood—studying physics at the school perhaps most central to its modern legacy. It was a purely emotional appeal, impractical to its very core, but there was no escaping its sway. Regardless of what might lie beyond the next four years, I couldn't imagine spending them doing anything else.

My inner voice wasn't my only vote of confidence. Despite the near squalor of my mother's life in America, and the menial work that seemed to have claimed her every waking moment since our arrival, she remained steadfast that my passion for science was not to be ignored. Years of hardship hadn't changed her. She was still the same unsung intellectual who encouraged me to read the classics when I was a girl, modest but immovable, even in the mire of what felt like inescapable poverty. My father, for his part, agreed without hesitation. It was a support that never made sense to anyone but us—certainly not the friends we'd made in Parsippany's community of immigrants, who saw my decision as a wasted lottery ticket—but it was enough.

If I needed more encouragement, I would find it in my surroundings, especially as I took my first steps into a physics lecture hall. It was cavernous, with an impressively high ceiling supported by gently curving rafters. Benches of solid hardwood descended from my place in the doorway toward the spot, like a stage awaiting its performer, where a professor would soon stand. An array of blackboards covered the wall, so much larger than anything I'd seen in high school, still smeared with the ghosts of previous lectures' equations. And gazing down upon it all, windows lit the room with pale columns of natural light.

My heart pounded out a rhythm about twice the pace of my steps as I made my way to an empty seat. Everywhere I looked, I saw students who seemed to know something I didn't. They sat, stood, and conversed as if they owned the place. Finally, just as I found what appeared to be a place to sit, the professor appeared. A hush fell over the hall.

"Welcome to Physics 105: Advanced Mechanics. This will be a demanding course, but for those willing to put in the work, it will be an illuminating one as well." The professor looked the part, with hastily combed gray hair, a tweed coat slung over his chair, and the kind of poise that only comes from decades spent mastering one's craft.

"Some students, I'm told, call it '*death* mechanics,'" he added with a smirk. "I suppose that's a fair summary of the attrition rate."

I sat back in my seat and took a shallow breath, as anxious as I was gleeful.

"Those of you with an interest in history may appreciate the fact that this room—Palmer Hall—was the venue of many of Einstein's lectures during his time here. This very place."

What? I sat up.

"In fact, not far from here is the Institute for Advanced Study, located at 1 Einstein Drive. It's said the location was chosen specifically for him, as he loved to stroll through the surrounding trees, pondering . . . well, the kinds of questions that call for such solitude."

It was almost too much. As if I wasn't already entranced by the school's centuries-old history and soaring Gothic architecture. As if I needed more confirmation that physics was the right choice. As if I wasn't already in love.

Everything around me seemed to further my feeling of enchantment. The scents of textbook pages, brick, and freshly cut grass. The way the instructors paced lazily back and forth before packed halls, cocking their heads casually as they stopped to lean against their desk. The way they wore their sweaters. The way they held their chalk. The lifetimes of knowledge that buttressed each word they spoke. The sparkle as their eyes lit up, even as they delivered lectures they'd surely memorized long before. I'd always felt that my passion had defined me, but these people *lived* theirs—to a degree I'd never imagined.

Particularly memorable was Eric Wieschaus, a professor leading a genetics seminar that exposed freshmen to the bleeding edge of the field. He was an expert among experts, but it was his tone that impressed me most; his voice was soft, even meek, but eternally excited. And he carried himself without a hint of elitism, sporting loose-fitting plaid shirts, shaggy hair, and a bushy mustache, looking more like a carpenter than a scientist. It suggested that even the most complex ideas were something to share, graciously, rather than secrets to hoard. Then, one autumn morning, he outdid himself.

"I really hate to do this, everyone, but I'm afraid that today's lecture will end about thirty minutes early, uh, because . . . well, I guess some of you might have already heard . . ."

A few students looked at one another nervously.

"I got the phone call this morning that Christiane Nüsslein-Volhard, Edward B. Lewis, and I . . . well, we've been awarded the Nobel Prize in Medicine this year."

The collective gasp was palpable, as was the hush that followed.

"Wooo!" shouted a student, breaking the silence, followed by a few claps. In an instant, the applause had spread across the room, eventually reaching a roar.

"Tell us what you did!" another voice added, further cutting the tension and sending a wave of laughter across the room.

"You can be sure I'll be teaching you about it this semester!" Wieschaus answered with a shy smile.

The class replied with a playful groan of disappointment.

"*Weeeellll*, all right," he conceded as the groans turned back to cheers.

"It all began with an attempt at cataloging abnormal phenotypes of *Drosophila*—fruit flies. We were looking for examples associated with the genes that cause fatal complications. But we stumbled upon something we didn't expect. Something big. You see, it turned out that many of these genes are also expressed in humans, and potentially responsible for all sorts of diseases.

"You have to understand," he continued, "this was a *huge* undertaking. We were screening thousands of genes to locate a very, very small subset that led to birth defects in fruit flies, of all things. Not exactly a smart career move, especially in those days. But what can I say? It's easy to be fearless when you're young. I guess it paid off."

Finally, there was a then-obscure astrophysicist named Professor Tyson—Neil deGrasse Tyson, as the world would later know him. His flamboyant teaching style was infectious, made even more potent by the affability that would become his trademark. Once a week, he'd take the train from New York, where he'd recently been appointed director of the Hayden Planetarium, his presence instantly transfixing the room as he walked through the door. He'd then make an almost theatrical show out of his pre-class ritual of getting as comfortable as possible: ceremoniously taking off his jacket, tie, and watch, removing his wallet from his pocket and setting it on the desk, and sometimes even stepping out of his shoes. It was clear he didn't want a single distraction to get between him and the obsession with astrophysics he'd come to share with us.

Particularly memorable was the final lecture of the class. He lowered the lights, projected the now famous photo of the Hubble Telescope's deep field imaging of the distant universe, and spoke to us with a voice so resonant it felt like a call from the depths of the cosmos.

"Take a breath, everyone. Just . . . let this photo wash over you." His words were carefully chosen and softly delivered. "Those tiny flecks of light aren't stars, or even star systems. They're entire *galaxies. Hundreds of thousands* of them. It's a scale our puny brains as individuals can't even process. But thanks to tools like the Hubble, we—as a species— are getting our first glimpses. That's why I'm showing you this image on our last day—because I don't want you to ever forget this feeling. Stay curious. Stay bold. Be forever willing to ask impossible questions. This specular exposure—the Hubble deep field—is a testament to how beautiful the answers can be."

Two worlds were forming. There was real life, in which I continued to worry about my mother's health, our ability to keep up with our finances, and my own status as an outsider (albeit an increasingly for- tunate one). Then there was Princeton. A place I could only describe as a paradise for the intellect.

Bridging the two were Mr. Sabella and Jean. With high school be- hind me, I was free to treat them as I would any other friends (although my mother stuck to a nickname for Mr. Sabella, both affectionate and formal at the same time: *dà hú zi shù xué lǎo shī*—"big bearded math teacher"). As the only adults in my life who'd actually experienced Amer- ican college, they made for invaluable confidants during my first clumsy months. Mr. Sabella and I stayed in touch with weekly phone calls that continued without exception, and visiting his family's home was a wel- come reprieve from a new life that I loved but often found overwhelming.

The Sabella children were growing fast, with the oldest now a teen- ager, and the entire family seemed to bond over a shared love for laugh- ing at my absentmindedness; my tendency to forget my gloves on even the coldest days was a favorite, as was my apparent inability to wear matching socks. But behind the phone calls and the dinner invites and the goofing off, they were my first American role models. They were modest, dedicated to their community, and unfailingly kind.

My attempt at living in separate worlds simultaneously wasn't meant to last, however, and the two collided before I'd even finished my freshman year. Though enigmatic, my mother's long-standing ailment, whatever it was, had worsened so steadily, and for so many years, that it was now a crisis. As I would soon learn, it was a fate my parents had anticipated for a long time—maybe my entire life—but remained ill-equipped to face. Now, it seemed, they no longer had a choice. It was time to fill me in.

As a teenager, my mother had endured a long bout of recurring rheumatic fever that silently eroded the tissue of her heart valves and left her with a chronically deteriorating cardiovascular condition in adulthood. She was even warned by her doctors that having a child— me—was too dangerous to be medically advisable. It was a detail that warmed and hurt my heart at the same time; I already owed so much to her renegade spirit, and it was fitting to add my very existence to the list. Now, however, the severity of her condition risked spilling over from an unpleasant chronic illness to an acute, and eventually deadly, threat. Without an operation, each new day could be her last.

"I'm . . . so sorry." Mr. Sabella's tone carried a vulnerability I wasn't used to hearing.

"What are we gonna do? The doctors are saying she needs this operation to *survive*."

The silence on the line lasted only a moment, but it was enough for my heart to sink. Even he didn't have answers.

". . . I wish I knew, Fei-Fei."

Panic began to set in.

A picture of the unthinkable was creeping into the periphery of my mind's eye: a life without my mother. It was a thought so dark, and so disorienting, that I couldn't entirely process it. It was pure, primal weight, formless but icy and suffocating. It burrowed into the pit of my stomach, deeper and deeper. It was a loneliness I simply wasn't prepared for.

Worse still—grotesque as it felt to acknowledge—our grief was accompanied by embarrassingly practical concerns as well. We thought we'd saved so much, pooling our wages and scrimping obsessively for years, only to learn that the costs of the operation were at *least* an order of magnitude greater than the contents of our checking account. As we scrambled to understand our options—or our lack of them—it became clearer and clearer that the costs of postoperative examinations and recovery alone would likely bankrupt us.

Visions of our family's future without my mother consumed me. I recalled how hard it had been to stay afloat even with her job, modest as it was, and how much closer to impossible it'd be without it. For all my father's warmth, he wasn't a natural provider; he was still that same perpetual child he'd always been, and needed my mother's seriousness as a counterbalance. And here I was, at Princeton of all places, studying physics of all things. Domino after domino was poised to fall. I couldn't even imagine what life would look like once the dust settled.

Then our luck changed. Although Mr. Sabella didn't personally know of any way around the cost of the operation, the situation came up in conversation a few weeks later with a fellow faculty member—my high school art teacher—whose neighbor knew of a care facility called Deborah Heart and Lung Center. Deborah not only specialized in the kind of operation my mother needed, but offered programs tailored for low-income families. It was even located near Princeton.

I immediately picked up the phone, my ardor dampened slightly by my usual role as translator, this time between the receptionist and my parents. Still, it was only a matter of moments before something astonishing began to dawn on me: the people here could actually help. They could provide the operation, and we appeared to qualify for them to subsidize it in full. I thanked them profusely, my hand trembling as I set the receiver back on the hook.

The date of the operation overlapped with the final exams of my first semester, but thanks to Princeton's Honor Code, the system of guidelines under which all exams are administered, I was able to arrange to take my tests at the Deborah clinic. I sat directly outside the sterilized area of the operating room itself, translating during and after the procedure.

I had to admit it was nice to have a distraction during the wait. Although the procedure was only minimally invasive, sparing us the fear of losing her before she could be revived, we were told that the entirety of her prognosis hinged on its outcome. If, for whatever reason, it wasn't as effective as we hoped, there would be no plan B. We had one shot at a recognizable future, and it was already underway.

As I finished my exam and my father paced the halls, I found myself reflecting on our place in America. We'd been so fortunate the last year, but it only papered over our total lack of roots in this country. I wondered what would await us when the lucky streak ended. We remained on the right side of the brink for the time being, but it was, nevertheless, the brink. And beneath everything was the simplest, deepest truth of all: I just wasn't ready to say goodbye to my mother. I wished I had more tests to take.

Finally, the doctor emerged, and gestured for us to join him on the bench.

"We have a lot to discuss, but let's start with the most important thing: the operation was a success."

I exhaled fully for the first time that day. I knew my father was excluded from much of the conversation, but my body language made the outcome obvious even before I had a chance to translate. I could sense the same wave of relief washing over him.

"She has many years ahead of her now, but only if she makes her health a priority from here on out."

"Okay, okay, sure," I replied, my voice still breathy and weak. "How can she do that?"

"Stress is the greatest enemy of a condition like hers. Both mental and physical. So, first things first: does she currently work?"

"Yes, full-time," I said, somewhat cautiously.

The look on the doctor's face grew stern.

"That'll have to change, unfortunately. Part-time work, at *most*. And even then, I urge extreme caution. You must understand: this operation helped a lot, sure, but her heart is still malfunctioning, *fundamentally*, and it's extremely fragile. She simply *cannot* exert herself."

Even in the midst of my gratitude, I couldn't help but feel frustration. Not at the doctor, of course—he meant well, and I had no doubt his advice was medically sound. But I felt it nonetheless.

"I understand, but for how long?" I asked.

The doctor paused for a moment, suddenly realizing the gulf between our expectations. "For the rest of her life, Fei-Fei."

Two weeks later, my mother was back to work full-time.

I had no doubt her rebellious streak was pleased to have a new edict to flout, but there was no sense in romanticizing things. Our prospects as a family were still an open question, which meant her job remained a risk she had no choice but to take daily—especially as she insisted, with even more conviction than before, that I remain at Princeton. She and my father had come too far, and risked too much, to give up now, no matter the cost.

The surgery, thankfully, did help. She had more energy than before, and seemed largely free of the chest pains that had plagued her for years. And I realized, after just a few weeks, that I was no longer catching her gasping for air when I returned home for the weekend. Nevertheless, it was clear that *something* had to change, and as long as my education was nonnegotiable, we didn't have the luxury of half measures.

The issue came up during a trip home not long after the surgery. We gathered around the secondhand dining table we'd found on a curb shortly after arriving in America, the site of countless conversations, arguments, and meals I'd prepared with my father in between homework assignments over the years.

"Fei-Fei, as you know, I'm finding it harder and harder to work a full shift in the gift shop each day. The time has come to make a change."

"What kind of change?" I asked.

"We need a better way to survive than relying on someone else. We're thinking about starting a small business of our own."

It was the kind of idea that seemed absurd on its face but started to make sense the more we discussed it. Years of reacting had instilled in us a hunger to stand up and take an action of our own. And unlike my mother's surgery, in which even the entirety of our savings wouldn't make a dent, a business was something we actually had a shot at buying our way into. We'd also be able to borrow from the friends we'd made in New Jersey's immigrant community, assuming our venture generated at least some revenue. This time, *we* would be the ones making the move.

Our first idea was to open a grocery store, specializing in the Chinese food items and ingredients we often drove for miles to find. It was a smart plan, knowing how many of our fellow immigrants faced the same challenge, but the promise of a popular shop was a double-edged sword for a staff consisting entirely of my ailing mother and a father who couldn't seem to focus on work beyond short bursts. And we knew delivery schedules would be demanding, with drop-offs generally arriving in the early-morning hours when New Jersey's winter temperatures fell to icy lows. With the cold becoming the primary trigger of my mother's symptoms, this alone was a deal-breaker.

We continued the search through the classifieds. Restaurants. Repair shops like the one where my father worked. Gift shops like the one where my mother worked. On and on. Most bore a similar balance of pros and cons, until, near the bottom of the page, an answer appeared— one that might as well have been served on a silver platter. A local dry-cleaning shop was for sale, and the more we considered it, the more perfect it seemed.

It was the kind of business we could imagine opening and closing at reasonable hours, protecting my mother from the elements during the winter. Dry cleaning was a fundamentally mechanical operation, relying extensively on boilers, pressing machines, and conveyor belts. It was the kind of environment where my father's aptitude for machines might finally come in handy. And because foot traffic tends to spike on weekends, I could help keep things running on my trips home. It checked just about every box we could think of (aside, perhaps, from the one about any of us having even a shred of previous experience).

Of course, there was the price tag to consider, and it was no joke: $100,000. But with a bit of strategy, even that seemed surmountable, if only just so. Although our savings only added up to a fraction of the total—just under $20,000—it was a fraction we could build on. And money wasn't all we'd amassed over the years; we'd formed a modest network of contacts as well—friends, neighbors, and employers, many of whom were fellow immigrants from China my father had met early on. It took some doing, but we cobbled together a total of nearly $80,000. It seemed like we'd be paying back each loan's principal for the next few centuries, to say nothing of the interest, but we were getting somewhere.

Unfortunately, our luck wasn't fated to last. The amount we'd raised was a staggering sum, especially for a family like ours, but it still wasn't enough to negotiate. We'd run aground. Weeks passed, and the idea began to fade from our minds. Princeton kept me occupied, of course, and my parents had enough on their plates either way. For the time being, my mother simply resolved to endure.

A month or so later, Mr. Sabella offered to pick me up for the weekend trip home. It wasn't an unusual gesture, as I occasionally stayed with his family when back in town, but the conversation felt strange from the moment I climbed into his Subaru. He sounded as if something was weighing on him that he didn't know how to express; as he so often did when the subject was important, he seemed to find the most labored, circuitous path to get to the point, as if he were begging me to drag the secret out of him.

"So listen, I uh . . . I had a talk with Jean the other night. I talked with her about, well, we discussed some things, and . . ."

". . . and what?" I asked.

"Well, I just . . . I didn't expect her to be so generous. She's . . . you know she's being very generous about all this, and I—uh . . ."

I had no idea where any of this was going.

"See, she and I, er, we decided that . . ."

"Mr. Sabella, I don't understand what—"

"I'm trying to tell you we're going to lend you the rest of the money you need to buy the dry-cleaning shop!"

Since our earliest interactions, my relationship with Mr. Sabella had been a verbose one. Conversation, debate, even good-natured arguments. For once, I was at a loss for words.

"Mr. Cohen! Hi! Your jacket is ready!"

The customer replied with a laugh, as amused as he was surprised. "You remembered me again!" He had the look of a man watching a stage magician. "I don't know how you do it," he said as he leafed through his wallet for the claim ticket. My mother returned the smile, matching his warmth. It was a side of her I didn't see very often—maybe ever—and an especially arresting sight given that less than six months had passed since the operation.

What Mr. Cohen didn't know, but would have surely appreciated, was that my mother had made a mental note of the dark blue Volkswagen Passat he drove and knew to get his jacket ready as soon as she saw it pull into the parking lot. "Mr. Cohen! Gray jacket!" she'd yell, prompting me to scramble for the garment and hand it to her before I heard the jingle of the door opening. The result was a kind of service that bordered on clairvoyance as far as our customers were concerned. She was the daughter of a Kuomintang family, born on the wrong side of the Cultural Revolution and plunged into a lifelong exile of the mind. Now, she was the friendliest face in New Jersey dry cleaning.

It didn't start that way. We racked up an impressive bill of mistakes early on, as misplaced and damaged clothing cost us more than we earned. Customers routinely lost patience as our slow, untrained performance added frustrating delays to their daily routines, and we found ourselves in frequent disputes over the parking lot with the restaurant next door. Finally, we (or, more precisely, I) achieved a dry-cleaning rite of passage—destroying a cashmere sweater—adding our heftiest penalty yet to the pile.

Eventually, though, we got our bearings straight. The business stabilized, evolving from a balancing act to something like a routine—coherent, deliberate, and even rhythmic—and our customers noticed. More and more of them became regulars, especially the young professionals commuting from their homes in the suburbs to the city each day. Although we wouldn't realize this until much later, we'd lucked out on both timing and location: the economy was booming during the second half of the 1990s, and our store just happened to face the bus stop that connected Parsippany to Lower Manhattan.

I thought about the Sabellas, and how they'd loaned us tens of thousands of dollars despite having modest salaries of their own and kids on the verge of college, for no reason other than a desire to see my family survive. It was a generosity I found hard to fathom, and made the thought of failing—of letting them down—all the harder to bear. But it made those early hints of stability all the sweeter, too. At the rate we were growing, we might be able to pay them back on something faster than a geological timescale.

Most heartening of all, I saw something I hadn't in years: my parents acting like themselves. Not merely reacting and struggling to survive but *doing* something. They were part of a community and were contributing, every day, on their own terms. I was reminded of their capacity for creativity and ingenuity and, at least in my mother's case, appetite for hard work.

My mother's cheery knack for customer service wasn't the only surprise. Realizing that dry cleaning is a fairly low-margin business but that alterations are a lucrative exception, she began offering the service to our customers—undaunted, evidently, by her almost complete lack of experience. Building on the modest sewing skills she'd developed making clothes for me in Chengdu, she took it upon herself to turn a hobby into a profession, learning diligently on the job. And it worked. Even our earliest customers—people who were, essentially, handing their clothes to a complete amateur—never knew. She developed the skill quickly and invisibly, keeping her cool and working methodically to fix the mistakes she made early on, earning repeat business and lasting loyalty within a year.

My father found a way to contribute as well. The shop's many machines were like a playground to him, and he made a regular habit of servicing the boiler, presses, clothing conveyor, and dry-cleaning machine. Over time, his passion for tinkering translated into thousands of dollars in savings on repairs, and even grew creative; among his more inspired touches was a network of wires and hooks installed throughout the shop to serve as scaffolding for ivy and other climbing plants. It made the interior unexpectedly lush and green, delighting customers while indulging his love for nature.

There were moments that I had to step back and simply watch. *These* were the people I grew up with in China: strong, resourceful, impressive. It'd been far too long since I'd seen them. I was proud to witness their return.

I never quite experienced college the way most Americans do. My obligations at home were the most obvious impediment, underscored by a still-guarded personality and a tendency toward solitary pursuits that made anything beyond academics difficult. There was something else, though: a sense of separation from my peers, reinforced by what remained of my language gap, any number of cultural differences, and, of course, a tremendous class divide.

Reminders of that divide were often superficial, even subtle, but they were always there. For instance, as if I were the proverbial cobbler's child, our newfound role in the dry-cleaning business didn't expand my wardrobe options. But this, at least, was a solvable problem; a perk of attending a school with such uniformly wealthy students was the discarded garments that practically overflowed in the dormitory's laundry rooms. Just as hand-me-down supplies got me through high school, secondhand clothes helped me get by as an undergrad.

Other divides were harder to bridge. I never joined one of the school's famous eating clubs, nor did I ever quite tap into that networking instinct that so many Ivy League students seemed to naturally possess. Looking back, in fact, I'm not sure I attended a single party. Ultimately, even admission to a place like this couldn't change the fact that I was the product of a world that many of my peers would have found incomprehensible. I found theirs equally hard to understand.

But there were advantages to living such a sequestered life. With free time already limited by my responsibilities, I found it hard to justify anything that threatened to dilute the richness of my studies. Every day brought me closer to the end of the university experience, and I couldn't stand the thought of regretting a missed chance to learn something valuable. So I packed my schedule as densely as I could, immersing myself in math and physics, scouring corkboard advertisements for lectures and workshops, and checking out stacks of books from the library.

I even developed a habit of wandering into the afternoon tea held for the staff at the Institute for Advanced Study every Friday. I had no business there, obviously, but the events weren't strictly private, and I'd occasionally run into a grad student I could chat with about our work. But all I was really after was a chance to absorb the feeling of *being* there, to walk among the minds that made this place so legendary to scientists and even catch occasional fragments of their conversations.

I lived for the moments when a clearing in the crowd revealed an unexpected glimpse of a pioneering physicist like John Wheeler, or a cutting-edge string theory researcher like Edward Witten. The sightings were made all the more surreal for how prosaic they were: titans of their fields rounding a staircase, reaching for a napkin while juggling hors d'oeuvres, or nodding along with small talk. Giants inhabiting a slice of life as mundane as any of my own.

Something was beginning to change by my sophomore year. Although the love I felt for physics was undiminished, I found myself questioning what the subject meant to me in the grand scheme of things, as if threads were beginning to unravel. I wondered if it was really physics *per se* that so inspired me, or simply the spirit that *motivated* physics—the courage that spurred some of history's brightest minds to ask such brazen questions about our world. I wanted desperately to follow in their footsteps—to help reveal some unknown truth—but I was no longer certain what kind of truth it'd be.

I kept reading in the meantime, with an ever-growing interest in the minds behind the ideas that had so captured my imagination. I devoured biographies of thinkers like Einstein, Feynman, and Bohr, studying their histories as intently as my own coursework. And while I learned much about their interest in subatomic particles and natural constants, I began noticing a pattern as well—peculiar, but strangely consistent.

One after another, the greatest figures in physics seemed to develop an unexpected late-career interest in the mystery of life itself, even taking abrupt shifts toward the formal study of biology. Erwin Schrödinger was among my favorite examples. Despite a career spent at the forefront of twentieth-century quantum mechanics, his short but profound *What Is Life?* examined genetics, the behavior of living organisms, and even the ethical implications of their study. The book had a lasting impact on me, and I was captivated by the idea of exploring the world through a more organic lens. After years of following the trail of physics to the outermost reaches of the universe, it was suddenly doubling back on itself, leading me to look inward for the first time—toward living bodies, beating hearts, and restless minds.

My reading list grew more and more eclectic. I dove into Douglas Hofstadter's *Gödel, Escher, Bach: An Eternal Golden Braid*, and was swept away by the range and depth of Roger Penrose's *The Emperor's New Mind*. In the case of both books, it wasn't just the intellectual heft of their ideas that challenged me, but the richness of the connections between them. They tapped into our millennia-old desire to understand the mind—indeed, to make sense of intelligence itself—wading further into abstraction than I'd ever ventured, all while they maintained an unmistakably humanistic thread. They exemplified the virtues of science—rigorous and hypothesis-driven—but without ever sacrificing romance or awe. In fact, for a reader like me, the discipline of their methods amplified that sense of wonder enormously.

What's more, both books were among my first exposures to the idea that the mind could be understood in discrete, mathematical terms. They made the compelling case that a full accounting of intelligence would, by its very nature, reveal not magic but *processes*—rules and principles—operating on measurable quantities over time in scrutable, even predictable ways. They were, in other words, my introduction to the philosophical implications of computation.

It wasn't until college that I realized how many of my peers had grown up with computers. Their identities were shaped by the archetype of the bedroom hacker, sleep-deprived and cast in a perpetual blue glow. Learning, exploring, experimenting. They created video games as kids using languages like BASIC, took programming classes as teenagers, and found like-minded communities on the internet. It was a hobby, an aspiration, and an endless opportunity to be creative. By the time they reached a place like Princeton, many of them were already fluent in the technology.

For most of my life, my infrequent run-ins with computers had suggested they were little more than tools. My father took advantage of a job he briefly held at a PC warehouse to assemble a desktop system of my own as a gift when I left for college, but I never saw it as anything beyond a way to write papers or access the early internet, like a more sophisticated version of the graphing calculator I used in high school.

As my studies progressed, however, my conception of a computer's value expanded. It was dawning on me that silicon wouldn't just help us decode the nature of the mind, but help us *model* it. And it stood to reason that as those models grew in detail and fidelity—as more and more of our intellectual capabilities were mapped, deconstructed, and even simulated by machines—they would, in essence, embody those capabilities themselves. What I once saw as mere hardware I now saw as a kind of ally in our quest for understanding. The idea that so entranced those early pioneers of AI—names I didn't yet know, but would soon learn, and soon revere—now entranced me. At the start of the next quarter, I enrolled in my first computer science class.

Physics prepared me well for the study of computation. I was once again learning a new language—a *programming* language known simply as "C"—but unlike English, it empowered me in a way I'd never felt before. It was pristine in its clarity and precision, allowing me to orchestrate computation in complex, abstract ways, and at a scale I couldn't have previously imagined. I was reminded of something my mother told me on our flight from China to the United States in an attempt to keep my spirits up. "Learning a new language," she said, "is like opening a door to a new world." I can't say I agreed during my first few years grappling with English. But the further I delved into computer science, the more her words resonated.

It was during this period that an opportunity presented itself—one that I instantly knew was potentially life-changing.

"You won't believe what happened today, Mr. Sabella. A classmate told me about an experiment being conducted at UC Berkeley this summer. I don't know all the details yet, but it's something to do with neuroscience and biology and how vision works. You know, within the brain."

"Wow, right up your alley, huh?"

I'd been talking about this stuff for weeks now, obsessively. I didn't have to explain my excitement about the news for Mr. Sabella to pick up on it.

"Yes! But here's the most exciting part: he said they need an assistant, and that they'd prefer an undergrad without a lot of experience."

"Wait, so you mean—"

"I think I'm going to Berkeley this summer!"

To trained and untrained observers alike, the early days of the 1990s must have seemed like the dawning of an entirely new age. Hinton's backpropagation technique appeared to provide the final piece of the puzzle of neural networks, and LeCun's success in reading handwritten digits delivered an unqualified validation of the algorithm in the real world. An almost magical paradigm in engineering had arrived, in which organic, human-like perception could be engineered as deliberately as a database or file server. But trouble was brewing, yet again. As the still-fledgling field of AI would soon learn, its days of false starts and dashed hopes were not yet over.

LeCun's achievements notwithstanding, a divide was emerging between the theory and the practice of machine learning. Despite the obviousness of their potential, neural networks quickly ran aground when applied to just about anything beyond reading ZIP codes, and the reasons were manifold. For one thing, although the algorithm bore a conceptual elegance when drawn on a whiteboard, the computation required to bring even a simple implementation to life was stagger-ing, and still well beyond the capabilities of even most corporations and governments. Equally damning was the state of digital data—a comparatively rare commodity at the time, especially when it came to *perceptual* data like images, video, audio, and the like. What did ex-ist was often fragmented and proprietary, inconsistently cataloged and trapped within the borders of private servers. Whatever neural net-works were fated to achieve, it was becoming clear their time had not yet arrived.

Before long, a period known as an "AI winter" had set in—a long season of austerity for a now unmoored research community. Even the term "artificial intelligence" itself—seen by many as hopelessly broad, if not delusional—was downplayed in favor of narrower pursuits like decision-making, pattern recognition, and natural language process-ing, which attempted to understand human speech and writing. "Ar-tificial intelligence" seemed destined to remain the domain of science fiction writers, not academics. Just as the history of physics follows a sinusoid-like pattern as the abundance of discovery ebbs and flows, AI was revealing itself to be a temperamental pursuit.

Yann LeCun and Geoff Hinton were, without a doubt, pioneers. But whether they would live to see their ideas change the world was yet to be decided. And although both kept their heads down and con-tinued their research, the world moved on, in search of simpler, more efficient, and less biologically extravagant solutions. Neural networks, simply put, were a good idea born at the wrong time.

"On behalf of American Airlines and our flight crew, we'd like to wel-come you to California! The local time is 3:46 p.m., and it's a comfort-able 71 degrees outside with clear skies. We ask at this time that you lift your tray tables and fasten your seat belts as we prepare for landing at Oakland International Airport."

It was my first trip within the United States, and I'd taken it alone. I smiled to myself as a flicker of realization came over me: the voice on the PA was no longer speaking a foreign language.

Arriving in California was exciting, but the decision to go wasn't without its complications. My parents still relied on my assistance to run the dry-cleaning shop smoothly, and it wasn't clear how we'd manage while I lived for eight weeks on the other side of the country. As always, however, my mother was insistent I go.

One of my fellow researchers was waiting to pick me up, and we went straight to the lab. There would be time to discuss accommodations and other practical matters later. Now, he seemed to share my eagerness to dive in.

"So where are you from? What's your background?"

"I'm studying physics at Princeton," I replied, feeling a bit out of place. I wasn't studying neuroscience or even biology, and I suddenly wondered if I'd be accepted by the team.

"Oh, cool. I'm an EE myself. I'm Garrett, by the way."

An electrical engineer? Really? So I'm not *the only one from another field?*

"Wait, you mean you don't have a bio background, either?"

"Nope. See, that's what's so fascinating about this project. We're not *really* going to be studying the brain. At least, not in a biological sense."

I was confused but intrigued.

"We're going to be studying it *computationally*."

As Garrett explained, our project was an attempt at taking a step beyond Hubel and Wiesel's seminal work on the mammalian visual cortex. Like the original, this new experiment would project imagery before a cat's eyes and analyze the neuronal response. This time, however, the more advanced technology of our age would afford a deeper look inside. Instead of projecting isolated line segments, we would play full-motion video clips. And instead of simply studying the brain activity the video inspired, we would attempt to *reconstruct* the imagery that caused it—from the inside.

What made the experience so unique for me, however, were the circumstances surrounding it. The lab was newly formed and run by a young assistant professor; I'd be in a supporting role alongside another undergrad and Garrett, a postdoc. The project was understaffed and underfunded, but also uniquely unconstrained. As a result, the responsibilities of a research scientist fell on me, years before I was even remotely qualified to perform them—and I found it all thrilling. My job included building the experiment's apparatus from the ground up: researching the hardware, tracking down the proper electrodes, comparison shopping for the amplifiers and loudspeakers we'd use to listen to their output, then putting it all together from end to end. It was intense, and often stressful, but never boring.

It wasn't all intellectual exploration, however.

"Uh, Fei-Fei?"

The lab phone rang, and Garrett was calling my name with a familiar inflection.

"I think it's your . . . mom?" he whispered, his hand covering the receiver.

"Thanks," I said, taking the phone.

"Hi, Mom," I said softly as I switched back to Mandarin. "Uh-huh? Yes, she's asking if—no, Mom, listen, I'm saying—no, no . . ."

I was mediating yet another conversation with a customer on the other side of the continent.

"Just put her on, okay? Okay. Thank you."

"Uh, hi, Mrs. Russo." Back to English. "It sounds like you're concerned about linen? Yes. Uh-huh. Yes, that's right. Uh, that should be fine. Why don't you put my mom back on the phone and I'll catch her up. Thank you—you, too."

If there was any concern that my West Coast adventure would go to my head, moments like these put it to rest. Having to drop everything to reassure a customer about shrinkage made it easy to stay grounded.

* * *

The brain remains the single most sophisticated object in the known universe—by a staggering margin—even in an era of mobile devices, spacecraft, and particle accelerators. It outpaces our most powerful supercomputers, all within a volume measured in cubic inches, powered by nothing more than a fraction of the calories we consume each day.

The story only grows more impressive as one peers into its folds. Despite the relative simplicity of the neurons that comprise much of its design, the brain is perhaps the greatest example one can imagine of the maxim that, at a large enough scale, quantity has a quality all its own. When these elementary mechanisms are replicated on the order of 100 billion times, with 10-to-the-11th-power connections between them, something transcendent happens. *Matter* somehow becomes a *mind*, giving rise to love, joy, sadness, anger, fear, and laughter, not to mention our capacity for science, art, music, and mathematics.

The same organ that allows us to discern color turns some of us into artists, some into critics, and billions more into appreciators. The same gray matter that interprets auditory vibrations can also summon the inspiration to write a song, treasure the experience of listening to one, and even recall the presence of a friend, in aching detail, the first time it came on the radio. This singular anatomical structure, composed entirely of organic compounds and locked for a lifetime in the darkness of the skull, makes possible *everything* we value about life.

With no previous exposure to neuroscience, I was transfixed by this idea. The question of how something so profound could emerge from such modest ingredients consumed me and permeated everything we did in the lab. It made complex, often tedious work exhilarating.

Specifically, the goal of our research was to explore the way sensory information is processed by asking a seemingly straightforward question: if a cat were shown a sequence of precisely controlled visual stimuli—in this case, brief movie clips of natural scenery—could we reconstruct the footage using nothing more than signals detected within its brain?

To find the answer, we set our sights on a section of the visual cortex known as the "lateral geniculate nucleus," or LGN. It serves as a waypoint between the optic nerve and higher levels of processing within the brain, and it's believed to play a role in focusing attention within the visual field and keeping track of changes in stimuli over time. For the purposes of our experiment, however, it also provided an accessible group of neurons that we could associate with corresponding regions of the retina. In other words, the LGN sits somewhere between what the eye senses and what the brain understands; our goal was to decode the signals that pass through it along the way.

That was the theory, anyway. In practice, things were more complicated. For instance, electrodes capable of probing the cortex are extraordinarily thin—on the order of micrometers, or the scale of a single human hair. We relied on a mechanical aid designed to lower them slowly and accurately into the cat's brain, their output connected to an amplifier capable of converting raw electrical signals to an audible form for playback on the loudspeakers. From there, we fed the data into a computer running specialized signal-processing software for later analysis.

Slowly but surely, it all came together. Finally, after a whirlwind of building, validating, and revalidating, a surprisingly sophisticated apparatus appeared to be ready to run. We lowered the lights, turned on the projector, and connected the electrodes.

"Is everyone ready? Three . . . two . . ."

Even now, the experience that followed remains hard to put into words.

". . . one."

With the flip of a switch, a frenetic crackle burst out of the loudspeaker. It was pure chaos at first—startling, even—but the noise gradually gave way to a faint sense of order, especially as we learned to correlate the images on the screen with the sounds we heard—a rhythmic whooshing that soon became unmistakable. We'd listen for hours, slightly modulating the projected visuals and paying close attention to changes in the audio. Over time, patterns emerged, as each seemingly uniform cluster of neurons revealed a unique tone and character. Given all the digital tools at our disposal, this level of hands-on experimentation was probably unnecessary. But it helped us train our ears, develop our intuitions, and connect with the work on a level deeper than mere analysis. It felt like pure science.

The exhilaration only continued as the results came into focus. Amazingly—to me, anyway—our method actually worked. With a bit of signal-processing finesse, we *reconstructed* the movies projected before the cat's eyes—albeit in a slightly blurrier form—with nothing more than signals intercepted in its brain. There were many caveats, of course, as in any experiment, but we'd demonstrated a real, functional understanding of how visual neurons respond to stimuli. We documented our process, tabulated our results, and submitted a draft for peer review. Within two years, our work saw the light of day as a published article in *The Journal of Neuroscience*. Not bad for a team of rookies.

Beyond the thrill of my first glimpse of true science, Berkeley helped me see Princeton from a new perspective. Life back home was regimented, consisting of daily classes at the university, weekend shifts at the dry-cleaning shop, and virtually nothing else. I was content with this, of course; I knew what my parents had sacrificed for me, and I considered my academic career an incredible gift. But I also knew the day was coming when I'd have to set my passion aside—maybe forever—in favor of something practical. A career in medicine, or finance, or whatever. Home was the place where I prepared myself for it, little by little. It was where I still felt like an immigrant.

In comparison, Berkeley was like an entirely new reality. My walk to the lab each day was a zigzagged tour through a city of astonishing color and depth, from the unrest of near-constant protests to occasional sightings of the now legendary "Naked Guy"—an endearingly rebellious fixture of campus life in the late '90s. Here, everything was different, including me. I didn't feel like an immigrant. I didn't feel isolated. I didn't even feel poor. I just felt like a scientist.

Most important, it was where I caught my first glimpse of the ideas that would soon dwarf all of my previous obsessions. Although the domain of physics was the whole of the natural universe, from the Planck scale to galactic superclusters, it was hard to imagine a more exciting playground for the mind than what we were studying. Somehow, the mysteries of intelligence felt more expansive and more intimate at the same time. So, despite the grueling workload and the pressure I felt as a first-time collaborator with no prior lab experience, I never felt exhausted. Instead, as I made my way back to my dorm each night, crisscrossing the streets of Berkeley under a sky that went dark long before I stepped outside, I was energized. All I felt was contentment.

Although the experiment lasted barely a summer, I returned to Princeton a different person. Physics had been my first obsession, but I was beginning to realize that its appeal wasn't in the equations, or even the concepts. It was in the chase, and the quest for understanding what it symbolized. What's more, I now *knew*, without equivocation, that I loved research. I could feel it. A newfound zeal washed over me every time I opened a spiral-bound notebook to jot down ideas, every time I heard the squeak of a dry-erase marker revising an equation, and every time the fan whirred as I booted up a lab computer to crunch numbers.

Research triggered the same feeling I got as a child exploring the mountains surrounding Chengdu with my father, when we'd spot a butterfly we'd never seen before, or happen upon a new variety of stick insect. Time lost its meaning in the lab, and I lost myself in the work. After an adolescence spent feeling as if I never really belonged, I was suddenly certain I'd found my place.

Part of me never left the dark of that Berkeley lab. The otherworldly sounds of its loudspeaker would roar on in my memory, each hiss and crackle hinting at a language science was just beginning to unravel. Even more than Princeton, it was the place that most fully demonstrated what my parents sought in coming to this country: the freedom to recognize a passion, and to live it, without compromise. Whatever my future held, those moments in the lab, our hearts pounding as we listened, were all the proof I needed to know they'd made the right decision.

The pursuit of opportunity without limits was my parents' North Star. It was a vision that animated them like nothing else, carving a path through their lives so deep that it came to define them as people. It was the same maniacal commitment that elevated my heroes from academics to scientists to legends. Now, still breathless from my first brush with real discovery, I found myself searching the skies for a North Star of my own: the kind of idea—a question, a hypothesis, a *bet*—that any scientist worth their stripes would chase to the ends of the earth. Beyond, even.

I just needed to find it.

5

FIRST LIGHT

Imagine an existence so bereft of sensation that it couldn't even be described as "dark," as no corresponding notion of light had yet been conceived. Imagine a world in which nothing is seen, or heard, or felt, rendering the very idea of being alive little more than a metabolic distinction. Imagine a world of beings lacking even a basic sense of self beyond some rote, passionless instinct to feed and reproduce, to say nothing of more complex notions like identity, or community, or a larger reality. Now imagine all of that at a global scale—a planet teeming with organisms, but yet to realize its own existence.

This was the essence of life in the primordial oceans that covered much of the Earth 543 million years ago. By the standards of today, in which every waking moment bathes the senses and engages the intellect, these organisms, so primitive they bordered on the abstract, lived lives that Socrates might have described as perfectly unexamined. It was a truly unseen world, characterized by deep water but shallow instincts.

Of course, the simplicity of these distant ancestors of ours was only natural given the environment of their time. They inhabited a sparse, aquatic space in which even competition for food was a passive affair.

Organisms predating trilobites relied on little more than chance to stumble upon their prey, which took similarly aimless measures to avoid their predators—blind luck—and ate only when their next meal was so close that consuming it was all but involuntary.

Nevertheless, the implications of that sensory deprivation were profound. With nothing to see, or hear, or touch, there was, in turn, nothing for these early life-forms to ponder. With no connection to the external reality we take for granted in everyday life, they were so thoroughly denied stimulation that they lacked brains altogether. For all its mystery, a brain is, after all, a kind of organic information-processing system—all but unnecessary in a world of beings devoid of sensory input and, thus, the ability to collect information about that world in the first place.

Truly imagining the inner life of such an organism is all but impossible, but the attempt can be instructive. It's a reminder that we've never known existence without *some* sensory connection to the outside world, even in the womb, and that we can't simply step back from that awareness to contemplate an alternative. After all, what *are* thoughts if not reactions to stimuli, whether direct or otherwise? Aren't even our most abstract deliberations—even something as ephemeral as mental arithmetic—built on a foundation of reasoning acquired through years of experience navigating physical spaces? No matter how sophisticated our minds may be, there's little going on within them that can't ultimately be traced to some intrusion from what lies beyond their borders.

Then, during a period so brief and yet so transformative that evolutionary biologists still puzzle over it, the world turned upside down. The complexity of life exploded—with one estimate suggesting that the rate of evolution was accelerated to an incredible *four times* that of all subsequent eras—spurring an atmosphere of unprecedented competition. It was a perpetual battle for dominance, each new generation pressured to adapt in tiny increments as the challenge of survival intensified. Bodies hardened in response to a world of mounting hostility, fortifying soft tissue with brittle, defensive exoskeletons and developing offensive features like teeth, mandibles, and claws.

The Cambrian explosion, as it's now known, was a furious reshuffling of the evolutionary order. But although it constitutes a pivotal chapter in the history of life on Earth—perhaps the most consequential of all—its precise cause is not yet a settled matter. Some imagine it was triggered by a sudden change in climate, while others have speculated about a historic shift in ocean acidity. Zoologist Andrew Parker saw something different, though, and while many biologists are skeptical about his hypothesis, it has deeply influenced my thinking about AI. It was less an exogenous force than an internal one, according to Parker, who identifies the fuse that ignited the Cambrian explosion as the emergence of a single capability: photosensitivity, or the foundation of the modern eye.

At the heart of this burgeoning sense was a single class of proteins, known as "opsins," which exhibit unique properties such as changing shape upon the absorption of a photon—in essence, physically reacting to exposure to light—and connecting in chains known as "ion channels," which translate that reaction into a bioelectric signal that can be transmitted elsewhere in the body.

As simple as these early developments were, at least compared to the remarkable intricacy of today's eyes, they provided an evolutionary toehold that sparked a rapid ascent. The next step was a shallow divot surrounding the photosensitive region, making it possible to discern not just the brightness of a nearby light source, but its direction as well. Further evolutionary iterations saw the depth and narrowness of this depression increase, eventually taking the form of an aperture not unlike that of a pinhole camera.

First described in the writings of Chinese philosopher Mozi around 400 BC, and later independently observed by Aristotle, the pinhole camera is a simple exploitation of the camera obscura effect, a natural phenomenon in which light filtered through a small hole on the side of a chamber projects a strikingly clear image of the outside world into its interior. Apertures dramatically increased photosensitivity, expanding the experience of vision from a simple awareness of light to the absorption of entire scenes.

Finally, the foundation of modern vision was complete with the advent of the lens, which increased the amount and clarity of light coming into the eye. How exactly the lens came into being remains a topic of some speculation, with many hypotheses centering on the notion that it evolved from a purely protective manifold originally unrelated to sight. Whatever its precise origin, though, the lens emerged again and again in the evolutionary record, developing independently in all phyla of living organisms. It soon took on the form of a delicate transparent surface, adapting nimbly across generations to explore a tremendous range of optical properties, rapidly accelerating the evolution of the eye.

Photosensitivity was a turning point in the history of life on Earth. By simply letting the light in—to any degree, no matter how dim or formless—our evolutionary predecessors recognized, for the first time, that there was something *beyond* themselves. And, more urgently, they saw that they were engaged in a struggle to survive, with more than one possible outcome. They were awakening to a harsh environment in which threats and opportunities alike abounded, competition for resources was increasing, and their own actions meant the difference between eating and being eaten.

The perception of light was the first salvo in what would become an evolutionary arms race in which even the slightest advantage—a nominal boost in depth or a near-imperceptible increase in acuity—could propel its lucky possessor and its progeny to the front of the pack in an eternal hunt for food, shelter, and suitable mates. Such slim competitive margins are the playground of evolutionary pressures, iterating with abandon through mutation after mutation and producing a near-immediate impact on the ecosystem in the process.

Most of these changes do nothing, of course, and some are harmful. But those few that confer even a minor edge can be engines of devastating change, upending the natural order in a flurry of upheaval before settling into a new baseline upon which yet greater capabilities will soon be erected. This process hastened as the generations passed, and, in a period of only about ten million years—what Parker wryly dubs an evolutionary "blink of an eye"—life on Earth was born anew.

Mediating this competitive dynamic was the relationship between sensory awareness and the capacity to act. Even the earliest forms of vision conveyed glimmers of information about an organism's surroundings that didn't just guide its behavior but *drove* it with an immediacy that had never existed before. More and more, hungry predators were empowered to *locate* their food, rather than merely waiting for its arrival, and even to take active steps to pursue it. In turn, would-be prey harnessed their own inchoate awareness to react with evasive maneuvers.

Soon, these flickers of biological innovation blossomed into a collective dance, the balance of power swaying back and forth as an expanding taxonomy of life battled its way into a new epoch. Today, fossil records lay bare the fruits of natural selection during this frenzied period; evidence suggests the evolution of the trilobites alone peaked near the end of the Cambrian era with tens of thousands of species spread across ten orders.

Further complicating the picture was the simultaneous emergence of a sense of touch, which quickly fell into a complementary balance with an evolving sense of vision. Mirroring those early flickers of light sensitivity, nascent nerve endings swept across the surfaces of primitive bodies to carry tactile signals as well.

Those nerve cells grew and interconnected to create what are called "nerve nets," decentralized precursors to the central nervous systems that would eventually characterize more advanced life-forms. Nerve nets are simple but potent bioelectric systems, merging control of motor and sensory functions into a single reactive design suitable for basic tasks like responding to physical aggression and finding food. Although primitive, nerve nets were an evolutionarily expedient way to keep pace with a world of mounting competition, and can be found even today, especially in aquatic organisms like certain jellyfish.

But it's not enough to simply connect eyes, nerve endings, and limbs, especially as those eyes evolve to deliver a broader and more nuanced view of the world and those limbs develop new degrees of freedom and deepening powers of articulation. Effective action in a complex environment requires more than reflex, posing yet another challenge of adaptation that spurred the development of an increasingly sophisticated intermediate step between what an organism sees and feels and how it reacts.

As the depth and quantity of information provided by the senses grew, an organism's tools for processing that information were pressured to grow as well—analogous to today's need for more and more sophisticated computing devices to manage the excesses of data found in the modern world. The result was a centralized hub for processing the dizzying ins and outs of a growing nervous system, its components compressed with greater and greater density into an organ we now call the brain.

The brain, therefore, was not the product of some mysterious intellectual spark from within, but rather a reaction to an ever clearer, ever more chaotic image of the outside world, reaching inward through the senses. The ability to perceive our surroundings encouraged us to develop a mechanism for integrating, analyzing, and ultimately making sense of that perception. And vision was, by far, its most vibrant constituent.

The drama reached even greater heights as the first of these newly awakened creatures made their way onto dry land, emerging from the waves to find an alien landscape in which the very rudiments of mobility were unfamiliar and demanded an entirely new paradigm. Movement, for instance, was no longer effortless and omnidirectional, but constrained to flat surfaces and throttled by the intrusion of physical forces like gravity and friction.

On the other hand, the range of sight was profoundly extended, as the unobstructed atmosphere above the surface of the ocean admitted views that dwarfed the claustrophobic dark of the deep sea. The world was no longer a sphere of hazy fluid, but an open vista, awash in brightness and clarity reaching from the edges of shorelines to the peaks of mountains and beyond. The horizon had grown from inches to miles, and the minds of these early land dwellers were challenged to expand accordingly.

This had an especially profound effect on the notion of planning, as actions could now unfold over far greater ranges, all while dealing with more uncertainty. Minds had no choice but to adapt with greater intellectual capabilities as the scope and reach of vision expanded, gradually incorporating an awareness of causality, the passage of time, and even the effects of manipulating the environment itself. The stage was set not just for potent predators and nimble prey, but for true intelligence—and for the foundation of the human race as we know it today.

Hundreds of millions of years later, it's hard not to be impressed by the world produced by this evolutionary turning point. Millennia of civilization have seen our species grow from primates to nomadic tribes to agricultural communities to industrialized cities and now, finally, to technological, information-processing superpowers.

Intrinsic to this astonishing progression, even now, is our sensory connection to the world. Although massively aided by technology, from the mobile devices in our pockets to the satellites in the Earth's orbit, we remain dependent on our connection to everyday reality to navigate our lives.

Appropriately, what began in the fossil record has come to influence our own cultural record. The history of art is a testament to the primacy of vision—and to our growing appreciation of its nuances over the course of centuries, from the cave paintings that heralded the dawn of a new form of communication, to the flood of creativity that burst forth during the Renaissance, to today's world of photography, film, television, and even video games.

We can see the gears of visual understanding turn in the piercing contrast between the chiaroscuros of Caravaggio and the soft shadows of Vermeer and Zorn. We can transcend realism to distill the iconography of everyday life with van Gogh and the stylized portraiture of Kahlo. We even feel its presence in the comparatively opaque statements of modernists like O'Keeffe and abstract expressionists like Motherwell and Rothko. Whether realistic or conceptual, sentimental or political, art harnesses those hundreds of millions of years of hard-won evolution to linger on the sheer joy of interpreting the world through the eyes—and, thus, the sensibilities—of the individual.

"So, Fei-Fei! How's it feel to be a college grad? Well, almost."

Jean had finished clearing our dinner plates from the table and was cutting into a pan of brownies she'd left cooling on the counter. The dessert became a ritual after my first visit to the Sabellas' home nearly four years earlier; it was my first memorable exposure to American sweets, and the look on my face as I took a bite delighted Jean so much that she insisted on serving brownies every time I returned. The fact that it was a simple store-bought mix didn't matter. As far as I was concerned, her brownies were the height of indulgence.

"It's very exciting. But I wasn't expecting the choice of what comes next to be so difficult."

"Have you thought any more about the options we talked about? Grad school? A job? Maybe a bit of traveling first?" Mr. Sabella asked.

"Give her a second, Bob!" Jean laughed as she served our desserts.

"No, no, it's fine. It's all I've been able to think about, actually."

It was 1999, and my time at Princeton was coming to a close. Once again, I faced a choice between my scientific ambitions and the realities of life, as the allure of grad school collided with the pressure to start a career. And with the dot-com boom in full swing, it was a genuine dilemma: the financial world was eager to recruit anyone with a mind for numbers and a fancy degree from the right school, making even physics geeks like me the target of aggressive recruiting efforts from a revolving door of Wall Street players. I was courted by Goldman Sachs, Merrill Lynch, and other firms with names one could imagine engraved in stately slabs of marble. And they offered everything: perks, leadership opportunities, eye-watering starting salaries, and, of course, real health insurance. They promised relief from our debts, an end to the toil of dry cleaning, and security for my family in the face of my mother's worsening health. In return, all they asked was that I give up science.

After mulling it over for the better part of a week, I finally brought the topic up to my mother during a quiet hour in the dry-cleaning shop. We were in our usual positions: she was at the sewing machine, a couple of pins held between her lips and a look of one-eyed determination as she studied her work, and I was next to her, assuming my role as the tailor's assistant, unstitching a pair of pants she was preparing to lengthen.

"Mom, I'm thinking about my options. I had an interview with all these . . . 'firms,' I guess you call them? Big Wall Street types. I have to admit, they're tempting."

"Big . . . Wall Street types?"

I realized I'd already stepped beyond her familiarity with the jargon of American culture.

"You know, stocks and trading. Investments. That sorta thing. Obviously I'd have a lot to learn, but I think it's something I could do if I really set my mind to it."

"Huh," she replied flatly. "Is that what you want?"

"Well, I mean . . . the salary alone would be life-changing for us, and—"

"Fei-Fei, is it what you *want*?"

"You know what I want, Mom. I want to be a scientist."

"So what are we even talking about?"

My mother had a way of slicing through my equivocating so fast it would take me a second to recognize it. Checkmate in barely three moves. I was going to grad school.

My Princeton professors often said that postgraduate studies weren't just another academic milestone but a turning point, representing the first transition from being a student to becoming something like a true scientist, turning a passion into a journey and an affinity into an identity, tempering an education to become the foundation of a career, a reputation, and a life. It was an encouraging thought that clarified the question I faced, but made it all the more vexing as well. I knew I wanted to be a scientist, but what kind? For what purpose, exactly? How would I know?

My experience at UC Berkeley brought to life the mystery of intelligence and showed me that a greater understanding of vision might be the key to unraveling it. Two paths extended from that realization, however: one neuroscientific, promising greater and greater insights into the brain's capabilities, and the other computational, in which the fundamentals of engineering could be applied to modeling, and perhaps even replicating, those capabilities.

I decided to pursue both.

The study of neuroscience and computation made for an unconventional pairing, at least among the master's programs of the time. A handful of institutions could accommodate it, though, even if it took some legwork to track them down. In fact, in a stroke of rather remarkable luck, two of the world's top-ranked schools offered exactly the program I was looking for.

The first was a dual-track Stanford program that blended neuroscience with electrical engineering, helmed by Professor David Heeger—the rare academic with substantial experience in both fields. Every detail of Heeger's curriculum seemed tailor-made for me, with one inconvenient exception: he'd completed his last year at the school, and the program would not continue in his absence.

Scratching Stanford off the list, I turned to an alternative program at MIT that felt even more aligned with my interests. It was the brain-child of Dr. Tomaso Poggio, among the first generation of researchers in a relatively obscure field called "computer vision." Poggio's work was impressive to me even then, and my admiration has only grown in hindsight as I realize how far ahead of its time it really was. He took direct inspiration from the architecture of the brain to build a family of algorithms termed "connectivist models"—densely interwoven information-processing systems not unlike neural networks—to recognize the contents of images.

Still, I had one more option to consider: the California Institute of Technology, more commonly known as Caltech. Although the school had a storied history of its own and a rather glamorous connection to NASA by way of its world-famous Jet Propulsion Laboratory, there was no denying the fact that it was the underdog in terms of rankings. Stanford and MIT were among the most prestigious academic institutions on earth, and it seemed hard to fathom turning down an acceptance offer from either of them—let alone both. But Caltech punched far above its weight when it came to association with my heroes, with Feynman, Millikan, and even Einstein himself lecturing there over the years. At the very least, I couldn't resist a chance to visit.

From the moment I touched down in Pasadena, it was clear that Caltech had the advantage when it came to climate. It was my first trip to Southern California, and the weather lived up to its sunny reputation, with a dry heat that felt like instant refuge from the humidity of New Jersey. I was struck by its photogenic charm as well, from its flowers that appeared to bloom in every direction to its turtle ponds and their lazily sunning inhabitants. MIT and Stanford were unimpeachable when it came to scholastics, but this place felt like paradise.

Although the campus was small—dwarfed even by Princeton, itself considered diminutive—I was overwhelmed by the vibrance of Caltech. The colorful, airy Spanish Colonial architecture felt like another world to me after spending so many years amidst the cathedral-like weight of my alma mater's buildings. And the physics-related sightseeing opportunities were endless. I immediately spotted the site where Einstein was famously photographed riding his bicycle, casually passed the Millikan library, and happened upon the auditorium that served as the venue for Feynman's legendary lectures.

Everything I saw and felt during my visit to Caltech suggested this was where I belonged. And although it may sound trivial, I couldn't pretend that the opportunity to escape years of shivering through Northeastern snowstorms wasn't a selling point all by itself. But what began as an inclination to study there turned into certainty when I met the people I'd be learning from.

The first of my would-be advisors was Pietro Perona, who exuded Italian charm and had no sense of boundaries when it came to interdisciplinary research; he was situated in the electrical engineering department but loved cognitive science and shared my desire to blend the two. Even conversationally, his interests struck me as unusually well-rounded from our first interaction.

"Out of curiosity, Fei-Fei, what do you think about the piece on the wall?"

Pietro gestured toward a framed poster covered in bold primary colors, divided into squares and rectangles by irregularly spaced orthogonal lines.

I had made time for a handful of art classes at Princeton and was excited to recognize it as a Mondrian.

"I've always loved his work," Pietro continued. "The simplicity of the geometry never fails to make me stop and think."

"About what, exactly?" I asked.

"About whether there might be rules guiding it. Or at least capable of explaining it."

"Rules? You mean . . . like, an algorithm?"

He smiled, then continued. "Aren't you curious? What if it turns out that if you measure the proportions of every painting by Mondrian, some kind of pattern emerges? Wouldn't that be fascinating?"

I smiled back. I couldn't tell how serious he was—I was almost certain he was kidding around with me—but I loved that he'd even taken the time to develop such an idea. Intelligent, adventurous, and silly, all at once. I felt like I'd waited my entire life to meet thinkers like this.

The second was Christof Koch, a computational neuroscientist. As I had with Pietro, I saw in Christof that first day the hallmark of every good scientist: an imagination without limits, and a fearlessness in the face of the challenges such an imagination naturally seeks out. He was highly accomplished in biophysics, but had a track record of continual reinvention that impressed me. Like Perona, he was eager to blur the lines between disciplines, and encouraged my impulse to do the same. He came from physics, a background we shared, and was a former student of Poggio. But I was to learn in that first meeting that a deep philosophical passion had wrapped itself around his mind, and it dominated our first conversation.

"Fei-Fei, have you ever thought about how you might explain color to someone who suffers from color blindness? How you'd put the experience of seeing red into words?"

Hmmmm. I hadn't.

"Isn't it strange that our familiarity with color doesn't seem to translate into an ability to describe it? We can really only *refer* to it; you might know what I mean when I say 'blue' or 'red,' but only because you've already seen these colors yourself. My words are merely invoking your memories; they aren't imparting new information."

This was certainly thought-provoking.

"So when you imagine some future generation achieving a *total* understanding of how vision works, do you think their mastery will include an ability to, say, *describe* the quality of redness from first principles?"

I thought for a moment before responding.

"Hmmm . . . Well, wouldn't it have to? I mean, if you really mean 'total' understanding."

"That's a perfectly reasonable answer. But it presupposes there's an explanation for such experiences to be found in a reductionist accounting. What if, somehow, there *isn't*? What then? What are we to do with that contradiction? Vision may be a complex phenomenon—maybe among the most complex—but it's still a *physical* process: matter behaving in accordance with physical laws. And yet, subjectively, don't our experiences feel *nonphysical*? Why should seeing red *feel* like anything subjective at all?"

These weren't questions I'd considered before, and his fixation on them told me everything I needed to know about his ability to challenge me.

The two made for an interesting pair. They were both tall and appeared to be about the same age—somewhere in their forties, I estimated—but with contrasting builds, Pietro being the sturdier of the two, and Christof quite lean. Both had heavy accents—Italian and German, respectively—but spoke with a humor and an easygoing confidence that softened their intensity. And while Pietro looked the part of an academic, with tucked-in button-downs and beige Dockers, Christof took pride in an aggressively splashy wardrobe, from piercing fluorescent shirts to hair dyed comic-book colors like green and purple.

What they had in common, however—to an uncanny degree—was a curiosity that could only be described as gleeful, imbuing everything they said with an infectious energy. They asked probing questions about complex subjects without hesitation or even a hint of self-consciousness, as if the answers to life's deepest mysteries were never more than a conversation away. Christof in particular often seemed so captivated by his own thoughts that he was more interested in exploring them in a monologue than in talking to me, even in one-on-one conversations. But his preoccupation came from a place of innocence, not aloofness, like a child helplessly distracted by daydreams. It reminded me of my father's absentmindedness, and I found it charming.

After so many years of doubting myself, struggling with a second language, and growing more than a little guarded as a result, it's strange that I'd be drawn to such brash personalities. But as I'd discovered with Mr. Sabella, a shared love for science could make me feel like anyone's peer, even if only for the duration of a friendly chat. The world as I knew it faded to near silence when I found myself in dialogue with people like Pietro and Christof, as if our ideas alone were doing the talking, unencumbered by our language, status, or age. They were a new kind of role model: immigrants who hadn't just made it, but had made it as scientists.

My visit to Caltech was among the most memorable afternoons of my life. These were intellectual giants, and it was an honor to simply converse with them for a few hours, let alone contemplate the chance to become their student. My decision was made before my return flight got off the runway.

Given the scope and intricacy of its evolution, it's no surprise that the human capacity for vision has defied decades of attempts at automation. But what if that changed? What if we could share a human-like awareness of the world with our machines, with their automated speed and tireless precision? Imagine drones or even satellites that fly over forests, glaciers, and coastlines to generate expert assessments of the environment's health on a global scale. Imagine intelligent nonhuman assistants that help the vision-impaired negotiate environments of any complexity, just as a human assistant would. Imagine search and rescue made safer by robotic first responders that pair the judgment of an EMT or firefighter with a machine's stamina and resilience, or automated medical diagnostics that bring a specialist's insights to patients all over the world through their mobile devices.

Opportunities abound in the digital world as well. After more than a hundred years of visual media, including photography, film, journalism, and television, the consumption of imagery has become a fixture of modern life. But unlike text and numeric data, both of which have been searchable since the earliest days of computers, even a cursory search of images remains a manual affair, demanding the time—and, often, the wages—of a human. How might visually intelligent machines help us make sense of a collective data burden that has long since surpassed any hope of manual curation?

Possibilities like these have tantalized AI researchers since the earliest days of the field. What they soon realized, however—and what every generation since has only confirmed—is that visual understanding is a challenge of astonishing complexity, starting from the data itself. Because digital imagery is stored in the form of pixels—individual points of color encoded numerically—it appears to a machine as nothing more than a long list of integers. To see the image as a human might, in terms of meaningful concepts like people, places, and things, an algorithm must sift through this list and identify numeric patterns that somehow correspond.

Unfortunately, defining these patterns for even simple concepts like straight lines or geometric shapes is difficult. Doing so for something as organic and protean as a human face—in all its colors and proportions, and across an infinite range of angles, lighting conditions, and backgrounds—is vastly more complex.

And the puzzle only deepens from there. For instance, where exactly does one draw the line between the passive act of *seeing* from the related but far deeper act of *understanding*? How often is the purely perceptive experience of sight—blobs of color given form by edges and textures—made coherent by our ability to impose meaning on those shapes, even before we've had time to consciously process what we see? It soon becomes clear that there's no separating the two; to see *is* to understand, making the challenge every bit as intellectual as it is sensory. Vision, therefore, is not merely an application of our intelligence. It is, for all practical purposes, *synonymous* with our intelligence.

This is the magic of sight. It's a skill so finely tuned that although we see the world through nothing more than the light that happens to land on the surfaces of our eyes, what we derive from that light expands to fill the entirety of our experience. This almost miraculous translation, from sensory input to robust, actionable knowledge, is among the most impressive capabilities of our brains. The computational cost of this task alone remains orders of magnitude beyond what even warehouse-sized supercomputers can muster, all delivered by a wet, organic lump about five inches in diameter. And its conceptual depth continues to humble even the luminaries of the academic world.

The puzzle of vision is about much more than understanding how we see. It isn't simply a question of colors or shapes, or even of number crunching at ever-larger scales. It's an investigation into a phenomenon at the very core of our cognition, from which so much of who and what we are springs forth, biologically, interpersonally, and culturally. It's a journey to the most foundational layers of our experience. So often, to see is to know. Understanding *how* we see, therefore, is to understand ourselves.

My career as a grad student began with the purchase of an especially large textbook. It'd been published just a year before I enrolled, making its contents almost as fresh as its binding. It was heavy and sharp-edged, and it cracked audibly the first time I opened it. I was excited every time I saw its cover, which wove together each thread of my academic journey into a single artifact.

It was titled *Vision Science*, two words that seemed handpicked to describe the path I'd been trying to follow since the UC Berkeley experiment. An inch or so lower, in italics, its subtitle anticipated my curiosity even further: *Photons to Phenomenology*. And above both, a full-bleed depiction of van Gogh's *Starry Night* filled nearly two-thirds of its surface. It was a dense and comprehensive work, destined to serve as a standard for decades to come. I wanted to learn everything it had to teach me.

Two years had passed since that life-altering moment in a darkened lab—those crackling and whooshing sounds that yielded my first glimpse of the inner workings of a mind other than my own. Two years of a pursuit that had only just begun. I was intrigued and challenged by the art of engineering, but I didn't want to be an engineer. And although I was enthralled by the mysteries of neuroscience, I didn't want to be a neuroscientist. I wanted to draw on both while constrained by neither.

My timing couldn't have been better, even if it was nothing more than happenstance. I didn't know it yet, but the study of vision was an outgrowth of artificial intelligence itself—one community among many in exile, fractured and driven away from the banner that once united them, now a decade into the deep freeze of another downturn. The fizzling of once exciting prospects like neural networks and expert systems had brought about another round of alienation, as start-ups closed their doors and academic interest faded. It was another AI winter, and I was in the thick of it. But the thaw was coming fast.

6

THE NORTH STAR

The shimmer of a Pasadena dawn was creeping up the horizon, cast in a palette of warm colors I'd come to recognize as distinctly Californian. Its call to venture outdoors and disregard the obligations of the day was tempting, but no sky was blue enough to compete with the promise of discovery. Today was the first day of a new experiment I'd been preparing for months, and it was waiting for me underground.

Our work would take place in the psychophysics section of the Koch Lab, a shadowy basement world hidden beneath Caltech's sun-baked lawns and cycling paths. Devoid of natural light, and routinely deprived of the artificial kind as well, it was a place of near perfect sequestration: three identical booths, separated by blackout curtains, each large enough to insulate the senses of a single seated occupant.

Once inside, our subjects would place one hand on a mouse, another on a keyboard, and stare into the dark. After a momentary lull, a monitor would light up, displaying a sequence of images so incoherent they could have been curated by a Dadaist: letters arranged like alphabet soup; photographs of random, disjointed scenes; sudden flashes of colored noise, all timed down to the millisecond and eliciting precisely measured responses of clicks and key presses. Then, within a matter of seconds, the darkness would return. Another moment of stillness would hang in the air, and the sequence would repeat. Again, and again, and again.

Chaotic as it must have seemed, not a single detail was arbitrary. It all added up to an attempt, however contrived, at reading a mind—or at least inferring some fragment of its contents. A few frenzied seconds of a subject's twitching fingers, shallow breaths, and dilating pupils captured in a thicket of data that might take days, weeks, or even months to fully disentangle. The secrets of the senses are deeply hidden; coaxing them into the light for even an instant can be a strange affair.

Evolution bore down on a single photosensitive protein for a half-billion years, pushing relentlessly as it blossomed across eons into an apparatus so exquisite that it nearly defies comprehension. Now, at Caltech, the fruits of that labor were to become our teacher—the entire visual cortex, reaching from the glassy surface of the eye to the deepest recesses of the mind. As far as my advisors were concerned, an essential first step toward the promise of machine intelligence was a better understanding of the human kind.

I didn't know exactly what I hoped to get out of my postgraduate years apart from the opportunity to immerse myself in the field that had stolen my heart. But I hoped that somewhere along the way I'd find a pursuit that I could follow with the zeal of my role models—the spirit that drove Eric Wieschaus to turn an obsession with fruit fly abnormalities into a Nobel Prize, or Neil deGrasse Tyson to spin the cosmos into numerical poetry. I wanted a North Star of my own. But until I found it, I was content to wrap my mind around the question of how the ineffable experience of vision really works—or, in the puckish words of my textbook's subtitle, how photons become phenomenology.

An early step toward that understanding came from the pages of my textbook *Vision Science*, with the introduction of the Princeton psychologist Anne Treisman. A wunderkind of experimentation and a giant of twentieth-century cognitive science, she combined charmingly simple tools with raw ingenuity to probe human perception, decades before the digital technologies that would have accelerated her research dramatically.

Treisman's "feature integration theory of attention" became an almost universal foundation for understanding the nature of visual awareness. By presenting subjects with a momentary flash of an abstract arrangement—say, a single red circle mixed into a jumble of green and red squares—she was able to disentangle the time it took them to make sense of the image at varying levels of depth. She found that it was possible for people to identify the *presence* of red almost instantaneously—to simply know the color is contained within the image, somewhere—but that it took them longer to find the red *circle* in particular, as its identity was a combination of two distinct features: color and shape, coinciding in the same spot. In other words, the ability to *integrate* the perception of red and the perception of a circle not only took longer, but appeared to comprise an entirely separate, more intensive stage of visual processing.

Treisman's work was grand in its scope and dense in its explanations, but it was unified by the idea that human vision begins by identifying small details, then establishes the relationships between them until they reveal a complete picture. It was an intuitive thesis, and it suggested a metric for understanding vision at work: simple objects defined by few features can be recognized quickly—an orange ball on gray pavement, for instance—while more complex scenes, such as a winding forest path or the details of a friend's face, require more time.

It was a paradigm I saw repeat across the study of computer vision, as researchers wrote and refined algorithms that could identify fundamental details in photographs and other images—sharp edges, changes in light and color, fragments of texture or patterns—then built higher-level algorithms to recognize the connections between them and associate them with more meaningful things, like people and objects. What little I knew about vision made sense. But the picture was soon to grow far more complicated.

"I've got something for your reading list, Fei-Fei," Pietro said, dropping a copy of an article on the desk in front of me.

"This?"

I picked it up and flipped through it, noticing it was less than a quarter of the length of most published papers. Pietro smiled knowingly.

"Trust me. You're gonna want to read this."

He wasn't kidding.

Submitted by the neuroscientist Simon Thorpe to the Letters section of a 1996 volume of the journal *Nature*, the article was short—only three pages—but thunderous in its findings. Even its matter-of-fact title, "Speed of Processing in the Human Visual System," undersold the impact it would have as it threw the accepted orthodoxy of an entire field into question. It was an example of the greatest tradition in all of science—the disruption of established ideas, intuitive and familiar as they may be, by a more intricate reality.

Using an electroencephalogram, or EEG, Thorpe measured electrical signals across the surfaces of human subjects' brains while they observed images on a computer monitor. When a photograph was flashed on the screen for only 27 milliseconds—the time it takes for a honeybee to flap its wings a few times—his subjects could identify its contents with remarkable accuracy. But he dug deeper, pinpointing the moment of recognition within their brains: just 150 milliseconds after the image appeared, or roughly the time it takes to blink. It was the most precise investigation into the speed of human visual processing ever conducted, and the numbers were drastically smaller than what Treisman's theory would have predicted.

Thorpe's subjects were processing entire photographs, teeming with detail, perspective, subtle lighting, and meaning—and all in the time it took Treisman's subjects to identify basic colors and shapes. A single question burned in the mind of everyone who read the article: *how?* I could see why Pietro was so eager for me to read it, too, and why, more than three years after its publication, it remained a constant source of discussion and debate between him and Christof. I instantly shared their fascination.

For me, the work was made all the more surreal by how recently it had been published, just a handful of years before my arrival at Caltech. It's easy to forget how young the modern study of human vision really is even today, with its earliest publications dating back only a few decades. In contrast to physics, with its storied history stretching across centuries, populated by legends from Galileo to Newton to Bohr, vision was—and is—largely uncharted territory. The study of *computer* vision is even younger. It felt like the map was being drawn even as I held it in my hands, and it electrified my early days as a grad student. I couldn't help but gush about it in my weekly calls to Mr. Sabella, which continued from Pasadena.

"I've never seen anything like it," I said. "This field is so complex, and so exciting, and yet . . . it's practically brand-new! Most of the biggest contributors are still doing active research as we speak!"

The more time I spent with Pietro and Christof, the more I appreciated the sense of adventure that defined their careers as academics. Though they hailed from physics and engineering, both wore their love for fields like psychology, cognitive science, and neuroscience on their sleeves. They read computer science journals as regularly as anyone else in the department, but they pored over publications like *Psychological Review*, *Proceedings of the National Academy of Sciences*, and the especially prestigious *Nature* just as intently.

That fascination translated into strong opinions and an eagerness to advance the frontiers of knowledge, which meant confronting the disparity between Thorpe's and Treisman's findings head-on. The evidence was strong that at least some aspects of vision—namely, the ability to recognize real-world scenery—were all but effortless. But what gave rise to that effortlessness? Could it be quantified somehow? What were the implications for our understanding of the brain as a whole? They were questions worth finding answers to, and, conveniently for my advisors, attempting to do so would be more than enough work to keep their particularly persistent new grad student occupied for a while.

How does one read a mind?

In the lab, accurately capturing a test subject's perception, expectations, and even decision-making is commonplace. Devising an experimental method for doing so, however, requires a combination of engineering, psychology, ergonomics, and even something akin to sleight of hand. It's ironic that while our experiments looked no different from what you'd expect to see in many other laboratories—test subjects festooned with electrodes, assistants wrangling reams of data, and so on—designing them was nothing short of an art form.

Our goal was unusually nebulous: determining whether test subjects could accurately recognize the contents of a photograph displayed for just a fraction a second, but *without* focusing their attention on it. Thorpe had established the speed of such a task, but he hadn't explored the role that conscious attention played. Is deliberate focus required? Or is our ability to recognize perpetual and unconscious, sensing the world around us whether or not we take notice? We suspected the latter, but we wanted to prove it.

The idea for how to go about doing so came from Achim Braun, a visiting postdoc in Christof's lab. Braun was researching a similar hypothesis—that our brains process extensive visual details without our conscious awareness—using what he called the "dual-test method," in which he engaged a subject's attention with a central task that required deliberate focus while presenting a peripheral task requiring only passive observation, the high level of attention demanded by the first task ensuring the second won't be processed consciously.

The ingenuity of the method is the way it lays bare the focal point of the subject's senses. Because the central task has an objective response that requires effort to produce, it can be determined with high certainty over the course of multiple rounds whether the user was fully engaged with it or not. Although comparatively simple, the peripheral task also has a correct response, making it possible to reliably measure the subject's secondary awareness. Because both tasks are presented during a period of only around two hundred milliseconds (only slightly longer than the blink of an eye), the possibility of performing them both consciously, one after the other, can be ruled out.

Our experiment used this precise control over the subjects' attention to ask a simple question: having viewed a randomly chosen photograph of outdoor scenery—one we were certain they'd seen only peripherally—did it, or did it not, contain a depiction of an animal? Their answers would speak volumes about the nature of attention as it relates to visual perception.

From the subjects' perspective, the pace of the experiment was breathlessly fast, filled as it was with lightning-quick glimpses of images and patterns requiring near-instant responses. But the task of administering it was considerably less so. From one day to the next it felt more like babysitting than scientific inquiry, as we waited for the bleary-eyed undergrads we'd lured with the promise of some weekend spending cash to emerge from their booths. Because willing subjects were never quite as abundant as we'd have liked, we were at the mercy of their schedules. On more than one occasion, my primary responsibility for the day was meeting a stranger at the entrance to the lab at six in the morning. But I loved even that. In its own way, it, too, was a part of science.

As important as our experiment was, Pietro and Christof made it clear that a good scientist needs to keep up with the literature as well. And the more I read, the more I realized that Thorpe wasn't Treisman's first challenger. A bread crumb trail of sorts revealed itself to me, buried in decades of articles, suggesting a growing collection of exceptions to her ideas.

Perhaps the most distinctly incongruous findings came from a vision researcher named Irving Biederman. He and his colleagues arranged an experiment in which subjects were shown quick glimpses of photographs rather than abstract shapes and colors, and then asked to identify what they saw. Despite the significant increase in the complexity of the stimuli and the vanishingly short length of its exposure, the subjects' answers were consistently accurate. In less time than it took one of Treisman's subjects to, say, recognize a lone letter *A* amidst a field of multicolored *B*'s, Biederman's subjects could somehow absorb enough detail from a photograph to tell if it was a picture of a shopping plaza's parking lot or a home kitchen.

The next wrinkle came from a psychologist named Molly Potter. Using an early computer monitor, she presented passages of text to her subjects, flashing them one word at a time in large type at the center of the screen. Their comprehension was impressively high, even when the words appeared at a rate of twelve per second—twice the speed at which the average college student reads under normal conditions. As convincing as Treisman's demonstrations were that visual perception works its way up from the level of small details, reading appeared to represent a powerful exception.

The research was all the more impressive in light of the comparatively primitive tools with which it was carried out. Lacking a direct view of their subjects' cognition, thinkers like Treisman, Biederman, and Potter extracted decades of fascinating hints through the clever use of behavioral observations under tightly controlled circumstances. But the approach had limits; at the end of the day, it's only possible to infer so much about the brain from the outside. To understand these phenomena from within required a new generation of technology.

That technology finally arrived in the form of neuroscientific tools like the EEG and functional magnetic resonance imagery, or fMRI, arming researchers with higher grades of clinical precision than ever before. Thorpe's paper was among the most notable, but it was far from the only one. Equally important was the work of the MIT cognitive neuroscientist Nancy Kanwisher and her students, who used fMRI analysis to identify a number of brain regions associated with precisely the kind of processing that was necessary to deliver the fast, accurate feats of perception that researchers like Thorpe and Biederman had uncovered. Whereas EEG measures electrical impulses across the brain, which are exceedingly fast but spread diffusely over its surface area, fMRI measures blood oxygen level changes when specific patches of neurons are engaged.

An early breakthrough was the discovery of the "fusiform face area," a cortical region in the temporal lobe, no more than a cubic centimeter in size, which appears to be tailor-made to recognize human faces. Next came the nearby "parahippocampal place area," which plays a similar role for identifying familiar locations, like one's kitchen or a frequently traveled road. Another discovery was the "extrastriate body area," which helps us perceive the physical orientation of those around us by reacting to the presence of arms, legs, and the like.

There's something special about these structures, known as the "neural correlates" of vision: they appear to be purpose-built. Each recognizes a single category of thing, and *only* that thing—faces, familiar locations, body poses, and the like—thus explaining the astonishing speed of our perception in specific recognition tasks. Rather than attempt to decode them from scratch, detail by detail, a dedicated feature of our neural anatomy springs into action to recognize them almost instantly. From our perspective, it feels effortless.

Biologically, the role of effort in a process says a lot. Evolution is parsimonious to a fanatical extent, responding only to environmental pressures so extreme that the alternative to adaptation is extinction. For a capability to be refined to such an extent—to render something so complex all but *automatic*—it must be of fundamental, even singular importance.

Vision, therefore, isn't just a question of the details of what we see. While images can be broken down and examined in the granular terms proposed by researchers like Treisman, especially in tightly controlled lab conditions, the vision we rely on to survive in a chaotic world deals in *things*—objects, people, and places. Indeed, from the earliest stages of processing, we perceive our surroundings not as an assemblage of colors and contours, but in terms of *categories*.

As exciting as these findings were on their own, they connected to each other in a way that felt even more profound, like the coastline of an undiscovered continent. Each new idea pointed to something big—historic, maybe—just waiting to be discovered, and it made me all the more impatient to see the results of our experiment. Were we on the verge of a clarified understanding? Or a more complicated one?

Pietro had a midmorning cappuccino at the campus's Red Door Cafe on most days, and I'd begun tagging along with him. My personal finances didn't quite support a fancy coffee habit for myself, but I enjoyed watching his process, from the custom order he imparted to the barista, to the care with which he added just a hint of brown sugar, to the delicate stirring that followed. After my years of hustling, it was a welcome reminder that the simpler moments of life are worth savoring.

Today, however, my reason for coming was more strategic: the results of the experiment were in, and I wanted to share them immediately. For all the attention Pietro paid to his ritual, it was easier to talk with him over coffee than lunch, as he'd developed a habit of arranging our trays into colorful tableaus he likened to the work of pop artist David Hockney. Although amusing at first, his "Hockney collages," as he called them, were mostly an opportunity for him to entertain himself while I grew hungrier and hungrier, remembering how sophisticated his love for art history had once seemed.

As he took his first sip of cappuccino, I opened the notebook in which I'd transcribed the latest results and began reading them out loud. I was proud to have something tangible to share after so much work, but as I went down the list of numbers, Pietro became as excited as me.

"Fei-Fei, these figures . . . I mean, they're—"

"I know! They're incredible!"

In test after test, the numbers painted a shockingly clear picture: our subjects recognized photographs of real-world scenes, even when their attention was focused entirely on something else. We knew the response times would be fast, but we were caught off guard by how quickly, and how consistently and accurately, the subjects performed. This unique feature of the brain, capable of identifying countless visual concepts with surprising discrimination and breakneck speed, wasn't just powerful—it appeared to be all but automatic.

It was a privilege to contribute to research that seemed to be making an impact in the field, but the greatest reward was a philosophical one. Our results joined the ranks of decades of work suggesting there was a simple idea at the heart of human visual perception: that above all else, our vision is based on an awareness of well-defined categories. On the recognition of *things*. Pietro's demeanor—one of subtle but unmistakable glee—told me he agreed. I was increasingly convinced that we were on the verge of unlocking the secret to everything.

As the end of my second year at Caltech approached, I felt I'd read enough literature, attended enough seminars and symposia, and, with the publication of our experiment, seen enough firsthand to appreciate a powerful fact: that visual perception relies on categorization; that our brains naturally sort the details of what we see into broader terms that matter to us, like objects, people, places, and events. The sight of a tree against the sky, for instance, is so much more than a simple pattern of green and blue. Vision works at a higher, more meaningful level, arming us with *knowledge*—the awareness of leaves we can imagine swaying in the breeze or holding between our fingers, or a branch with a texture and weight that we can instantly estimate, both of which differ dramatically from the untouchable atmosphere and colored light that hangs miles above.

The ability to categorize empowers us to a degree that's hard to overstate. Rather than bury us in the innumerable details of light, color, and form, vision turns our world into the kind of discrete *concepts* we can describe with words—useful ideas, arrayed around us like a map, reducing a complex reality to something we can understand at a glance and react to within a moment's time. It's how our ancient ancestors survived an environment of pure chaos, how generations of artists extracted beauty and meaning from everyday life, and how, even today, we continue to find our way around a world defined by ever-growing complexity.

So much of what I read seemed to reinforce this idea. While Treisman revealed one way we recognize complex objects, Biederman, Potter, and Thorpe complicated the picture with a striking alternative: that in some cases, such intensive, bottom-up processing is bypassed altogether. Our own lab's research explored the extent to which recognition operates in the absence of conscious attention. Especially illuminating was Kanwisher's suggestion that this incredible capability is facilitated by purpose-built neuronal correlates that map to specific things in the world—powerful evidence that the brain is physically inclined toward fast, robust detection of well-known visual concepts.

It felt like we were trying to reverse-engineer clockwork crafted with meticulous patience by some unknowable colossus. We were still far from completely understanding it—its smaller gears remained mysterious, even as they ticked away before us—but we'd stolen a glimpse of something remarkable. Biological evolution is the only force in the universe capable of creating true intelligence from scratch, and I felt like we were recovering its blueprint, or at least a few scraps of it.

It was changing the way I saw my own field of computer vision as well. Although ingenuity abounded, it was scattered across an eclectic range of research projects. Nowhere could I find a shared, unified effort, analogous to the single-minded force that had patiently shaped the development of our own minds over the millennia. I couldn't help but wonder what the world would be like if that changed—if researchers banded together to understand and re-create the core idea that seemed to lie at the very heart of human cognition.

I could hardly imagine the discoveries that might await such coordination. There's no limit on what artificial intelligence might ultimately become, but that began to feel like a secondary point; I was increasingly convinced that *this* particular challenge—making sense of the visual world by understanding the myriad categories of objects that fill it—was an ideal first step toward unlocking it. It appeared to have worked for our species, after all. I now believed it could work for our machines as well.

I thought of my role models, from the legends of physics to my own professors. For years I'd admired the power of the ideas that motivated them as scientists, and the galvanizing effects they'd had on their fields. Now, only a couple of years into my grad school education, I believed I was seeing a glimmer on my own horizon—something distant and hazy but bright enough to light my path forward. One way or another, we were going to make the visual world familiar to machines. Surpassing even the standards of a life prone to fixation, I had developed an obsession that was more intense that any I'd ever known.

I'd found a North Star of my own.

An image of a jetliner appeared on the screen as the algorithm set about its task. It was a challenge even a toddler could manage: to spot the presence of an airplane, anywhere in the photograph. But in 2003, it remained a question machines could answer only after absorbing huge amounts of example material. Even then, their odds of success were modest. That afternoon, Pietro and I were testing an idea that we hoped might change those odds, perhaps dramatically. I looked closer, eager to see what the algorithm would do.

Pink dots began to appear on the screen, visual aids meant to highlight details within the photo that caught the algorithm's eye, so to speak. I winced a bit as the first popped up in a patch of grass just off the tarmac. The algorithm was looking in the wrong place. But the trend reversed quickly as the next two appeared on the jet's wings. Then another, somewhere in its tail section. Then three more near the cockpit. Finally came the last dot. The landing gear. *That counts*, I thought. *It's technically part of the plane!*

I exhaled excitedly. So far, so good.

Next came the really hard part. Since each highlighted feature accounted for only a few pixels, the algorithm was designed to group them into clusters representing larger parts of the object it was meant to identify. A proxy, in other words, for a dim form of visual comprehension. Colored circles would be drawn around each part—blue and teal for different segments of the fuselage, red for the vertical stabilizer, and green for the area where the two met. Sure enough, the algorithm placed them almost precisely where they belonged.

Airplane recognized.

It was a thrilling moment, but not because it worked—because of *how* it worked. Rather than immersing the machine in hundreds of photos of airplanes covering as many variations of color, style, perspective, and lighting conditions as possible, we had shown it precisely one. We did, however, show it hundreds of images of completely unrelated subjects— spotted jungle cats, motorcycles, human faces courtesy of our smiling lab mates and Pietro's fancy new digital camera, and some random selections we'd downloaded from Google Images. Our hypothesis was that by exposing the algorithm to a broad cross section of the visual world first, it would be better equipped to learn something specific. So while it had been trained on a wide variety of things, the airplane it had just recognized was only the second it had seen. Ever.

Our creation was just a proof of concept, and still made its share of mistakes. But our goal was to demonstrate that algorithms, like humans, benefit broadly from seeing more of the visual world. The North Star was now a fixture on my horizon, and we'd taken a genuine step in its direction.

We called the technique "one-shot learning." It was a significant departure from the status quo of image recognition, but the ability that inspired us is well-known. As humans, we're naturally adept at recognizing things after even a single glimpse: a new kind of musical instrument, an animal we've never seen before, the face of a recently elected politician. A number of explanations for this ability can be invoked, but among the simplest and most powerful is the fact that even when we're seeing something new, we're bringing a lifetime of previous experience to bear on it. No matter how novel, virtually everything we see draws so heavily from past experiences—familiar details like contours, light and shadow, textures and patterns—that it's hard to imagine seeing anything in true isolation.

Our technique brought this concept to machines, and it appeared to be working. If the results were a pleasant surprise, however, the reception that our paper received was overwhelming. It was something of a breakout success, not only being accepted to the International Conference on Computer Vision (ICCV) in Nice, France, but earning us one of only a few oral presentation spots. Although the paper was coauthored with Pietro and a fellow researcher named Rob Fergus, I was the lead. That meant the honor of the trip, and the responsibility, was mine.

Speaking at ICCV was a rare opportunity, especially for a grad student, and my near-total lack of experience presenting before such an important audience was weighing on my mind. To make matters worse, Pietro wouldn't be able to come with me. He and his wife were expecting the birth of their first child, and their due date was approaching. It was my first academic conference, and my first onstage presentation. And I would be going alone.

Nerves might have been an issue on the flight to Nice in the absence of the task in front of me. My responsibilities at Caltech had kept me in a state of nonstop hustling, and thirteen quiet hours at thirty thousand feet ended up being my only free window to put together the talk that I'd be delivering. I kept my head down for most of the trip, writing up an outline and cobbling together slides as fast as I could.

Upon arrival, however, I felt Pietro's absence keenly. It's customary for advisors to attend a student's first conference alongside them, whether they're presenting or not, as a show of support and to help with networking. It was beginning to sink in that I'd been left to fend for myself in an event hall full of hundreds of strangers. If I were going to get nervous, now was the time.

"Fei-Fei?" a voice called out behind me. I turned to find an unfamiliar face looking down at me.

". . . Yes?" I cautiously replied.

"It's wonderful to finally meet you! I'm Jitendra."

"Jiten . . . Oh! Jitendra . . . *Malik*? Are you—"

"I suppose you know me as Pietro's former advisor, yes," he said with a laugh. "He asked me to keep you company. You didn't think we'd let you do this alone, did you?"

Although I'd known Jitendra's name, and certainly his reputation, this was the first time we'd met face-to-face. I tend to think of academic relationships in familial terms, and so I considered him—my advisor's advisor—my "academic grandfather." He lived up to the appellation, with a presence that was both calming and encouraging. After my talk, when I was set upon by a mob of researchers eager to learn more, he was a lifesaver. Simply having him by my side turned an overwhelming day into something manageable, and began what grew into a lasting bond.

Despite the flurry of conversation following my talk, something subtle occurred to me—that every question I was asked was about the algorithm itself. *How did you set up the Bayesian equations to estimate the posterior probability? How did you estimate a prior distribution of images? You mentioned using a recently proposed variational inference algorithm to optimize the model parameters—can you talk more about that? What are your plans to expand it in future revisions? How might it perform under different circumstances?*

Again and again we were asked about the mathematical core of the machine learning algorithm we chose—a probabilistic technique called a "Bayesian network"—but not a single question about the data we trained it on. While that wasn't unusual—data was not so subtly dismissed as an inert commodity that only mattered to the extent that algorithms required it—I began to realize that we'd underestimated something important.

The defining feature of our algorithm—its ability to learn new categories of objects from as little as a single exposure—was critically dependent on data. It was, ultimately, the diversity of other things our algorithm had seen that gave it a kind of perceptual experience and allowed it to perform so well when presented with something new.

In fact, the more I thought about it, the more I wondered why this topic—the subtle but intriguing power of data—wasn't getting any attention. After all, we'd achieved rather surprising results from an absolute dearth of the stuff—a smattering of a few hundred images spread across just a few randomly chosen categories. It raised a question that seemed more provocative every time my mind returned to it: *if so little data could make such a powerful capability possible, what might more data enable?*

How about a lot more?

* * *

"Almost done . . . Just a second . . ." Another lunch at the Red Door Cafe, another waste of a few perfectly good minutes of eating time as Pietro arranged our platters into the next in his series of Hockney collages. "There!"

"Uh-huh. Very nice," I said. I wasn't even pretending to look anymore.

Pietro smiled at his work, clearly picking up on my impatience and clearly unbothered by it. I grabbed my tray back from him and began eating.

"I keep thinking about our one-shot learning paper," he said, changing the subject. "I'm proud of what we accomplished, but we both know the data was the real star of the show."

I nodded, still chewing.

"So, what if we created a completely *new* data set? A bigger one. I think we could do the whole thing ourselves, from scratch."

I continued nodding.

"I mean, what if all this new data—*entirely* on its own—is the key to reaching that next level?"

It was an audacious idea, and just enough of a long shot to keep things interesting.

"So, let's start with the most obvious question: how many image categories should this new data set of ours include?"

I set my fork down and pondered the question for a moment. Knowing that the biggest collection ever assembled at Caltech offered seven rather randomly chosen categories, rounding up seemed like a sensible place to start.

"How's, uh . . . ten?" I offered.

Pietro furrowed his brow.

"That'd be an improvement, I suppose, but I wonder if we're being too incremental."

I liked the spirit of his suggestion, but I couldn't help but consider the reality as well. Knowing that the actual work of collecting, labeling, and organizing the images would fall on me, I did my best to balance the needs of our research with the practical concerns of daily life.

"Okay. Um . . . fifteen, then?"

Pietro grinned wryly.

"Fine. Twenty!"

He didn't budge. *Seriously?*

Pietro would later tell me I was getting close—he was thinking something on the order of thirty categories would suffice. But noting the way the conversation appeared to be devolving into a negotiation— and a rather guarded one at that—he felt compelled to go on the offense.

"Let's do a *hundred*, Fei-Fei."

As Pietro would later put it, I looked as if he'd sentenced me to death. Given the work this would no doubt require, I would likely lose some of my sanity, not to mention any semblance of a social life I might have aspired to over the next few months (admittedly less of a loss). But he was right, and I couldn't deny my excitement at the thought of how our model would perform given such a resource. Rather than give him the satisfaction, however, I did my best to take the idea in stride. Improving my poker face would be a longer-term effort.

As the brinkmanship of the conversation faded from memory, I began to think differently about the plan. Yes, curating a hundred categories of images—each containing a wide variety of examples—would be a more laborious undertaking than anything I'd ever attempted in my life, weekends at the dry-cleaning shop included. But it was exactly what I wanted. My North Star was glimmering over the horizon, brighter than ever.

"Hi, Fei-Fei."

"Hi, Mom. How's Dad? How's the shop?"

"A customer is asking for an alteration but he keeps using a term I'm not familiar with. I think it's a type of fit, but . . ."

A strange pause followed.

"Fei-Fei, I . . ."

Her breathing got more labored. I could hear her on the other end of the line, but she couldn't seem to summon a response.

"Mom? *Mom?* Are you okay?"

There's no good time to learn that your mother has suffered congestive heart failure. But two years into a grad program that's already stretching your fortitude to the breaking point, the feeling is hard to put into words.

In hindsight, it had been clear for weeks that she wasn't feeling well. Given the sheer strain of running the shop more or less alone, she'd simply needed a break, I assumed, and I invited her to come for a visit. But when she arrived at the airport struggling to breathe and paler than I'd ever seen her, I could tell something far more serious was going on.

It was an emergency, undoubtedly, but my parents' lack of health insurance left me unsure exactly how to react. In a panic, I called everyone I could think of, and was referred to a Chinese-speaking doctor working out of a private clinic in Irvine. It was a nearly two-hour drive, but she was the only one willing to see us for an out-of-pocket fee, mercifully discounted as well. Her diagnosis was quick: my mother's heart's health was dire.

Mr. Sabella remained my go-to source of comfort. "How's your mom, Fei-Fei?" he asked.

"The doctor says she'll survive. We caught it just in time."

"Thank God. How are *you* holding up?"

I let out a sigh as it all poured out of me. Our latest, most desperate plan. After seven years of running the dry-cleaning shop, we had no choice but to sell it. It'd been our lifeline when all other options seemed beyond our reach, but my mother had simply grown too sick to keep going, even with my father's help. And although the business was solvent, we were still nowhere near the kind of profit margin that would have allowed us to hire employees. The time had come to move on.

Even more drastic was my decision to move my parents across the country to join me in Pasadena, where we could once again face the challenge of surviving as a family. My dorm was even smaller than our place in Parsippany, but it was our only option for the time being.

There was a moment of silence on the line as Mr. Sabella took it all in. "You're going to continue your studies, right?" He seemed to be sensing something even I hadn't quite faced yet.

"I don't know."

Another moment of silence lingered until I broke it with a laugh.

"Do you think I can declare my parents as dependents, at least?"

A new reality was emerging, so complicated that it destabilized every decision I'd made since the day I walked into that lecture hall at Princeton as a physics major. A lifetime of curiosity had led me to a field known for fierce competition, low pay, and no guarantee of a lasting career, all while my parents needed a level of support I wasn't capable of providing. Every day I spent pursuing my dreams felt selfish at best, and reckless at worst. The more I thought about the difference between my own family and those of my lab mates, most of whom were middle class at least, if not wealthy, the harder it was to deny the truth: I just didn't have the luxury of being a scientist.

But the story wasn't over yet.

A few weeks had passed when a fellow student mentioned that a partner from McKinsey, the world-renowned management consulting firm, was in town to recruit. They were looking to fill an intern-level analyst position that promised extensive on-the-job experience, which meant that researchers from Ivy League schools with even tenuous connections to math and computer science were ideal candidates. In a moment of genuine desperation, it felt like an opportunity worth considering.

I'd been here before, of course, and it was tempting to write it off as just the latest skirmish in the long-simmering conflict between my academic goals and life in the real world. But the voice of my inner scientist was different this time. Shaken by the latest blow to my mother's health, it had grown less insistent, as if even that special, guarded part of me was beginning to yield to a reality I knew I couldn't ignore forever. Pushing my hesitation aside—an act I now found disconcertingly easy—I bought an outfit way beyond my budget, carefully hid the tags beneath the collar in anticipation of returning it immediately after, and arranged for an interview.

It all felt about as unnatural as I expected, but I couldn't ignore the fact that fate appeared to be on my side from the start. It was perhaps my first opportunity to present myself as a fully formed person outside the academic world, and it filled me with a conviction I didn't normally possess. I was unabashedly nerdy, sure, but there was more to me than that: years of struggle had tempered me, fostering a scrappiness my fellow candidates had never had reason to develop, alongside an instinct for pragmatism I only now realized made me unusual. Then came an almost comical stroke of synchronicity.

"We like to organize our interviews around a hypothetical business scenario," the McKinsey representative began. "No one expects you to actually know the industry, of course, so think of this more as a creative exercise than anything else. We're just trying to get a sense of your instincts. You know, analytical reasoning and stuff."

Simple enough, I thought.

"I want you to imagine you're a manager in . . . let's say . . . the clothing industry."

Wow.

What began as a routine assessment blossomed into an unexpectedly rich conversation, from my love for physics and my fascination with the mysteries of intelligence to the world of laundry-supply vendors and my amateur career as a dry-cleaning executive. Against all odds, it actually seemed like it was going . . . well.

The recruiter agreed, apparently. The response was immediate and aggressive, with the news that McKinsey had decided to turn the internship into an official offer of a permanent position.

My feelings were so mixed I'm not sure they even registered. On the one hand, my stomach turned at the thought of leaving so much behind—Caltech, Pietro, Christof, Jitendra, my fellow students, everything I knew, really, and worst of all, the utterly cosmic opportunity to pursue an idea that felt historic. My North Star. On the other hand, after seeing my parents living on the brink for so many years, and increasingly feeling as if they were there because of me, it was as if I were finally being relieved of a burden so oppressive I'd never fully appreciated its weight. My mother had given everything for me to be here, and now, when I knew she needed me most, I could finally repay her. I headed straight home, ready to share what I thought was good news.

"This is how you dress for the lab, Fei-Fei?"

I looked down at myself. I'd forgotten I had my interview outfit on.

"Oh, right," I said with a half-hearted laugh. "Don't worry, I got a great deal on it," I added, revealing the tags, still intact.

"What's going on?" she asked, now even more confused. Life had been such a blur that I'd yet to mention any of my plans to my parents.

"Mom, we need to talk."

I explained the interview, the job offer, and everything else. I told her about the perks, and the starting salary, and the way they'd already sweetened the offer before I'd even had a chance to respond. I explained that it was, for all intents and purposes, a fast track to the kind of career every immigrant mother imagines for their child. She listened politely, but I saw a familiar look on her face well before I finished speaking.

"Are we really going to have this conversation again?"

"Mom, I know, but listen—"

"I know my daughter. She's not a management consultant, or whatever you called it. She's a scientist."

"Think about your health, Mom! Think about the expenses we have to look forward to. How is an academic career going to help us—"

"Fei-Fei. We didn't come this far for you to give up now."

"This isn't giving up! This is a dream job—a *career*—and it could free us from *all* of this. I mean, look around! We're three adults living in *a dorm*!"

I'm not sure if I believed the words coming out of my mouth, but they seemed like the right thing to say. Whatever my mother thought about them, she paused for a moment, perhaps to mull them over, before responding.

"Fei-Fei, you keep talking about this 'selfish' journey you're on. As if science is something you're *taking* from us."

"How can I not feel that way? I could be earning a living for all of us right now, and—"

"You're not hearing me. This has never been *your* journey. From the very beginning, this has been *our* journey. Whether you were fated to be a scientist, a researcher, or something else I can't even imagine, and whether or not you'll ever make more than a pittance doing it, we've been working toward it as a family since the moment our plane left that runway in Shanghai."

I didn't know what to say.

"I'm going to say this one last time: we didn't come this far for you to give up now."

She was right. She was always right. This time, for whatever reason, I finally heard her. I would never question my path again.

"Hey, what's that dog breed called?" I asked a fellow student from across the mostly empty lab as we ate lunch.

"Which one?"

"You know, it's brown and white and . . . also black, I think . . . and it's got these really cute floppy ears. God, I've completely forgotten its English name."

We were pondering the kinds of cosmic questions only graduate students dare confront.

"I know it starts with a *B* . . . Actually, don't tell me . . ."

I reached for the English dictionary I still kept on my desk. Nearly a decade into my life as an American, and even as the internet grew to replace so many of the objects in our lives, it served as an occasional lifesaver. I flipped through the pages, then scanned down until I saw . . .

"Ah! Yes! *Beagle!*"

"Okay, so? What about beagles?"

I stopped and looked back at the page. I'd forgotten why I'd even brought it up, but it didn't matter. Something else entirely was dawning on me.

Pietro and I were aiming for a data set with a hundred image categories, but we'd been struggling to devise a good way to decide which exactly to include. We worried that the selections might be biased if we did it ourselves—that even subconsciously, we'd gravitate toward categories of images we knew our algorithms would be more likely to succeed in recognizing.

I squinted, looking more closely. There was something elegant about the way the dictionary illustrated certain words. Most were nouns, with an emphasis on tangible, visual stuff—objects, in other words, or, in the case of the beagle, animals. They seemed like exactly the kind of categories we'd want. And they appeared to be spread more or less evenly across every letter, which sounded pretty unbiased to me. I wondered: what if we just let the dictionary make the choices for us?

It was perfect. The doorstop of a book I'd been lugging around for years had become the most useful tool in my world as an aspiring computer vision researcher. Every now and then, being an immigrant pays off.

Early revelations aside, curating the full data set was a long, slow, unglamorous slog. Months were spent manually querying image search engines, picking out the best of the results, then cropping and resizing them to consistent dimensions. A small team of undergraduate labelers pitched in, three or four in total, and even my mother, now a local, found ways to help.

As arduous as it could be, there was something illuminating about the process. After thinking so much about the variety of the visual world, I was seeing it in a way I never had before: as a single real-ity that includes accordions, blenders, cell phones, crayfish, lobsters, pizza, stop signs, umbrellas, and so many other things. There was a kind of poetry to it; it made me appreciate how rich and unpredictable the world is, and how little of its detail we notice.

Finally, it was done. At the time of its completion in 2004, it was the largest collection of images ever assembled for machine learning: more than nine thousand of them, spread across a hundred categories. It was unprecedented, and I couldn't wait to see what it'd unlock. We felt empowered in a way we'd never been before, as if we were suddenly in possession of a supernatural artifact, ready to endow our creations with greater capabilities than we'd ever imagined. But there was one detail left I couldn't resist: working on my own, I threw in yet another category as a playful way to thumb my nose at my mentor, albeit at my own cost. If Pietro wanted 100, I'd give him 101.

We immediately published a follow-up to our one-shot learning paper, now featuring a model powered by a staggeringly diverse set of training images—a data set now officially known as "Caltech 101"—and boasting significant performance gains to match. Due to its admittedly incremental nature, it wasn't the breakout success of the first paper, at least not initially. But it established a more lasting legacy as a model for others to follow. The performance curves we drew to graph our results became a benchmark; within six months, researchers from all over the world were citing our paper as the standard to beat—which many of them did. As exciting as it was to publish our own research, feeling as if we were contributing to the ideas of others—and playing even a small role in their success moving the field forward—was an even greater thrill.

It was clear that life at Caltech would never be easy, but my gratitude for simply being there ran deeper than ever. We managed to sell the dry-cleaning shop, affording my mother a much-needed chance to rest for the first time since we'd come to this country. (I couldn't pretend that the prospect of never again fielding a long-distance call about an over-starched dress shirt didn't please me, too.) Most of all, I was passionate about my studies, to the point of an almost daily sense of exhaustion.

Thankfully, Caltech is the kind of place where fellow obsessives aren't hard to find. I encountered one in particular outside Pietro's office, when I heard what appeared to be *two* conspicuously Italian voices, rather than the one I was used to. I soon learned that the second belonged to a fellow grad student I'd yet to meet. He was tall, with an accent so impenetrable it made Pietro's practically vanish in comparison, and boasted a head of wildly curling hair that stood out from across the room. He also happened to be in a hurry that day, making for a forgettable first encounter even as Pietro introduced us. But it allowed me to put a name to the voice: Silvio.

Silvio's presence in our lab meetings soon caught my eye. Like me, he often kicked off his presentations by discussing artwork. He was drawn to pieces like Escher's *Hand with Reflecting Sphere* and Vermeer's *Girl with a Pearl Earring*, both of which lingered on aspects of the visual world he explored through his research—the warped contours of curved reflections, the gleam of metallic surfaces, and the three-dimensional nature of everyday objects. Of course, the eye candy quickly gave way to mountains of equations. The more time we spent together, the more I realized we shared something familiar: an inability to turn off our curiosity, no matter the circumstances.

"Look! Look at that motorcycle!" He was excited enough to completely derail what had begun as a relaxing stroll across the campus.

"What about it?"

"Okay, see the chrome exhaust? See the reflections? They contain *so much* information. You see? The way they curve and warp?"

"Yeah, I see what you mean."

"But here's the catch—what *is* a reflection, exactly? It's just a distorted picture of the world *surrounding* the surface! It's almost a contradiction, and yet it tells us enough about the shape of that motorcycle part that we can imagine it in our minds, effortlessly. *This* is the kind of algorithm we're trying to design."

My God, what a nerd this guy is, I thought. *But he's the same kind of nerd as me.*

I was a student in two labs—electrical engineering with Pietro, and computational neuroscience with Christof. I met with each once a week, attended journal clubs reviewing the latest literature in both neuroscience and computer science, and, because both labs offered free food, was eating better than I might have expected. Then there was Silvio. Whenever time permitted—which, given our schedules, wasn't often, especially by the standards of a giddy new relationship—we had each other.

But as my years at Caltech passed, something else took root within me. I reflected on everything we'd done: our psychophysics experiment, our research into one-shot learning algorithms, our work demonstrating the power of the Caltech 101 data set, and the decades of literature we'd pored over. Despite the unorthodox path of my education, bifurcated at the hands of two advisors, I was beginning to appreciate the elegance of our work. It was no accident that we'd done all these things; I was more convinced than ever that *categorization* was the idea connecting them, and that its role in understanding vision—and maybe even the whole of human intelligence—would soon prove paramount.

So why was progress still so slow?

In a word, our algorithms were "overfitting," as it's called in data science. That is, no matter how cleverly designed—and we explored every variety we could find—even those that performed best during testing quickly faltered when exposed to new stimuli. Again and again, algorithms that appeared to have been trained effectively lacked the ability to apply what they'd learned—or were supposed to have learned—in the real world. It was, in essence, the opposite of human perception, which is defined by its ability to generalize. Generalization makes us flexible, adaptable, and even creative, ready to harness the power of new ideas rather than languish within the confines of past experience. Any creature lacking such an ability would be quickly overwhelmed by the unpredictability of the natural world, making it a key feature of a biologically evolved mind. But it remained largely out of reach for machines.

In our attempts to unravel the puzzle of overfitting, the algorithm itself was a natural place to start—specifically, the means by which it learned from its training data. Most of the algorithms we explored were so complex—so "computationally intractable," to put it more technically—that they couldn't be configured manually. The range of permutations for their countless parameters was simply too great, like a control panel of knobs and switches stretching beyond the horizon. Instead, automated techniques allowed them to approximate the ideal balance of those parameters through a long, iterative sequence of trial and error. For years, the refinement of such techniques was a pillar of computer vision research.

But Caltech 101 encouraged us to think more deeply about data as well, which, in turn, encouraged us to wonder how this side of the equation might contribute to overfitting. After all, without data, what does the "learning" in "machine learning" refer to? Despite its obvious importance, the topic lacked the precision we'd come to expect in physics, mathematics, or statistics. Researchers like Pietro and Jitendra were among the few who'd explored it with even nominal depth, and they had developed what I felt were the best intuitions for understanding it. Our publications seemed to demonstrate that as our data sets got bigger, the capabilities of our algorithms grew—relatively speaking, anyway. Even so, the curation of data felt more like a black art than a science.

I began to wonder what we might be doing wrong. Should the training images be oriented differently? Did we need more variety? Was it a question of resolution or camera quality? Or maybe—and I almost hesitated to entertain the notion, let alone speak it aloud—was it possible that even 101 categories weren't enough? The more I considered these questions, the more obvious, even pressing, they seemed. But as far as I could tell, no one else in our community was asking them.

Even the question of quantity—our specialty—seemed enigmatic. I had to admit it was reasonable to wonder what made a number like 101 so special. It wasn't an empirically proven result, or even some principled estimate derived from theory. It was the outcome of a game of chicken with my advisor over lunch trays arranged like Hockney paintings. Was it really so surprising that this wasn't the prelude to a breakthrough? I returned to the literature again, this time with a vengeance. If not 101, what? 200? 500? 1,000? *Please, not 1,000*, I thought. I was determined to find a clue, somewhere, somehow.

It took some digging, but I eventually found something. It even came from a familiar source—a paper by Irving Biederman, one of the central contributors to our modern understanding of vision, published all the way back in 1983. It'd been years since I'd read it, no doubt skimmed alongside a stack of other literature at two in the morning. Now, after everything we'd learned from our adventures in one-shot learning and our dream of achieving true visual categorization, I saw it in a new way.

The paper explored an interesting but not directly relevant topic: the way we use our knowledge of basic geometric shapes to recognize complex objects. In the process of building toward his conclusion, Biederman attempted to answer a deceptively simple question: roughly how many unique categories of "thing" exist in the world? That is, if you add them all up—"rocking chair," "penguin," "sports car," "Labrador," "mountain," and everything else—what would the total number be?

It sounds more like a riddle than a scientific challenge. But I was impressed with the ingenuity of Biederman's approach, which he based on an analysis of the English language. Words play a foundational role in helping us categorize what we see, and he reasoned that a tally of those we dedicate to discrete, quantifiable things—known as "count nouns"—would be a good place to start. He then imagined how many truly distinct variations of each such noun existed, the way a single category of object like "cup" may include a white tea set with ornate handles, a brightly colored coffee mug, and a transparent, featureless glass. Because some categories lend themselves to more variety than others, he streamlined matters by assuming a sensible average. From there, calculating the total was a simple matter of multiplication.

The logic was straightforward enough, but it was the *scale* of his idea that made it so disruptive. It instantly revealed how limited our research had been—how limited our *imaginations* had been—and how sprawling the world beyond both truly was. The paper was a hazy, photocopied relic, but it felt as if Biederman were speaking directly to me: *you want a breakthrough? This is the price. This is what it takes.*

Nevertheless, Biederman's number—a potential blueprint for what our ambitions as researchers demanded—was big. Really big. It wasn't 1,000, 2,000, or even 5,000. And it certainly wasn't the 101 we spent months cataloging.

It was *30,000.*

I had no idea what to do with the number. The creation of Caltech 101 felt like a herculean effort, and here I was faced with an estimate that dwarfed that by two solid orders of magnitude. But there was no looking away from it now. There was something there—true insight— its heat all but coursing through the digits printed on the page. What's more, I knew that wherever this number was fated to take me, I'd be going alone. My field was fixated on algorithms, full stop. But the more I thought about data—especially data at large, perhaps *massive* scales— the more I realized it was an entirely unexplored frontier. The world had chosen its direction. But my North Star was leading me in another.

7

A HYPOTHESIS

Beads of sunlight, piercing and white, flickered through the greenery streaking past my car as it sped along Route 206. The two-lane road was an easy drive, carving gentle curves through a canopy of trees that periodically broke to reveal glimpses of small towns on the horizon. I hardly saw any of it. My thoughts were worlds away, and while I could muster enough attention to stay between the lane markings, that was about it.

Although it'd only been a year since I graduated from Caltech with my doctorate, just about everything in my life had changed. My mother got sick again. Sicker than ever before, in fact, then abruptly stabilized. I also got my first real job—a junior faculty position at the University of Illinois Urbana-Champaign—and the health insurance that came with it. Silvio and I got married. Then he got a job, too . . . in Michigan. I had a lot to be thankful for, but I was a walking symbol of the turbulence so common in early academic careers. I was somehow married, alone, and living with my parents, all at once.

Still, my research into the categorizing nature of vision remained the center of my world, and I'd been invited back to Princeton to present my latest work to the computer science department. I'd grown accustomed to delivering lectures by this point, but I'd picked up hints that this invitation might be something more—the first step in a recruitment process, and potentially a faculty position. Those were higher stakes than I was used to, and I was grateful for my habit of beginning my trips to New Jersey with a visit to the Sabellas. The winding route that led from their neighborhood to my alma mater gave me plenty of time to mull things over.

It wasn't the lecture, though, or even my career, that preoccupied me most. My life simply hadn't been the same since I'd stumbled upon Biederman's number—his estimate that something on the order of 30,000 unique concepts might provide a complete foundation for understanding the visual world. Those unassuming five digits had become a black hole in the center of my mind, ensnaring my thoughts virtually every waking moment.

On the one hand, my intuition was aligned with Biederman's. His number just *looked* right, in a way I could feel in my gut. It had the veneer of evidence, a datum I could somehow put to use. At the same time, it was clear that he never intended it as a particularly empirical quantity. It was a classic back-of-the-envelope calculation, meant more as an illustration than a hypothesis. And yet, for some reason, years after I'd originally laid eyes on it, I couldn't let it go.

It inspired a shift in my thinking toward a sense of scale I'd never imagined before but offered little insight beyond that. The number 30,000 was certainly intriguing, but 30,000 *what*, exactly? I was confident the answer wasn't as simple as creating a new data set with 30,000 randomly chosen categories instead of 101. Surely, such a collection would be much more than a set of illustrated concepts from a desk dictionary. It might even begin to *model* the world holistically, rather than merely describe its features, to trace out a complete picture of life on Earth, object by object, and hint at the relationships between them. True meaning. But I was still only guessing.

As the minutes passed by, I began to daydream. The yellow and blue logo of a Sunoco station caught my eye, triggering a cascade of memories: an impressionistic flash of previous drives along the route. Colors and moods. A sharp detail here, a fuzzier one there, all surrounded by half-remembered shades, rich and evocative, but forever out of focus. I smiled involuntarily as my chain of thought arrived at something concrete: the way Mr. Sabella talked about his daily commute on this very road from his home in Budd Lake to Parsippany High, and how he meticulously tracked the price of gas to minimize the dent it made in his public-school teacher's salary.

It may seem trivial, but moments like these were exactly what motivated my obsession. They're what vision is truly about. It's not merely a "sense," at least not in the way a thermometer or Geiger counter "senses," but rather the catalyst of an *experience*. A flood of information and emotions alike, unleashed by the color of a gas station sign speeding by at fifty miles per hour. It's among the capabilities that define a mind at its most human—a point of entry to a whole universe of memories, associations, concepts, and reasoning, all woven into our visual connections to the world around us.

My thoughts returned to the presentation at Princeton. At least that was a problem I had a chance of solving.

"I don't know how a linguist wound up at a computer vision talk, Fei-Fei, but I'm glad he did."

Seated across the table from me was Christiane Fellbaum, a computational linguist, and one of the many Princeton faculty I met in the days following my lecture. She hadn't attended herself, but a colleague of hers had wound up in the audience and had a feeling she'd appreciate my work, connecting us immediately after.

Christiane's work in linguistics bore only the most tenuous connection to mine, but what we did share was pivotal: a strong cognitive science influence and a special interest in understanding—even mapping—the way a mind conceptualizes its world. The notion that had so captivated me during my own study of human vision, the way we categorize the contents of our perception, was integral to her work, and in ways very similar to mine. Both of us believe that categories are the intersection between vision (the things we see) and language (the way we describe them). Twenty minutes into the conversation, it dawned on me that I didn't even know if we were supposed to be discussing a job offer. Either way it was the last thing on my mind, as she was about to ask a question that would change my career, and my life, forever.

"Have you heard of a project called WordNet?"

WordNet, as I was about to learn, was the brainchild of George Armitage Miller, a legend in psychology and cognitive science. Born in 1920, he was one of the most influential of a generation of psychologists who looked past the surface of human behavior in an attempt to establish models of the mental processes that drive it. As such, he was naturally drawn to the structure of language and the role it plays in thought. With WordNet, he sought to map it at an astonishing scale.

Two questions, equally ambitious, inspired the project: what if every concept a human could articulate through language was organized in a single, massive database of words? And what if, in contrast to the alphabetical organization of a dictionary, those words were connected to one another on the basis of their meanings? For example, rather than pairing "apple" with "appliance" because of the accident of their spellings, "apple" would be paired with a whole cluster of related words—"food," "fruit," "tree," and so on. It would be like a map of everything humans value—everything we've come to describe with a word—arranged in one connected space. This, in a nutshell, was WordNet.

The project had grown to an almost incomprehensible size since its inception in 1985, including well over 140,000 English words and expanding rapidly into new languages. For Christiane, who was serving as president of what had become known as the Global WordNet

Association, it was almost a full-time job. I was in awe of its scope, its longevity, and the coordination that must have been required to guide its growth so precisely and over so many years. I practically blushed as I remembered the effort it took to wrangle a handful of undergrads for a few months to collect enough images for the Caltech 101 data set—its own categorical depth more than a thousand times smaller. But I was also inspired to a degree I hadn't felt in a long time.

WordNet was a revelation. It provided an answer, or at least a hint, to the questions that had consumed so much of my waking life in the nearly four years since stumbling upon Biederman's number. It was a map of human meaning itself, uncompromising in both the scope of its reach and the veracity of its contents. I didn't yet know how computer vision would achieve the scale Biederman imagined, but now, at least, I had proof such an effort was conceivable. There was a path before me for the first time, and I could see the next step.

Then, as if to drive the point home even further, Christiane mentioned a related project that sought to illustrate every concept WordNet contained with a single visual example, like a photograph or diagram. Although the initiative had been abandoned, I was intrigued. Even its name—ImageNet—was almost perfectly suggestive. Yet another nudge, and not a particularly subtle one.

The dots began to connect before I left the campus that day. First, there was WordNet: a lexical database of almost indescribable ambition that seemed to capture the entirety of the world's concepts, organized in a natural hierarchy of human meaning. Then there was ImageNet: an attempt to assign a single picture to each concept. Both projects seemed like responses to the yawning, mysterious space that Biederman's number had created in my thoughts.

I asked myself a question as absurd as it was obvious: *what if a data set like Caltech 101 were created on the scale of WordNet?* Ignoring the impossible logistics of such an undertaking—and indeed, "impossible" was the only word that sprang to mind—there was no denying the power of the idea. And it wasn't merely a question of size; although the data set would be astronomically huge, of course, its numbers would be a side effect of something deeper: diversity at a scale never before imagined, as messy and unpredictable as the world it would reflect.

After the years I'd spent immersing myself in this field, and the decades of history I'd studied with Pietro and Christof, this felt like something truly novel. Divergent, even disruptive. The next step in pursuing a mystery that haunted my days and kept me up at night. If there was even a nominal chance this might get me closer to discovery—*any* discovery—I had to consider it.

My thoughts raced as I imagined the wealth of visual cues an algorithm trained on such a data set might internalize. The hard edges of plastic, the sheen of lacquered wood, the texture of an animal's fur, the reflections on the surface of an eye, and so much else—perhaps *everything* else. I envisioned our algorithms growing ever more flexible in their ability to separate foregrounds from backgrounds, to distinguish where one object ends and another begins, and to separate light and shadow from surface and volume.

What if the secret to recognizing *anything* was a training set that included *everything*?

Barely a year after I'd become an assistant professor at Urbana-Champaign, Princeton offered me a job. It was the biggest break of my career, and I took it. The Sabellas were so excited about my return to New Jersey that they showed up in force to help unpack: Mr. Sabella, Jean, and their second son, Mark, now a college graduate himself, all waiting at the entrance to Princeton's faculty housing community on the day I arrived. It was an unexpectedly beautiful spot on Lake Carnegie, with a three-bedroom floor plan that felt positively palatial after the dorm-sized homes my parents and I had lived in since arriving in America. It was such a leap in square footage, in fact, that we soon realized a three-person moving team was overkill. With Silvio still in Ann Arbor and my parents used to living in cramped quarters, we'd barely shown up with enough furniture to fill the place. But it was a joy to reconnect with the people who'd grown to mean as much to me as my own family.

"Hey, by the way, I've been meaning to ask you something," Mr. Sabella said, catching up to me as I walked to the car to grab the last box. "When are you gonna start calling me 'Bob'? You've been calling my wife 'Jean' all these years. Isn't it time?"

It took a second to even process what he meant. It seemed such a strange way to address the man who'd been a mentor and a kind of second father to me for so long. "Bob," as if he were simply some guy I knew.

"I'm not your teacher anymore, Fei-Fei," he said with a grin. "I think we can drop the formality. Unless you'd prefer I call you 'Dr. Li,' of course."

I caught up with Christiane a few weeks after relocating, eager to let her know what an impact our meeting had had. WordNet, ImageNet, and the ridiculous but stubborn ideas they inspired. Fate, or something like it. And now, joining the ranks of the Princeton faculty myself, I felt encouraged to take a step toward making those ideas real, to organize them into something audacious, perhaps to the point of madness.

Whether I was on the verge of a breakthrough or a failure, I was excited. Science may be an incremental pursuit, but its progress is punctuated by sudden moments of seismic inflection—not because of the ambitions of some lone genius, but because of the contributions of many, all brought together by sheer fortune. As I reflected on all the threads of possibility that had had to align to spur this idea, I began to wonder if this might be just such a moment.

One last thought occurred to me on my way out of Christiane's office.

"You know, I was thinking about ImageNet, and how you said it was never finished."

"Yeah, unfortunately. A little too boring for the undergrads we hired. And it was hardly meaningful research, so no PhD student wanted to touch it."

I chuckled as memories of downloading images for the data sets I curated with Pietro flashed in my mind. She wasn't wrong. But that wasn't why I'd brought it up.

"So . . . does that mean I can use the name?" I asked with an awkward laugh. "It's kinda perfect."

"What are we watching?" I asked from the couch as Silvio knelt over the DVD player. I could hear the whir of servos as he pushed a disc in.

"It's called *Wild Strawberries*. Don't worry, you'll love it. It's a classic."

Visits to Silvio's campus in Ann Arbor were an escape for both of us from the pressures of two suddenly evolving careers. He cooked meals from scratch and tried to impart some of his film buff's knowledge to me. Best of all, we got a chance to talk—or even just think—about something other than the work that defined so much of our lives.

"Hey, I need to talk to you about something," I said as the film ended. "An idea for a research project. It's been weighing on my mind for the last few weeks."

"So you weren't paying attention to the movie, then," he said with a knowing smile.

I laughed, but he wasn't totally wrong.

"I don't think I've *ever* felt more conviction about something."

"Well, isn't that a good thing? What's the problem?"

"Yeah, it's just . . ." I let out a heavy sigh. "God, it's gonna be a *gamble*."

Silvio had proved himself a confidant without equal. We were both young assistant professors in highly competitive departments facing years of publish-or-perish as we attempted to get our careers off the ground. We were both coming to grips with the pressure to deliver quality *and* quantity, nonstop, knowing that anything less would mean we could kiss our tenured professorships goodbye—along with our best chances of a stable livelihood. He knew the stakes better than anyone in my life.

I laid everything out from the beginning, despite the years I'd already spent chewing his ear off about it. Biederman's number, Word-Net, ImageNet, and a dream that made perfect sense until I tried to imagine actually *doing* it.

"You've spent years trying to get here, Fei-Fei. You've got the degree, you've got the job, and it sounds like you've got some inspiration. And hey, your husband is six hundred miles away, so you'll definitely have the time."

I giggled, appreciating his attempt at keeping things light.

"Yeah, but, you don't think this is all just too . . . out there?" I asked.

He thought for a moment before responding.

"Isn't 'out there' exactly the kind of idea you've been looking for?"

What good is a data set with tens of thousands of categories? Most models are still struggling to recognize one or two!

Do you have any idea how long it'd take to train a model on so many images? Fei-Fei, you're talking about years *here.*

How's anyone even going to download it? You're describing a collection of images bigger than most hard drives.

Do you actually have a plan for putting this together? Who's going to label millions *of images? How long is it going to take? How would you even verify the accuracy of it all?*

I'm sorry, but this just doesn't make any sense.

The more I discussed the idea for ImageNet with my colleagues, the lonelier I felt. Silvio's pep talks notwithstanding, the nearly unanimous rejection was a bad sign at the outset of an undertaking defined by its sheer size; I might need a whole army of contributors, and I couldn't seem to find a single one. Worst of all, whether or not I agreed with them, I couldn't deny the validity of their criticisms.

There was no escaping the fact that algorithms were the center of our universe in 2006, and data just wasn't a particularly interesting topic. If machine intelligence was analogous to the biological kind, then algorithms were something like the synapses, or the intricate wiring woven throughout the brain. What could be more important than making that wiring better, faster, and more capable? I thought back to the attention our paper on one-shot learning had enjoyed—the instant conversation-starting power of a shiny new algorithm richly adorned with fancy math. Data lived in its shadow, considered little more than a training tool, like the toys a growing child plays with.

But that was exactly why I believed it deserved more attention. After all, biological intelligence wasn't designed the way algorithms are—it *evolved*. And what is evolution if not the influence of an environment on the organisms within it? Even now, our cognition bears the imprint of the world inhabited by countless generations of ancestors who lived, died, and, over time, adapted. It's what made the findings of Thorpe and Biederman, and even our own lab at Caltech, so striking: we recognize natural imagery nearly instantaneously because that's the kind of sensory stimuli—the *data*, in other words—that shaped us. ImageNet would be a chance to give our algorithms that same experience: the same breadth, the same depth, the same spectacular messiness.

Finally, after enough discouraging conversations to last me a lifetime or two, I crossed paths with my first supporter. As a leading thinker in microprocessor architecture—the art of arranging millions upon millions of nanometer-scale transistors into some of the world's most sophisticated devices—Professor Kai Li understood the power of exponential thinking better than most. He believed I was onto something, and while he wasn't in a position to contribute directly, as our fields were only loosely connected within the computer science department, he knew we'd need serious computational power to get off the ground. Without a second thought, he donated an initial set of workstations to our cause. If nothing else, it was exactly the show of support I needed.

Kai was the only other Chinese immigrant among Princeton's computer science faculty. Born in the 1950s, he was part of a generation that put him among the first class of students to attend college in the aftermath of the Cultural Revolution, ultimately coming to America to attend grad school in the 1980s—a period during which such immigration was rare and relatable peers were scarce. The experience left him with a colorful personality, blending the intellectual intensity of my mother with the self-effacing humor of my father. Kai had the nondescript look of a professor, with black hair parted broadly at the side and an austere wardrobe. But he had a warm smile and a generous spirit. We quickly bonded.

The more I learned about Kai, the more I began to understand why he saw my ideas in a more favorable light than others did. He'd built a reputation as a pioneer in efficiently connecting microprocessors with huge stores of memory, cofounding a company to commercialize his research that eventually sold for more than $2 billion. He wasn't just an early believer in the power of large-scale data, but an expert in harnessing it. Unfortunately, he was also on the verge of an extended personal leave, cutting short my time as his protégé. The silver lining to his departure, however, was his need to find a new advisor for an exceptionally bright student named Jia Deng. Kai described him as the perfect collaborator: a young mind with engineering talent to spare, eager for a new challenge.

Kai and Jia were polar opposites in many ways. Where Kai was cheery and outgoing, Jia was reserved. While Kai wore his passion on his sleeve, Jia's attitude was so emotionless I worried I'd be unable to sense whether he was even interested in our work. I could tell from our first conversations that he was nothing short of brilliant—that much would have been obvious even without Kai's recommendation—but

I'd never met anyone who could conceal the heat of their intellect so completely.

Brainpower aside, Jia's status as a newcomer to the field caught my attention. His unusual background not only endowed him with engineering skills of a caliber the average computer vision student would be unlikely to have, but spared him the burden of expectations. This was an unorthodox project, if not an outright risky one, and far out of step with the fashions of the field at the time. Jia didn't know that.

So we dove in, a team of two, embarking on a project that seemed to call for thousands of contributors, if not more, all in the service of a hypothesis that most of my colleagues had dismissed out of hand. On paper, none of it made sense. But for the first time in my life, I felt a confidence I didn't have to question. No matter how long it would take, I was sure we were onto something big. Maybe historically so.

I leaned back and exhaled, loudly, swiveling my chair to survey the bare walls of my new office in Princeton's Computer Science Building. Despite my having had the job for close to four months, partially opened cardboard boxes still took up the majority of the floor space at my feet. Jia sat across from me on the couch, which represented the extent of my interior decorating efforts so far.

"All right. Let's see if we can wrap our heads around the scale of this thing."

Using WordNet as our starting point, we began by trimming the fat from it. Although its selling point was its incredible size and detail, we knew we wouldn't actually need most of its contents. ImageNet was meant to capture the world of *things*, not actions or descriptions, which made our first cuts obvious: verbs and adjectives. But even nouns were complicated; abstract concepts like "truth" or "awareness," for instance, can't be photographed. Only nouns referring to physical objects—generally speaking, things tangible enough to be counted: *one something*, *two somethings, a hundred somethings*—would be included. Everything else was stripped away.

All told, we cut the majority of WordNet's 140,000 entries, leaving a visual, countable subset just north of 22,000. It was still many times larger than any collection of training images for machine learning I'd ever heard of, but it was a dramatic reduction from what we'd started with. And it was strikingly close to Biederman's estimate of 30,000.

"What about variety?" Jia asked. "How many different images do we need per category?"

Ah, I thought. *Now we're getting somewhere.*

"Let's think biologically," I said. "How do children grow? How did our species evolve? The real world is just a mess, right? Nothing's ever black-and-white. Everything's changing. And yet we learn to make sense of it. We live inside all this detail, and we naturally become experts." I picked up a mug that was sitting on my desk. "But you asked about numbers. So tell me—how many different ways might this mug appear in a photograph?"

Jia thought for a moment. "There's size, for one thing. It might look bigger or smaller depending on how close it is to the camera."

"That's right. But I want a *quantity*. How many different sizes?"

He thought again, then shrugged. "Well, it'd be infinite, right? There's no specific number."

"Correct again," I said, this time with a smirk. Jia knew exactly where I was going with all this, but he was willing to let me draw it out to make the point. "So we've got infinite sizes. What else?"

"Lighting? The mug might be brightly lit or in shadow. And color, too. Mugs can come in just about any shade, and some have pictures and words on them."

"Good, good. And how many variations for each of those?"

"The same. Both are infinite."

"And we're still just getting started," I said. "What about perspective? Where's the handle pointing? Are we looking down at the mug or head-on? What about occlusion? Is there something in front of it? A stack of books? A cat's tail? Another mug? And what about backgrounds? Is the mug in front of a wall? A window? Is it inside a cabinet?"

"Infinite, infinite, infinite, infinite," Jia summarized, quite accurately.

The more I thought about it, the more I saw a developmental quality to our work—an attempt to synthesize the formative years of a child's perception in the form of data. I imagined the way kids play with things—how they reach out, groping and touching, prodding and poking. They become comfortable with changes in lighting and perspective by picking things up, turning them around, and viewing them from every angle. They play games like peekaboo, learning that objects persist even when momentarily hidden. All instincts our algorithms sorely lacked.

"Okay, but we still haven't arrived at a number," Jia wondered aloud. "So far we've just multiplied infinity by itself. What do we actually *do* with that?"

"I guess that's my point," I replied. "No amount of images will be enough. So whatever we think the number is, we should probably think bigger. Then think even bigger than that. We're guessing either way, so let's guess big."

We settled on a goal of one thousand different photographs of every single object category. One thousand different photographs of violins. One thousand different photographs of German shepherds. One thousand different photographs of throw pillows. On and on we'd go, for more than twenty-two thousand categories. Something on the order of *twenty million images*. And even that figure told us only about the finished product; we'd likely have to start with hundreds of millions, if not close to a billion candidate images to get there.

Jia looked skeptical. "I get the theory, but you're talking about an astronomical amount of work. This goes way beyond a few Google searches."

He was right, of course, but we needed to embrace that fact, not hide from it. We were trying to capture the fullness of the real world. The numbers were *supposed* to scare us.

"Jia, *everything* we want our algorithms to see is out there, somewhere. Every detail is being photographed, even as we speak. Everyone's got a flip phone these days. Everyone's getting a digital camera for Christmas. Just imagine what you'd see if you could somehow put all those photographs in one place. It'd be a mosaic of the whole world! The entirety of everyday life, from one end to the other."

"Provided we can organize it somehow," he added. "The images don't do anything on their own, right? They all need to be labeled before we can use them to train a model. And every label has to be accurate." Jia paused, as if the gravity of his own words was dawning on him. "That sounds like a whole other conversation."

"Yeah, yeah, yeah," I replied. "One miracle at a time."

Jia and I watched from the corner of the lab as the row of undergrads produced a steady beat of mouse clicks and key presses. The response to the email we'd sent out earlier in the week had been quick. *Wanted: Undergrads willing to help download and label images from the internet. Flexible shifts. $10/hr.* It seemed like a fair trade: we'd take a step toward a new age of machine intelligence and they'd get some beer money. It was a satisfying moment, but it didn't take long for reality to sink in.

"Is it me, Jia, or does this all look a little . . . slow?"

"Yeah, I was worried about that. In fact, I timed a few minutes of their pace and did some extrapolating."

Uh-oh.

"At the rate we're going, we can expect ImageNet to be complete in . . ."

I swallowed hard. He noticed.

"Yeah: *nineteen years*, give or take. Fei-Fei, I believe in this project—I really do—but I can't wait that long for my PhD."

Fair point, Jia.

"So, what do we do?" he asked. "Do we just hire more undergrads?"

"That's one option, sure. But it'll cost us, and if our time horizon is nineteen years, I'm not sure our lab budget is going to be big enough to buy our way out."

One way or another, it was clear we'd need more than a handful of teenagers to solve the problem. That had been barely enough for Caltech 101, which was all but a rounding error in comparison to ImageNet. Fresh tactics, it seemed, were in order.

I thought about the work Jia would have been doing with Kai Li before joining my lab. Theirs was a world of complex systems—staggeringly complex—and they lived for the pursuit of efficiency. Higher performance. Lower cost. The shortest path. Surely the protégé of one of the world's foremost microprocessor designers could think of a way to boost the productivity of some kids.

"Jia, hold on a second." I gestured at the undergrads. "This is all a *process*, right? I mean, on some level, isn't this essentially an *engineering* problem?"

He thought for a moment, then shot me the look of a man about to roll up his sleeves.

"All right," he said with the faintest hint of a grin. "Let's talk optimization."

The following months fell into a rhythm, though not a particularly graceful one. ImageNet was a wild animal that refused to be tamed, lashing out every time we got too close. We kept at it, scoring our share of victories—little ones, at least—alongside accumulating scrapes and bruises. But every time we thought we'd finally backed it into a corner, it summoned a deeper, more guttural roar, and sent us scurrying.

Luckily for me, Jia was the kind of partner who reacted to a frustrating problem by thinking harder. Human participation was the costliest part of our process, both in terms of time and money, and that's where he began his counterattack: making it his personal mission to reduce that cost to the absolute minimum. For example, when one of our labelers set about curating a collection of photos for a particular category, say, "Pembroke Welsh corgi," we initially expected that each step would be carried out manually: typing the query into a search engine like Google Images, combing through the results to find clear examples, applying the label to each, then placing the final selections in the proper directory. But most of those steps didn't require human intelligence.

The first thing Jia automated was the downloading phase, writing a program that submitted each WordNet category to an image search engine as our labelers had been doing. But since search engines are meant for human users, not machines, they don't return a set of images directly; instead, they present a web page that organizes the resulting hits as a scrolling grid of thumbnails, the source code of which Jia's program would then parse to extract links to the full-sized images themselves. It was a messy solution, but it gave us the ability to download candidate images at maximum speed, day and night, for as long as we wanted—months, if necessary. And the resulting images were automatically organized on our own machines.

Our repository began filling up like magic. Granted, the wide net we'd cast was catching a fair amount of junk—low-quality photos, clip art, and the like—but we were accumulating plenty of good stuff, too. Somewhere in our network of rapidly filling hard drives, the first glimpses of that mosaic were coming together—a crude but authentic depiction of the *entire* visual world. At least, it was for a while.

"Uh-oh," I heard Jia say from across the lab.

"What's the matter?"

"Looks like we've hit a bit of a speed bump. Uh . . . yep. Google's banned us."

"What? *Banned?* Why?"

"Evidently they cap the number of requests a single user can submit in a specific period. About a thousand or so, from what I can tell."

"How long is this period?"

"Twenty-four hours. It resets at midnight. That's the good news."

"Okay, how fast are we burning through the daily allotment?"

"Well, that's the bad news." Jia pulled up the log file and did some mental arithmetic. "About nine minutes."

Oof.

The growth of the repository stalled. And that wasn't our only problem. The pipeline was cartoonishly lopsided; our collection of raw images was exploding, with thousands upon thousands added each day before Google blocked us, but only a small fraction of them had been accurately labeled and organized. We'd known the labeling process would be a bottleneck from the beginning, but as the weeks went by, we were continually discouraged by how much of a burden it was.

Jia and I met to discuss the issue in the campus's Mathey Dining Hall, a place I'd grown reliant on as ImageNet's mental hold on me made the idea of taking time out for cooking all but unbearable. It was also a welcome change of scenery after so many days and nights in the lab, with its high ceilings, rustic chandeliers, and stained glass that suggested we'd found refuge in a monastery.

We talked through every step our labelers followed to identify, categorize, and label each image, streamlining them wherever we could with shortcuts and bespoke tools. If a process took three clicks, Jia would find a way to do it in one. Less typing. Shorter mouse movements. Faster everything. I caught myself studying the objects on the table as we talked, silently wondering whether or not they were among our twenty-two thousand categories. Surely there'd be an entry for "napkin," but did we differentiate between cloth and paper napkins? What kind of knife was that? How many varieties might there be beyond, say, "steak knife" and "butter knife"? "Butcher knives," I guessed. "Bread knives"? Maybe. There really were a lot, now that I thought of it. Did we have them all? I made a mental note to check when we got back to the lab.

"Oh and by the way, do you know what a dynamic IP is, Fei-Fei?"

Another trick up Jia's sleeve.

"Think of it as an intermediate step between our machines and Google's servers. Our lab computers stay put, but a dynamic IP connects us to middlemen that continually change, so Google thinks they're coming from different users."

"And this will keep us under the limit?"

"Way under it."

We were back in business, at least to an extent. Labeling was still an issue, but it was a relief to watch as our supply of candidate images kicked back into gear. Even minor victories were worth celebrating now.

ImageNet seeped into my very core as the months passed, becoming the lens through which I saw almost everything. Whether at work in the lab or walking across the quad, my private game of visual identification continued. If I saw someone walking a breed of dog I didn't recognize, I'd wonder if we'd dedicated a subcategory to it. A student riding a unicycle might make me wonder if "unicycle" was included at all, let alone all the different kinds of unicycles. For that matter, *are* there different kinds of unicycles? The garage sale experiences my father loved had become my world. Everything had been blown up to an incomprehensible scale, but it was the same spirit—insatiable curiosity, the lust for novelty. I wondered if there was a gene for it in our family.

The struggle bore on, each step taken in response to some new puzzle. When we found the images in a given category looked too similar, thus diluting the variety we sought, we used international translations of WordNet to submit the query in different languages in the hopes that images from around the world would vary more widely. When we couldn't find enough images at all, we'd add related terms to the search query, turning "corgi" into "corgi puppy" or "corgi dog park." And when the search engines subtly redesigned the layouts of their results pages, thus changing the location of the links to each image and breaking one of Jia's many auto-downloader programs, we reprogrammed them to match—and began checking for such changes on a regular basis.

For a guy who'd been designing microprocessor architectures only a year before, these were awfully prosaic engineering challenges. Still, we both knew our efforts were in service of something worthwhile. They may have been Band-Aid fixes, simplistic and often crude, but each brought us closer to the vision of an entire world laid bare for machines to see, and soon, I hoped, maybe even understand.

"Penne?" I asked.

"Very good!" Silvio replied, delighted, as he set the still-steaming bowl of pasta before me.

"But wait, what'd we have last week? It was also tube-shaped, but bigger, and the edges weren't cut diagonally."

"That was *rigatoni.*"

"Right! Yes! 'Rigatoni.' I liked that one, too."

"Are you asking because you're actually interested in my country's food? Or because you're wondering if ImageNet includes enough types of pasta?"

I took a bite to delay answering the question while he sat down and crossed his arms, clearly proud of his detective skills.

"It can't be both?" I finally replied.

We were a year into ImageNet, and I felt like we'd hit our stride. Between the work of our labeling team and Jia's endless efforts to optimize their process, I was sure we'd at least made a dent. I was curious how we were doing, and, as he often did, Jia knew what I was thinking.

"Wondering how long it's gonna take to finish ImageNet now? I've recalculated our estimate."

I was just about to ask. Excitedly, I hurried to his desk.

"All right, so—taking *everything* into account: all of our optimizations, shortcuts, plus the images we've already labeled—we've managed to cut that nineteen-year ETA down to . . ."

I suddenly lost my nerve. This was gonna be bad. I could feel it.

". . . about eighteen years."

Jia was a man of many talents, but softening the blow of bad news wasn't among them. For the first time in a long time, I had no idea what to do next.

Desperation inspires a baroque kind of creativity, and we ran the gamut of questionable ideas as the bleakness of our situation became harder to ignore—a gamut that even included aiding our human labelers with . . . machines. This involved some circular reasoning, of course—if algorithms were capable of recognizing objects accurately enough to help us label them, then we wouldn't need ImageNet in the first place. Nevertheless, we wondered if there might be some advantage to be gained by letting them play a marginal role—for example, employing the one-shot learning technique I'd developed with Pietro to crudely but quickly label large batches of images, allowing our human team to serve more as editors or proofreaders. It made a kind of perverse if debatable sense, but we never got the balance right.

More important, the real argument against automating the labeling process wasn't technological but philosophical. Even a subtle algorithmic shortcut, we realized, would be antithetical to ImageNet's mission. Our goal was to embed *unalloyed* human perception in every image, in the hopes that a computer vision model trained on the complete set would be imbued with some similar spark of acumen. Machine influence threatened to dilute that.

If humans were the bottleneck, and there was no way to reduce their involvement any further than we already had, our only remaining option appeared to be brute force: expanding our team of labelers enough to drag our ETA from nearly two decades away to the much-nearer term. An increase of a factor of ten might do it—given the work already done, we might get there in as little as a year and a half. But the funds simply weren't there. It was infuriating to think that after so much emotional investment, this would all come down to a question of money.

"Hmmm," I said, leaning back and staring up at the lab ceiling. A thought had occurred to me. A strange one.

"What?" Jia looked up from his workstation.

"I dunno. Well, maybe. Look—I do have one idea for raising some extra funds. It'd be *modest*, but something. It's *absolutely* a measure of last resort."

"I'm listening," Jia replied as he leaned in.

I sunk farther into my seat and breathed out slowly. I couldn't believe what I was about to say.

"How much do you know about dry cleaning?"

I squinted into the setting sun as I flipped down the visor. Vision is blurrier at seventy miles an hour, but no less rich in content. Reflector posts and mile markers flew by to our right, surrounded by cracks in the asphalt, rocky debris, and the occasional plastic bottle or crumpled fast food bag. Signs of all kinds whizzed by, reminding us of the speed limit, announcing the approach of an exit, or crediting a local chapter of the Unitarian church with maintaining the next mile of road. License plates and bumper stickers. A dog riding shotgun.

We were on our way to Minneapolis, where CVPR 2007—the Conference on Computer Vision and Pattern Recognition—was being held. ImageNet was on the rocks as our cash reserves dwindled, but rumor had it that a world outside our lab still existed—and it was summer. The conference felt like the perfect excuse for an escape, and I looked forward to twelve hundred miles of blissfully monotonous driving that I could spend thinking about anything—*anything*—other than our work. I rented a van and filled it with a few students from the lab. For the next couple of days, our only concerns would be diner food, bathroom breaks, and arguments over the radio station.

Unfortunately, there was no shutting off the part of me that obsessed about the visual world. We drove through forests, and I wondered what species of trees we were passing. Maple? Ash? Birch? We saw college towns like Madison, with their neon signs and busy sidewalks. A student in sunglasses was lying on a bench. A trio with an acoustic guitar, a stand-up bass, and a harmonica was busking. We passed through bustling cities, their skyscrapers soaring over us, reflective and geometric. We watched the sun sparkling on the water as we drove along one of the Great Lakes—Erie, or maybe Michigan. Waves lapping against the shore. Kids chasing the tide in and out. A couple tossing a frisbee.

I was again reminded of my father, as I often was these days, as he'd wander from one garage sale display to another, examining a secondhand bread maker or a VCR, his fascination indefatigable, his joy infectious. I wondered if I had that same look on my face.

There's just so much to know about life, I thought. *And so much of it comes in through the eyes.* I felt it in my gut and in my heart. ImageNet may have been doomed, but its goal was no less worthy. Sooner or later, someone would crack it. And when they did—when the whole of this world of ours came spilling into the minds of our machines, with all its color and chaos and mundane magic—everything would change.

"So Fei-Fei, now that you've got a lab of your own, what are you working on these days?"

It was a question I was dreading, but it came from Jitendra—Pietro's advisor and my "academic grandfather"—the person I was most hoping to run into. It'd been years since we'd spoken in person, and I knew he'd be at an event like CVPR. With ImageNet languishing and my future as an academic hazier than ever, I needed to see a familiar face. It wouldn't be the first time he raised my spirits in a place like this.

"Honestly, Jitendra, it's a bit of a sore subject."

"Uh-oh."

I told him everything. My conversation with Christiane. Laying eyes on WordNet for the first time. The decisions Jia and I made, each more fraught than the last. And the embattled year we'd spent struggling to get something impossible off the ground.

"Wow. That's, uh . . . quite a story," he responded, his tone uncharacteristically detached. If he had an opinion on what he'd heard so far, he was keeping it close to the chest.

"Yeah. And the worst part is, it all comes down to a problem of logistics, not science. I'm as sure as ever that ImageNet is exactly what computer vision needs, if we could just *finish* the damn thing."

"Well, Fei-Fei . . ." he began, choosing his words carefully. "Everyone agrees that data has a role to play, of course, but . . ."

He paused for a moment, then continued. "Frankly, I think you've taken this idea *way* too far."

I took a shallow breath.

"The trick to science is to grow *with* your field. Not to leap so far ahead of it."

I wasn't expecting this. Hearing Jitendra of all people join the chorus of detractors was a blow, and not just on a personal level: when the day came for me to collect letters of recommendation for a tenured position—an increasingly dubious prospect with such a grand failure hanging over my head—his would be among them. For many reasons, his opinion mattered.

I could almost see my North Star growing dimmer, my path cast back into darkness. A frightening idea was beginning to sink in: that I'd taken a bigger risk than I realized, and it was too late to turn back.

* * *

I wasn't sure what to do with ImageNet in the months following CVPR. There was plenty to worry about, but my thoughts kept returning to Jia. He'd entered the world of computer vision talented but naive, and he'd trusted me to guide him. Now, I could sense his frustration growing—justifiably—and I knew he was worried about his own path to a PhD. After all the struggles I'd faced in grad school, the thought of leading my own student astray was enough to turn my stomach.

The scientific heartbreak was no less gutting, of course. With such a long journey already behind me, I couldn't bear the thought that my instincts had steered me so wrong. We were suddenly rudderless, adrift on black waves beneath an empty sky.

Still, it wasn't over yet.

"Excuse me, uh, Fei-Fei?"

I was running late for a faculty meeting when Min, a master's student, popped up in front of me. He could tell I was in a hurry, but seemed insistent, even fidgety, as he spoke.

"Hi, uh, do you have a second?"

He didn't wait for an answer. I knew him well enough to know he was generally soft-spoken. Something big was clearly on his mind.

"I was hanging out with Jia yesterday," he continued, "and he told me about your trouble with this labeling project. I think I have an idea you two haven't tried yet—like, one that can *really* speed things up."

I instantly forgot about my haste as my ears perked up. *Jia has a social life?*

"Have you heard of crowdsourcing?" he asked.

He explained that online platforms were proving useful in organizing remote, ad hoc workforces that could range from individual contributors to teams of millions, automating the process of distributing tasks and collecting results. "Amazon is offering it as a service, if you're interested. It's called Mechanical Turk."

It was a clever name, taken from the original Mechanical Turk, an eighteenth-century chess-playing automaton that toured the world for years as both a marvel of engineering and a formidable opponent, even for experienced players. The device was actually a hoax; concealed in its base was a human chess master, who controlled the machine to the delight and bewilderment of its audiences.

Centuries later, the emerging practice of crowdsourcing was predicated on the same idea: that *truly* intelligent automation was still best performed by humans. Amazon Mechanical Turk, or AMT, built a marketplace around the concept, allowing "requesters" to advertise "human intelligence tasks" to be completed by contributors, known as "Turkers," who could be anywhere in the world. It made sense in theory and seemed to promise everything we wanted: the intelligence of human labeling, but at a speed and scale on par with that of automation. Amusingly—and quite perceptively—Amazon called it *"artificial artificial intelligence."*

I raced through the halls to find Jia, although his enthusiasm didn't *precisely* match mine when I did. After so many setbacks, he had good reason to be wary of yet another shot in the dark. But after all that we'd been through, he could see that this really could be the lifeline we'd been waiting for. With what seemed an even mix of hesitation and relief, he finally agreed: AMT was worth one more attempt.

My North Star was flickering back to life, and once again, I had to marvel at the timing. ImageNet owed the very possibility of its existence to so many converging technological threads: the internet, digital cameras, and search engines. Now crowdsourcing—delivered by a platform that had barely existed a year earlier—was providing the capstone. If I ever needed a reminder that the default position of any scientist should be one of absolute humility—an understanding that no one's intellect is half as powerful as serendipity—this was it.

AMT changed everything. It turned our workforce of undergrad labelers into an international team of tens, then hundreds, then thousands. As our support expanded, Jia's estimated time to completion plummeted—to fifteen years, then ten, then five, then two, and, finally, just under a year. And it cast our budget in an entirely new light, inverting the economic calculus of ImageNet. A dollar amount once woefully inadequate to build a big enough team of labelers under one roof could now be effectively spent on a crowdsourced team spread across the world and connected through the internet.

Along the way, I drew more and more on my experience in experimental psychology to help Jia create a system that put our workers' time and attention to ideal use, while minimizing the chance they'd be misled, confused, or tempted to game the system. At times, AMT felt like the human psychophysics experiments Christof and I conducted at Caltech—attempting to extract some subtle but essential piece of information from a stranger's perception—blown up to a global scale. In some ways it was easier; rather than reading minds, I just needed the right label applied to an image from our collection of bulk downloads. At the same time, however, it was vastly more complex; as simple as labeling an image may seem, it ultimately entails choosing precisely the right category from a predefined list of tens of thousands.

Not every challenge was technological, however. There were human issues, too, like the concern that crowdsourcing might be exploitative. Although the possibility wouldn't spark widespread discussion until many years later, it was hard to avoid the thought, even then. It encouraged us to pay as much per image as our funds allowed, a decision made easier by the fact that ImageNet was a purely scientific endeavor with no concern for profits to consider.

Research into the matter was heartening, too, at least at the time. A 2007 demography of AMT found that most contributors saw the service as a hobby or side income, not as an attempt to make their primary living. Of course, with the rise of the gig economy in the years since, the picture has grown considerably more complex. Today, it's hard to disentangle the power of big data from its human cost.

On and on it went, with thousands upon thousands of new images labeled every single day. At the peak of ImageNet's development, we were among the largest employers on the AMT platform, and our monthly bills for the service reflected it. It was expensive, but it was *working*.

Our budgetary woes weren't over, however. As affordable as AMT was, ImageNet was so big that we soon found ourselves uncomfortably close to the margins—yet again. In the strictest sense we knew we could afford to finish the job, but we couldn't rule out the possibility of collateral damage. ImageNet may have been our biggest and most expensive single project, but it was far from the only one; we continued to research algorithms as well, with grad students and postdocs alike exploring new techniques for recognizing objects in photographs and even identifying human movements in video. Each researcher was entitled to a living stipend, which we provided alongside the cushion of "rainy day" cash every lab is expected to maintain. ImageNet was closer to completion than ever before, but it was pushing everything else closer to the brink in the process.

After two more years on the knife-edge of our finances—an agonizing stretch in which even a minor bump in the road might have sunk us for good—ImageNet was finally maturing into the research tool Jia and I had always envisioned. Naturally, our lab was the first to put it to use, and we were all encouraged by its impact even in an unfinished state. With completion close at hand, we no longer had to use our imaginations; for the first time, it was obvious to everyone that we were building something worth sharing with the world.

It was a period of unusual stability outside of my work as well. My mother's health continued to decline, as expected, but her retirement from dry cleaning spared us the kind of heart-stopping crises we'd all been conditioned to anticipate. She even took up a few hobbies, with a particular interest in photography. My father's lifestyle grew more recreational as well, free for the first time in years to cook for the simple pleasure of it. The distance that separated me from Silvio remained an irritation, but our alternating trips between Ann Arbor and Princeton had been honed to the point of reflex. Silvio's route to see me was so consistent, in fact, that pilots started recognizing him.

I'd also begun making occasional trips to the San Francisco Bay Area to visit an accomplished cohort of machine learning and computer vision pioneers, including Andrew Ng, Daphne Koller, and Sebastian Thrun, all at Stanford. The meetings began as a friendly exchange of ideas, including some positive conversations about ImageNet—among the few I'd had. As had happened at Princeton a few years prior, however, the dialogue soon took on a more formal tone. Finally, I got a call from Bill Dally, chair of the computer science department, that made things official. He wanted to know if I was interested in bringing my lab to California.

Taking another job seemed unthinkable after spending less than three years in a faculty position at Princeton. But I'd never experienced a university quite like Stanford, or a place like Silicon Valley. After growing up in an immigrant neighborhood of New Jersey and spending the intervening years cloistered in academia, I knew little of the business world beyond Chinese restaurants and dry cleaning. Stanford, in contrast, was at the very heart of the tech industry, where the ideas our research explored were put into global practice. Although it wasn't a world I'd aspired to join myself, I was impressed by the reach of Stanford's influence on it, with companies like Hewlett-Packard, Cisco Systems, Sun Microsystems, Google, and so many others tracing their roots to the school. Everyone I met seemed personally inspired by the possibility of touching real human lives.

Still, I was conflicted about the idea of moving there. More than any other institution, Princeton had made my career possible. It had changed my life in a single afternoon with a financial aid package when I was a high school senior, the memory of which still gives me goose bumps, then had taken a second chance on me as an unproven assistant professor, outfitting me with my first lab and my first doctoral student, and surrounding me with colleagues I'd grown to love and respect.

There were people to consider as well, and more than before. My parents' needs pushed me in one direction, as life in Pasadena had demonstrated how much gentler West Coast weather was for my mother. But thoughts of the Sabellas pulled me in the other; they were no longer my "American" family, but simply my *family*, without qualification, and the thought of putting thousands of miles between us again—perhaps permanently this time—stung. Somewhere in between was Silvio. He'd remain in Michigan either way, but my relocating to California would make our long-distance relationship even longer.

As a scientist, however, the decision was much simpler. I was part of a young, fast-evolving field poised to change the world, maybe within my lifetime, and the people I met at Stanford believed that as sincerely as I did. Princeton felt like home, but I couldn't deny that Stanford seemed like an even more hospitable backdrop for my research. In fact, the more I thought about it, the more I worried that a place like "home" might be too comfortable for times like these. Moving somewhere new appealed to me precisely because it *wasn't* comfortable. It felt uncertain—maybe even risky—and I needed that.

And so, in 2009, I made the decision to once again head west, with Jia and most of my students transferring along with me. We arrived to find a new academic home on a sprawling campus—big enough to dwarf Princeton and Caltech combined—clad in an arresting architectural style of sandstone, arches, and bike paths, baking in nearly year-round sun. And just beneath it all lay historically deep roots in a world that was rarely spoken of at the time, but closer to my work than even I had yet to fully appreciate. Bigger than machine learning. Bigger than computer vision. A nearly forgotten field that once subsumed them both, and many other worlds as well, called "artificial intelligence."

Among the many people I met as a new member of the Stanford faculty was John Etchemendy, who was the university provost at the time. I'd known a number of administrators by that point, but it was immediately clear to me that John was in a class of his own. He was a philosopher and logician who'd spent decades as a professor before joining the administration, lecturing on topics like semiotics, logical truth, and the philosophy of language. As smart as he was—and he seemed to radiate intellect without even trying—he was friendly and a good listener. And my heart skipped a beat when he casually invoked John McCarthy, one of AI's founding fathers, and a key organizer behind the Dartmouth summer project that gave the field its name.

"You know, John was a friend of mine," he said.

I wasn't sure what was more surreal: that my new provost had been personally acquainted with such a legend, or that he mentioned it so nonchalantly. Either way, it was clear to me that I'd come to the right place.

By June 2009, due in large part to the infusion of new research funding provided by Stanford, the inaugural version of ImageNet was complete. In spite of the many challenges we'd faced along the way, we'd actually done it: fifteen million images spread across twenty-two thousand distinct categories, culled from nearly a billion candidates in total, and annotated by a global team of more than forty-eight thousand contributors hailing from 167 countries. It boasted the scale and diversity we'd spent years dreaming of, all while maintaining a consistent level of precision: each individual image was not just manually labeled, but organized within a hierarchy and verified in triplicate.

Quantitatively, we'd achieved our goal of building what was, at the time, the largest hand-curated data set in AI's history. But beyond the numbers lay the accomplishment that moved me most: the realization of a true ontology of the world, as conceptual as it was visual, curated from the ground up by humans for the sole purpose of teaching machines.

CVPR 2009 was held in Miami, and we'd arrived not just as attendees, but presenters. With its steamy heat and hyper-saturated colors, the city lived up to its reputation from our first steps out of baggage claim—it was a blur of neon swimwear, polished sports cars, and high-rise buildings set against a backdrop of natural blues and greens, tied together with a persistent texture of rhythmic sounds. The energy of our surroundings reflected our own impatience; after almost three tumultuous years, Jia and I were dying to reveal ImageNet to the world.

We were more than ready. The project's unusually long gestation had given us plenty of time to hone our ability to discuss it, and we were eager to put the skill to use. After living for so long with the polarizing effects of even mentioning our work, we were conditioned to expect curiosity, confusion, and confrontation in equal measure. We prepared accordingly, rehearsing an impassioned defense of its aims, as well as our best answers to common critiques. And although we already felt a bit like lightning rods, we figured we'd fully embrace our notoriety by splurging a bit with some of the last dollars of the project's budget.

"What's this?" Jia asked as I handed him a white cardboard box.

"Open it!" I said.

He pried open the flap securing the lid and looked inside.

"Uh . . . pens?"

"Pens with the ImageNet logo! I found a place online that does it."

"I mean, they look cool, I guess, but what are these for?"

"We can hand them out at the conference! It's what all the tech companies do. You know, merchandise. We need people to remember us."

Jia's expression somehow looked even blanker than usual. I remained undaunted.

We arrived with about as much confidence as an overworked team of nerds could hope for, but the mood was strange from the start. Our first setback was also the most consequential: that ImageNet was relegated to a poster session. In academic jargon, this meant we wouldn't be presenting our work in a lecture hall to an audience at a predetermined time, but would instead be given space on the conference floor to prop up a large-format print summarizing the project—hence "poster" session—in the hopes that passersby might stop and ask questions. We were lucky to be included at all, of course, as even this is a rare privilege at an event of CVPR's caliber. But we longed for a chance to explain our vision with more than a sound bite. After so many years of effort, this just felt anticlimactic.

We fielded the usual questions and enjoyed a handful of pleasant conversations but left with little to show for our presence. It was soon clear that whatever was in store for ImageNet—whether it would be embraced as a resource of uncommon richness or written off as folly—it wasn't going to get a boost at CVPR. On the bright side, people seemed to like the pens.

In the meantime, as I readjusted to a life without the challenge of ImageNet to contend with, the doubts I'd refused to acknowledge for years felt more real than ever. Were the naysayers right? Had this really all been a waste of time? ImageNet was more than a data set, or even a hierarchy of visual categories. It was a *hypothesis*—a bet—inspired by our own biological origins, that the first step toward unlocking true machine intelligence would be immersion in the fullness of the visual world. That an experience commensurate with the chaos and complexity that shaped our own evolution might have a similar effect on our algorithms. And I was as prepared for that bet to be proven right as to be proven wrong. Either outcome would be an opportunity to learn something. But I wasn't expecting it to be ignored.

What was I missing?

8

EXPERIMENTATION

A utumn had come to Kyoto. The afternoon was bright and lent a sturdy backdrop to the heartbeat bursts of green, orange, and red racing by, framed like a living portrait in the bullet train's windows. The countryside was lush and brilliant even at two hundred miles per hour, but, as was becoming a running theme in my life, I was too distracted to give it the appreciation it deserved. It had been a long, taxing journey, with all its attendant anxieties, and the months since ImageNet's disappointing third-tier debut at CVPR had been discouraging. Our critics remained dismissive, and interest from other research labs was scant. ImageNet's slide toward obscurity was beginning to feel so inevitable that I'd resorted to an impromptu university tour to counteract it, delivering live presentations wherever I could to lecture halls filled with skeptical grad students and post-docs. It wasn't much, but even delaying the inevitable felt like a small victory.

Now the next big opportunity to raise our profile was at hand: the International Conference on Computer Vision, or ICCV, in Kyoto. My travel companion for the day was Alex Berg, an assistant professor at SUNY Stony Brook and a like-minded computer vision researcher.

Alex had been an especially gifted grad student under Jitendra, exploring the challenges of object recognition in a spirit similar to my own work with Pietro, and his use of Caltech 101 in his PhD thesis made him not just a natural appreciator of the power of data sets, but one of ImageNet's few supporters. Although it was heartening to commiserate with a fellow believer, it only underscored how difficult the road ahead was shaping up to be.

All this stood in contrast to the excitement we felt in my lab, newly relocated to Stanford. At our fingertips wasn't just a data set, but a test bed that brought our ideas face-to-face with the entirety of the visual world—arming our algorithms with broader perceptive powers than they'd enjoyed, while testing them with more rigor than they'd ever faced. If image data sets can be thought of as the language of computer vision research—a collection of concepts that an algorithm and its developers can explore—ImageNet was a sudden, explosive growth in our vocabulary.

Everything we did as a lab felt energized. In one case, we used Image-Net to quickly train hundreds of instances of an image classification algorithm to recognize a collection of everyday things, then ran them simultaneously across a single photograph. Rather than simply detect the presence of individual objects, the experiment looked for *combinations* of objects that said something about the entire scene. For example, if the detectors spotted a person, a boat, an oar, and water, it classified the photo as a whole as a depiction of "rowing"—a deeper level of understanding that, arguably, verged on a primitive kind of visual reasoning.

As in many of our experiments from the era, the accuracy of the algorithms we used was spotty and much work remained to be done— even simple image recognition was still nascent, after all—but the rough edges only heightened the spirit of adventure that gripped us. Our work felt daring and forward-looking, unrefined but provocative. Much of it was conceptually simple, too. But it wasn't until ImageNet that it became feasible.

Meanwhile, Jia was coming into his own as a scholar. A year or so after ImageNet's release, he published a paper entitled "What Does Classifying More Than 10,000 Image Categories Tell Us?" in which he reflected on the fundamental ways image recognition was changing in the presence of ImageNet. Although a largely technical work, it had an undercurrent of philosophy that set it apart from the typical academic paper. It felt prophetic, even existential. His thesis was that ImageNet didn't simply represent an increase in scale, but a categorical shift—what a physicist might call a "phase transition," in which even the most basic properties of a phenomenon change. It massively broadened the range of possibilities our algorithms might face, presenting challenges that smaller data sets didn't.

Put a bit more technically, the "semantic space" ImageNet presented was expanding while growing more dense, with less breathing room separating correct answers from incorrect ones. In practical terms, this often meant that techniques that appeared to work well when distinguishing between a small number of widely varying categories performed poorly when tackling ImageNet's ten thousand, many of which could only be distinguished by subtle differences. Some techniques broke down altogether. It was a humbling, but ultimately invigorating sign that tomorrow's algorithms wouldn't just be better-performing versions of today's, but *different*, fundamentally, in ways we hadn't anticipated.

"You know what I liked most about Caltech 101?" Alex's words pulled me back into the moment. "It wasn't just the training data. It was the opportunity to compare the results of my own research with yours, using the same exact images. Apples to apples."

"A benchmark," I replied.

"Exactly. It made progress easy to measure. And what could be more inspiring to a researcher? It's like a challenge. A dare."

A dare. I liked that.

"Okay, so . . . what if we did the same with ImageNet?" I asked, still thinking out loud. "Even better, what if we organized an entire *contest* around it?"

"Something like PASCAL, you mean?"

The PASCAL Visual Object Classes data set, generally known as PASCAL VOC, was a collection of about ten thousand images organized into twenty categories. Assembled by a team of researchers in Europe, it was similar to Caltech 101, but with a crucial difference: it served as the basis for a computer vision competition that had been held annually since 2005. Each year, entrants from around the world submitted algorithms trained on the data set, which were then exposed to a new set of previously unseen images and ranked by the accuracy with which they classified them. The algorithm with the lowest rate of errors was declared the winner. Collaborative and competitive at the same time, the contest drew attention to the latest advances from across the field. And they did it all with a data set just a thousandth the size of ImageNet.

"Now *that* would be interesting," Alex replied. "'How does it perform on ImageNet?' I can imagine researchers asking each other that exact question about their latest idea."

A North Star for the field, I thought.

If the spirit of Jia's paper was correct, and ImageNet really did presage an imminent reshuffling of the deck—new rules, new intuitions, maybe even an entirely new paradigm—what better way to explore it than through a contest? The collective power of collaboration, energized by the pressure of competition. Exploratory but principled. Fierce. Even after years of work creating ImageNet, simply imagining the idea breathed new life into it.

It also meant the work of bringing ImageNet to the world wasn't over.

Preparations for the contest began as soon as I returned to the United States, and the premise seemed straightforward at first glance: take a collection of algorithms trained on ImageNet, test them on a set of never-seen-before images, evaluate their answers, and rank them by the number of mistakes they make. The one with the lowest total error rate would be the winner. In practice, however, turning a data set into a competition is a scientific challenge all its own.

In games like chess, poker, or basketball, the concept of winning is simple and self-evident. Declaring a winner in a scientific competition, however, is akin to making a commitment: not merely that the entrant performs well by some measure, but that its design makes a contribution to the field at large. That it can teach us something new, insightful, and maybe even transformative. That it's the next step toward the North Star. It's a grand claim, and it's essential that it be stated with confidence.

This made rigor and transparency fundamental, prompting us to draft extensive documentation explaining exactly how an algorithm would be analyzed and the precise formulae with which its performance would be quantified. But flexibility was a virtue as well. After all, when attempting to assign a single label to a photograph, even humans may disagree on which object is most relevant. Imagine, for instance, a picture of an arrangement of fruit in which both a strawberry and an apple are prominent enough that either could be considered its central feature. Would it be "wrong" to label the picture as one, but not the other?

To ensure we didn't declare a well-performing algorithm incorrect, each entry would be allowed to provide a rank-ordered list of five labels in total—making room for "strawberry" *and* "apple," in this case—an evaluation metric we came to call the "top-5 error rate." It encouraged submissions to intelligently hedge their bets, and ensured we were seeing the broadest, fairest picture of their capabilities.

As with the creation of ImageNet itself, the competition presented a steady stream of unexpected challenges. We spent weeks considering the logistics of sharing the data set with contestants, ultimately opting to distribute a scaled-down subset: about a tenth of the total imagery and a twentieth of the total categories, or about 1.4 million individual photos covering a thousand everyday objects, plants, and animals. To be sure we were providing novel tests to the algorithms, we recapitulated much of ImageNet's development process by downloading and labeling hundreds of thousands of new images, complete with yet another round of crowdsourced labeling. All told, it took months of work.

Along the way, Jia's efforts were supported by a growing team that included newcomers like Olga Russakovsky, a smart, energetic grad student looking for something interesting to throw her weight behind. She stood out instantly, with piercing eyes, curly hair reaching her shoulders, and an engaging speaking style. I liked her from our first encounter but was especially struck by the quiet contrasts that defined her: although bubbly and easily mistaken for a native Californian, she was, in fact, born in Ukraine, and spoke frequently of a grandmother still in Kharkiv. She was already a solid choice on intellectual grounds, but possessed a social adroitness that was rare in our department as well. I could tell she had the intellect to contribute to the project behind the scenes, but I began to wonder if, someday, she might tap into her natural savvy to represent it publicly as well.

"Excited?" Olga asked.

I was. The team had stayed late in the lab to wrap up some final details in preparation for the next day, when the website would go live and our contest would be announced.

"Tell me," Jia began. "What's your ultimate ambition here?"

It was a question I was more than prepared to answer, as I'd thought about little else since the darkest days of the ImageNet project. Given all the work we'd done, I found it reductive to think of ImageNet as merely a data set. Even now—especially now, with the contest close at hand—it was a hypothesis. It was a bet that what our field needed most was access to the diversity and variation that human perception had been weaned on for millennia.

I was optimistic that something like a breakthrough was on the table, but wary that the road leading to it would be a bumpy one. We discussed the menagerie of algorithms currently in fashion, and my belief that ImageNet's heft would prove too demanding for any of them to truly master. Support vector machines, random forests, boosting, even the Bayesian network Pietro and I employed in our one-shot learning paper would buckle under its weight, forcing us to invent something truly new.

"I don't think ImageNet will make today's algorithms better," I said. "I think it will make them obsolete."

Officially christened the "ImageNet Large Scale Visual Recognition Challenge," it would be a competition open to all, promising instant recognition to its winners, with its inaugural event held in 2010. Registration opened in May, results were to be calculated by September, and the winner would be announced at a workshop session of the ECCV—the European Conference on Computer Vision—to be held later that year in Crete. To the research community, the undertaking appeared to come together seamlessly. But behind the scenes, it took some outside help to make it happen.

Recognizing our lack of experience, not to mention ImageNet's still-flagging name recognition, we reached out to Mark Everingham, a founding organizer of PASCAL VOC. An Oxford researcher, Mark was a rising star in the world of computer vision in his own right, and kindly allowed ImageNet to begin its life as a new track within the PASCAL VOC competition, then in its sixth year. It was an especially gracious offer, giving us the chance to learn the ropes within the confines of something already established.

Given the relative rarity of computer vision contests at the time, the creation of a new one made enough of a splash to attract some early attention. We hit the ground running with 150 initial registrations, which culminated in thirty-five entries from a grand total of eleven teams. It wasn't a particularly crowded field, but it was a start.

In a way, the eve of the inaugural ImageNet Challenge was even more exciting than the launch of ImageNet itself had been a year earlier. Then, we were showing the world something we'd created. Now, the world would be showing us what they'd created with it. It was a fitting continuation of the biological influence that drove the entire project. ImageNet was based on the idea that algorithms need to confront the full complexity and unpredictability of their environments—the nature of the real world. A contest would imbue that environment with true competitive pressures.

Like our pre-trilobite ancestors, adrift in an ancient, global ocean, the computer vision algorithms of the modern world were about to descend into a crucible of their own. The submissions represented the first generation of research done with ImageNet, and we held it in our hands. I couldn't help but wonder if this was it—if we were about to catch a glimpse of some new frontier.

We weren't.

The winning entrant, from a joint team composed of researchers at NEC Labs, Rutgers, and the University of Illinois, was an example of a support vector machine, or SVM—one of the algorithms I'd assumed ImageNet would overpower. Its rather cryptic name is a reference to a feature of the high-dimensional geometry it utilizes, and emblematic of its abstract nature. SVMs had gained immense popularity in the preceding years, and by 2010 were beginning to feel like a de facto standard for object recognition. The entrant did indeed perform respectably, and we were appreciative of every contestant's efforts. But it amounted to only a slight improvement over cutting-edge work found elsewhere in our field; hardly the dawning of a new age.

It was a deflating moment, now one of many in the history of ImageNet. But if 2010 was anticlimactic, 2011 felt apocalyptic. The winner, this time from Xerox Research Centre in France, was another SVM, and its performance, although improved from the year before, represented another nominal gain of around 2 percentage points.

My miscalculation began to dawn on me. As I suspected, ImageNet was too much for most algorithms to handle. But the SVM in particular was more robust than I gave it credit for, offering a safe haven for entrants and forestalling the aggressive innovation I dreamt of. For two years running, well-worn algorithms had exhibited only incremental gains in capabilities, while true progress seemed all but absent. Worst of all, participation was already dropping, and precipitously: registrations fell from 150 to 96 in the second year, and the entries themselves fell from 35 to just 15. Perhaps unsurprisingly, fewer and fewer people seemed to think the effort was worth it.

To say it was "humbling" would be an understatement. We'd dedicated years of our lives to a data set that was orders of magnitude beyond anything that had ever existed, orchestrated an international competition to explore its capabilities, and, for all that, accomplished little more than simply reifying the status quo. If ImageNet was a bet, it was time to start wondering if we'd simply lost.

"Silvio! Look! I meant to show you!"

I heard my dad's voice down the hall, proudly calling Silvio over to see his latest garage sale scores. His favorite hobby remained alive and well in California, emboldened by an abundance of suburbs and year-round temperate weather. His fascination with objects that conveyed even a hint of Italian origin continued as well, and he was especially proud of a recently acquired belt that bore his favorite stamp: MADE IN ITALY. I wondered if, after all these years, he realized that his daughter had not only bested him with the ultimate Italian-made find, but had actually married it. And that he was currently showing it a belt.

"Ah," I heard Silvio respond. I smiled to myself. With a single syllable, he'd already exhausted most of his possible responses.

Home was now a town house in a faculty neighborhood just off campus, and while it was a perfectly comfortable place that my parents and I were grateful to inhabit, the experience was a fractured one. With so much of Silvio's and my time spent visiting the other, neither of us ever developed much of a local identity. Cross-country flights remained a frequent occurrence, diverting so much time to packing, unpacking, coordinating and commuting, and arriving and departing that we began to feel more like residents of the sky than of anywhere on the ground.

Still, there was an unusual calm to be found beneath the hustle. My mother's relative stability persisted, and for all the hassle of a long-distance marriage, Silvio's visits had the effect of accelerating his bond with my parents. He of course charmed them with his own cooking whenever he stayed with us, but they did a respectable job returning the favor. They developed a tradition of preparing a homemade Chinese meal to celebrate his first night in town, reviving the elaborate arrangements of rice, vegetables, stewed meat, wok-fried dishes, and soups I remembered from Sunday trips to my grandparents' house in Chengdu.

In turn, much of the conversation over the resulting dinner, largely mediated by me, the sole translator on hand, was spurred by his curiosity about the intricacies of Chinese cuisine. His admiration was genuine—far deeper than a stab at son-in-law diplomacy—and the respect was made mutual by their commitment to serving authenticity. No attempt was made to Westernize the recipes, and he enjoyed the results all the more for it. It was a dinner table populated entirely by immigrants, but one at which borders seemed to disappear.

It was all very nice while it lasted.

Just a few months later I was immobile, the invisible anchors of fatigue punching through the floor and digging into the bedrock. Weights on my feet, weights on my arms, weights on my eyelids. Rather than solve any of the problems of our long-distance relationship, Silvio and I made the eminently rational decision to complicate it: we were starting a family, and pregnancy was hitting me hard.

My third trimester was passing especially slowly, with the usual host of annoyances exacerbated by mysterious symptoms that worried my doctors enough to forbid all travel until after I gave birth. But there was no slowing down the world. The flood continued to wash over me—students, research, faculty, and the ongoing question of ImageNet—all symbolized by a glowing screen and a perpetually vibrating phone.

One of those vibrations felt out of place, however. Someone was calling at an oddly late hour, and the familiar name looking back at me—Jean Sabella—confused me.

"Jean? What's up?"

A momentary pause followed. "Fei-Fei, uh, Bob fell."

"What? What do you mean? Is he hurt?"

"No, no, I mean, something's really wrong. He can't seem to balance. He doesn't . . . He's just not himself."

It wasn't clicking. Jean sounded as if she were describing someone's grandfather, not Bob. Surely he was still too young for this kind of thing.

"Okay, um, have you taken him to the hospital?"

"That's where I'm calling from. They did a quick brain scan, and, look—we're still waiting for more details, but . . ." She sighed, slowly. "Fei-Fei, it doesn't look good."

I swallowed hard and sat up. I asked to speak with him. Her voice was muffled for a beat as she handed him the phone. "It's Fei-Fei," I could just barely hear her say.

". . . Hello?"

That's not Bob's tone.

"Bob? Uh . . . Jean said you fell. Are you okay? How are you feeling?"

He didn't give me the reassurance I wanted. He sounded distant and seemed to struggle to get the words out.

"Bob," I said, my voice growing softer as the gravity of the situation sank in, "do you want me to fly out there? I can leave immediately."

The pause on the line told me it was too strong a gesture. Bob knew my due date was just months away. He knew I'd been forbidden to travel. Both facts freighted my offer with a seriousness I hadn't appreciated until the words came out of my mouth.

Silence. Then a sharp intake of breath. Faint, scratchy, and trembling. It couldn't be what I thought it was. *Is he . . . crying?* Bob had never cried in my presence. I heard agitated fumbling and Jean returning to the phone.

"What happened? Fei-Fei, what did you say to him?!"

Twenty-four distracted hours followed, as I waited to hear back from Jean with news. Then it came.

Glioblastoma. Terminal stage. Nonoperable.

Bob was dying.

Dumbfounded, I began calling everyone I knew, desperate to find someone who could help. He'd been a lifesaver during my own family's many health scares, and I was determined to do the same for him. By chance, a contact I'd made through a fellowship program connected me to the neurobiology department of a nearby university hospital. The next day, he was transferred to one of the most advanced care units in the state.

It was a worthy gesture toward someone who meant so much to me, but there was little to be done. Bob deteriorated with terrifying speed, losing consciousness altogether just days after the tumor was discovered. The doctors did everything in their power, but he never woke up. Within three weeks, the man who'd been a third parent to me since high school, an extension of my family in all but name, was gone.

Grief rippled across my household. My father collapsed into tears from the moment he heard. My mother, reserved as always, reacted with solemnity. But I knew they were feeling the same thing. They, too, shared a special bond with the "big bearded math teacher," as they never stopped calling him in Mandarin, forged over the years they'd worked together to help an obsession-prone immigrant girl survive the throes of adolescence. Even Silvio was affected; he'd met Bob only a handful of times, but had grown to understand his singular importance in my life. On top of that, Bob's family came from Naples, just like Silvio's. Knowing that I couldn't attend the funeral—something he feared I'd regret forever, regardless of my doctor's orders—Silvio dropped everything to fly across the country and attend in my absence.

I remembered the rainbow spines of the books wrapped around the walls of Bob's office in Parsippany High—the "Math Lab"—and how our conversations provided me with a daily refuge. I remembered how he doled out fatherly advice, from his matter-of-fact scolding about my efforts on an exam to his tips on choosing a room when Caltech offered me graduate housing, and how our weekly phone calls traced an unbroken line across my life. I remembered how he pulled our family back from the brink with a loan for the dry-cleaning shop. And I remembered my last trip to New Jersey for Bob's retirement party, less than a year before, and how difficult it was to contain my emotions when he stood up to deliver a speech that not so subtly mentioned the pride he felt for "his two sons . . . and his daughter."

Something remained, however. Bob never realized his dream of being published in the sci-fi world, but he continued to write so prodigiously that he developed a habit of emailing me his personal journal entries at the end of each month. We became digital pen pals, corresponding in long-form detail like figures of some bygone era. They became the last remnants of the person I knew: pages and pages of his thoughts, from the profound to the prosaic, captured in black-and-white. To this day, they make me smile, laugh, and occasionally roll my eyes. And they always make me think. I'd dedicated my career to trying to understand the nature of the mind; among the greatest honors of my life was the chance to better know the nature of his.

Life showed no signs of slowing down, but even grief and the weight of a particularly immobile pregnancy couldn't keep my mind off ImageNet. It was a trifecta of intrusive thoughts that made me especially grateful for Silvio's visits.

"So," he asked during an unusually quiet dinner, "what's on your mind? Is it Bob?"

"Oh, Bob's always there," I said with a wistful smile. "But it's more than that."

"ImageNet?"

"Yeah. I dunno, this whole contest idea . . . It really seemed like the logical next step. But we're only two years in, and participation is already falling off. God, have I just been wrong about all of this? Is it that simple? I mean, that's the thing about hypotheses, right? Sometimes they're just . . . wrong."

"Sometimes, sure."

I looked up from my plate.

"But not this time. You know, there's a reason I've never tried to talk you out of this, from that first night you mentioned it. It's not just because you're my wife. It's because I believe in ImageNet, too! Maybe it's ahead of its time. Maybe Jitendra was right, and you've taken too big a leap here. But that doesn't make it *wrong*."

I smiled. He hadn't solved my problem, but his words were heartening.

"And by the way," he continued, "I think the tide is turning. Even in my own lab, where we're working on totally different kinds of vision problems, you know what people are starting to talk about? Bigger data sets. More variety. A broader picture of the world. That's *another* thing about hypotheses—sometimes they take time to win everyone over."

Even Silvio's warmest reassurances felt well-reasoned. He was good at this kind of thing. But I wouldn't need it much longer. Science has a funny way of defying expectations, even for those closest to it.

By August 2012, ImageNet had finally been dethroned as the topic keeping me awake at night. I'd given birth, and a new reality of nursing, diapers, and perpetually interrupted sleep had taken over my life.

I'd planned on skipping the presentation of the ImageNet Challenge results, this time in Florence, Italy, until I got a phone call from Jia. It was unusually late, and my first thought was that something was wrong.

"Hello?"

He was audibly animated, but didn't sound distressed. It was more like excitement, albeit the confused kind. Coming from Jia, that was enough to get my attention.

"Okay, so . . . we've been reviewing the results from this year's submissions, and one of the entries is just . . . I mean—"

He hesitated.

"What? What is it?" I asked.

"All right. Well, first of all, they're using a really unorthodox algorithm. It's a neural network, if you can believe it."

My ears perked up even more. If he didn't have the entirety of my focus a moment ago, he certainly did now.

"It's like . . . *ancient*."

I had to laugh. A twenty-first-century student using the word "ancient" to describe work from a couple of decades earlier was a testament to just how young our field was. (It may have also been evidence that I was getting older. I chose to ignore that possibility.) But he wasn't wrong. Our world evolved fast, and by the 2010s, most of us saw the neural network—that biologically inspired array of interconnected decision-making units arranged in a hierarchy—as a dusty artifact, encased in glass and protected by velvet ropes.

"Seriously? A neural network?"

"Yeah. But there's more. Fei-Fei, you won't *believe* how well this thing is performing."

The view out of the plane's window would have been pitch-black, even on the runway, but there was little to take in from the middle row beyond the seat in front of me. *You'll be in Florence before you know it*, I told myself, knowing full well that wasn't true. Dropping everything to attend ECCV had thrown my homelife into chaos, but Jia's news didn't leave much choice. And I had to admit that there was pretty significant upside to living with one's parents when an infant needs last-minute babysitting.

Recalling from my honeymoon with Silvio that there's no direct flight from San Francisco International to Florence Airport, I dug around to find the route that would get me home and back to the baby fastest. I settled reluctantly on a twenty-hour slog of sleep deprivation and cramped elbow room, with the only scheduled break in the monotony a layover in Paris, or Zurich, or some other iconic city I'd be in too much of a daze to recognize from an airport window. But there was no turning back now. The engines began to roar as we lurched into a slow taxi. That synthetic tone followed by a message over the PA. Tray tables up. Seat belts on. I wanted to sleep, but my racing thoughts kept me wired.

The object of my fixation was a submission that had clawed its way to the top of the leaderboard with an astonishing *10*-percentage-point leap in performance from the previous year's winner, setting an all-time world record for the field of about 85 percent accuracy. To put that in perspective, the research I'd seen suggested the accuracy of the average person would be something on the order of 97 percent—and that was for a far simpler binary choice, such as whether a photograph contained an animal. In contrast, the algorithm had to sift through a thousand options to find the correct response. So while it wasn't *quite* human-level, it was closer than any algorithm had ever come, and by a startling margin.

A beep, and then the captain's voice. We were at cruising altitude.

What was perhaps most startling about the submission was *how* it did what it did. Despite the decades of development and widespread interest in modern algorithms like the support vector machines that had won in the previous two years, its authors chose to bring the neural network back from the dead—and were absolutely *steamrolling* the competition with it. Second place wasn't even close. The winner was dubbed AlexNet, in homage to both the technique and the project's lead author, University of Toronto researcher Alex Krizhevsky.

The plane jostled as we passed through a choppy patch.

A 10-*percentage-point leap? In a single year? And from a neural network?* I turned the idea over in my mind as we passed from one time zone to the next. It was like being told the land speed record had been broken by a margin of a hundred miles per hour in a Honda Civic. It just didn't add up. Progress isn't supposed to look like this.

Or is it? I thought back to Jia's paper on what he'd learned training algorithms on ImageNet. How techniques that worked well with small data sets suddenly performed poorly when trained on large ones—and vice versa. Could it be that all this time, neural networks were better suited to make sense of ImageNet's larger, more densely packed space of possibilities? That they could handle a huge uptick in total categories paired with a dramatic narrowing of the differences between them, while their state-of-the-art competitors couldn't? Eager for more clues, I opened my laptop and pulled up the slide deck the AlexNet team had included with their entry, laying out the design choices they made.

AlexNet was an example of a *convolutional* neural network, or CNN. The name is derived from the graphical process of convolution, in which a series of filters are swept across an image in search of features corresponding to things the network recognizes. It's a uniquely organic design, drawing inspiration from Hubel and Wiesel's observation that mammalian vision occurs across numerous stages. As in nature, each layer of a CNN integrates further details into higher and higher levels of awareness until, finally, a real-world object comes fully into view.

The result is an algorithm that behaves like a retina, gazing out into the surrounding environment. Like a real eye, its outermost layer applies thousands of receptive fields to the pixels of a photograph, each tuned to a unique, tiny pattern and activating when it encounters it—a diagonal edge tilted at a certain angle, a fuzzy blend between two shades, a pattern of stripes or alternating intensities, and so on. At this level of awareness, these filters could be reacting to anything—the pattern of fur on a dog's coat, the edge of a kitchen counter, or the glint along the contour of a sunlit rose petal. In fact, AlexNet could catch *all* of those things—and many more—not just because it had been trained on ImageNet, but, crucially, because it remained faithful to the evolved spirit of biological vision. Rather than arbitrarily deciding in advance which features the network should look for, the authors allowed each of its hundreds of thousands of neurons to *learn* their own sensitivities gradually, exclusively from the training data, without manual intervention. Like a biological intelligence, AlexNet was a natural product of its environment.

Next, signals from those thousands of receptive fields travel deep into the network, merging and clustering into larger, clearer hints. Each new layer, operating at a more sophisticated level of perception than the last, responds when sensing something familiar—something it had been trained to recognize—lighting up with rising intensity like neurons in the throes of a biochemical rush. Tiny patterns become larger ones, which, in turn, connect like the pieces of a puzzle to form increasingly recognizable fragments—a tiger's stripes, wood grain, a shadow falling on the ground.

Finally, the few remaining signals that survived the trip through each layer, filtered and consolidated into a detailed picture of the object in question, collide with the final stage of the network: recognition. *Motor scooter. Leopard. Abacus. Hen. Television set.* Or any of a thousand alternatives. All from a single algorithm, and with an accuracy that was growing competitive with our own.

Of course, these weren't quite new ideas. Yann LeCun had remained astonishingly loyal to convolutional neural networks in the years since his success applying them to handwritten ZIP codes at Bell Labs. By the time AlexNet arrived, he'd spent two decades refining the algorithm and publishing his results, even in the absence of the resources necessary to realize them in full. Now, overnight, a commitment often written off as misguided seemed downright prescient. As if reincarnated, the spirit of LeCun's own CNN, appropriately named "LeNet," was clearly alive in AlexNet.

The connection made the team behind AlexNet, a trio of researchers from the University of Toronto, especially intriguing. The project was helmed by the eponymous Alex Krizhevsky and his collaborator, Ilya Sutskever, both of whom were smart but young researchers still building their reputations. The third name, however, caught my attention instantly: Geoffrey E. Hinton. The same Hinton who'd made his name as an early machine learning pioneer with the development of backpropagation in the mid-1980s, the breakthrough method that made it possible to reliably train large neural networks for the first time. The Hinton who had mentored Yann LeCun when he was still a student in his lab. The Hinton who, like his protégé, had refused to give up on the study of neural networks, even when it made him a near outcast among his colleagues. AlexNet, it appeared, was no mere contest entry. It was a moment of vindication a quarter century in the making.

The significance of the algorithm's roots became even clearer as I looked more deeply into its architecture. Though separated by more than two decades, the primary difference between AlexNet and LeNet appeared to be minimal. Both were implementations of the traditional neural network paradigm. But one key difference was immediately apparent: this new incarnation was much, much bigger.

AlexNet could process images about ten times larger than those fed into LeNet, scanning their contents with a convolution kernel—the "focal point" of the network, so to speak—of about twice the size. From there, the details it identified were filtered through a deeper network that had a few more layers than the original LeNet, allowing it to process what it saw more thoroughly and make more sophisticated inferences as a result. Finally, where LeNet was designed to route its analysis into one of ten possible results, corresponding to the ten handwritten dig-its it was built to recognize, AlexNet could identify a thousand object categories—the subset of ImageNet chosen for use in the competition.

But these were differences of degree, not of kind; at the level of theory, astonishingly little had changed. And yet AlexNet was per-forming like no other neural network in history.

How?

Part of the explanation was surely the hardware on which it ran. A defining flaw of neural networks—long considered fatal—was the dif-ficulty of training them. Even the far smaller networks of bygone de-cades often proved impractical. Indeed, training a network like AlexNet with the world's largest collection of images seemed incomprehensible. But technology had advanced significantly, especially when it came to cheap, high-performance computing hardware optimized for specific applications. Funnily enough, the world owed it all to the popularity of video games.

In yet another twist of fate, the style of number-crunching favored by neural networks is functionally similar to the kind used in ren-dering the graphics for video games—a multibillion-dollar industry that had been driving the advancement and commercialization of custom hardware since the 1990s, fueling the growth of megabrands like Nvidia, the company at the forefront of the field. By 2012, such hardware—specialized processors known as "graphics processing units," or GPUs—had attained affordable, consumer-level status. For Hinton's lab, that meant the silicon needed to bring AlexNet to life was no longer an investment requiring a government grant and con-struction permits. It was available off the shelf at Best Buy.

"Feasible" doesn't necessarily mean "convenient," however. Even with such powerful hardware within reach, training AlexNet on ImageNet required the use of multiple processors running twenty-four hours a day for an entire week. So, for a stretch of seven days in early 2012, while millions of GPUs all over the world were running hot to render jittering machine guns, charging hordes of zombies, and shrapnel-laced explosions, two of them, somewhere in Toronto, were bringing a new kind of neural network to life.

As dramatic as these advances in performance were, however, they weren't strictly novel. They simply allowed existing processes to be completed in more practical time frames. If one were to point to something truly *different* about the world of 2012—something categorically absent in the days of LeNet—it had to be the abundance of data used to train the network. After all, digital imagery was still in its infancy in 1989, and large-scale libraries of the stuff were rare. The idea of organizing a training set for neural networks—not just a collection of digital images, but a massive one, aimed at a specific application, each accurately labeled by a human—would have seemed all but nonsensical.

There was an exception, of course—the scanned images used to train LeNet to read ZIP codes—and it made for an arresting comparison. Even then, collecting a training set of handwritten digits was just barely feasible; unlike multi-megapixel, full-color photos, scanned digits were small, monochrome, and consumed relatively little memory. And it took only thousands of examples to sketch out the level of variety necessary to master their idiosyncrasies—not the hundreds of millions of examples demanded by the natural world. So it's unsurprising that the one application for which a training set could be found at the time stood for more than twenty years as the algorithm's sole achievement. Data, it seemed, had a way of breathing fire into the system.

Indeed, AlexNet came alive in the presence of ImageNet, greedily absorbing its contents, thriving on its scale and diversity. All along, neural networks hadn't needed fancier math and more exotic abstractions. They were simply waiting for a clearer picture of the world we expected them to understand. Something they could truly learn from. Just as big data trained LeNet to make sense of the intricacies of human handwriting, it was training AlexNet to make sense of everything.

I would later learn that Hinton had been working with renewed passion to prove the viability of neural networks for years leading up to 2012. In 2011, believing he was closer than ever to a turning point, he began to reach out to his colleagues in a style that was both confrontational and collaborative, soliciting advice on what he should do next in ways that sounded more like a challenge than a question. One of those calls was to Jitendra, a longtime friend who was skeptical of his project.

"What do I have to do to convince you that neural networks are the future?" Hinton asked.

"You really want to impress me, Geoff? Show me they can handle something serious."

"Like?"

"Like object recognition. In the real world." Whatever Jitendra thought about ImageNet, I'd known since my days at Caltech that he was a believer in the power of visual categorization. "Have you tried PASCAL VOC?"

"Yeah. No luck. It's just too small. There aren't enough examples, so the network doesn't generalize very well when we show it something new."

"All right, so you need something bigger. Have you been following Fei-Fei's lab, by any chance? When you're ready for a real challenge, take a look at what they're up to."

Whether Jitendra had truly had a change of heart regarding the project or was simply trying to get under an old friend's skin—and both seemed plausible—Hinton took the advice seriously.

As if every swirling thought aligned for a moment, snapping me out of the traveler's haze already setting in, something occurred to me: neural networks were a natural fit for ImageNet's representation of the world. LeCun's network did it with handwriting, discovering meaningful patterns at every scale of analysis, from the tiniest clusters of pixels to the texture of pen strokes to complete digits. It was a kind of perceptual fluency that emerged from the data all on its own, naturally organized into a hierarchy of awareness. Hubel and Wiesel saw the same idea play out across the visual cortex of a cat. We saw even deeper in that UC Berkeley lab. They'd *always* been capable of this. But it wasn't until this moment that they had the computational horsepower to achieve it.

Now, it seemed AlexNet had done the same with the world-spanning breadth of ImageNet itself. And that, simply put, was the biggest difference—the enormous increase in the sheer *scope* of the data now being explored. I marveled at the thought of what would be contained within AlexNet's layers once the training process was complete: shapes, edges, patterns, and textures, covering the people, animals, and objects we'd spent so many years capturing from the internet. Ghostly fragments of the real world, organized in just the right way to allow an algorithm to see.

The plane bounced gently as its wheels touched down in Florence. I still had trouble believing AlexNet was the advance it seemed to be. The leap seemed too great. But the more I thought about it, the more it seemed to bear the hallmark of every great breakthrough: the veneer of lunacy, wrapped around an idea that just might make sense.

Word had spread by the next morning. Something historic was going to be announced, or so the buzz suggested, and the vagueness of the rumors only piqued attendees' curiosity. By the time I arrived, the workshop was so crowded that LeCun himself had to stand against the back wall, having arrived minutes too late to find a seat.

The mood in the room was fraught from the moment the proceedings began, with the crowd split into three factions. The first was the small contingent of ImageNet supporters, including me, Alex Berg, and members of Hinton's lab. The second, by far the majority, consisted of neutral but intrigued observers. It was the third group, modest in number but bellicose, who was most vocal. They were the detractors who had been opposed to the very idea of ImageNet since its earliest days, and while I normally brushed off their attitudes, their presence was harder to ignore here.

Worse, we were hardly a unified front. Hinton couldn't attend because of a chronic back problem that made international travel almost impossible for him, so he'd sent Alex Krizhevsky in his place. Alex was immensely talented, and his status as lead author made him an appropriate stand-in. But as with many brilliant people, his personal presentation didn't quite live up to the gravity of his work—something I'm not sure even *he* fully appreciated. It took the form of an awkward flightiness not uncommon among academics, typified by his apparent inability to respond to my repeated text messages attempting to confirm our meeting before the workshop. (He did, thankfully, arrive when he was supposed to.) With audience incredulity at an all-time high, his matter-of-fact delivery made it all the harder to win over converts.

Tensions flared when the floor was opened for questions. We heard all the usual complaints—that ImageNet was too big to be practical, that there was no need to include so many categories, and that object recognition models were still too primitive to warrant such an extensive data set. The fact that AlexNet was demonstrating the opposite, more or less point for point, was oddly unconvincing. But there were new critiques as well, some of which were downright bizarre. One attendee—a rising star at a top university, no less—went so far as to suggest that the category of images depicting T-shirts, specifically, lacked the diversity necessary to train a model reliably. I was more amused than anything else by this point. *Really? T-shirts are the Achilles' heel here?* The rest of the room was simply baffled.

But those who listened were rewarded. Over the course of twenty-seven slides, most bearing little more than black-and-white text and diagrams, the nature of the neural network was demonstrated with a clarity we'd never seen, and it was revelatory. After Rosenblatt's perceptron, Fukushima's neocognitron, and LeCun's LeNet, it was a long-overdue next step, decades in the making, finally realized at a scale befitting its potential.

Of particular note was the process by which AlexNet learned.

Like all neural networks, AlexNet's initial state is shapeless and inert, like a tapestry in a void. Then the onslaught begins: one after another, a photograph is chosen at random from the ImageNet library and the network is tasked with correctly assigning it one of a thousand labels. It's an all-but-impossible request at first; its tens of millions of neurons are configured at random, lacking even a hazy understanding of the world, and yield only misfires. A picture of a mushroom labeled "bottle cap." *Incorrect*. A picture of a tow truck labeled "electric guitar." *Incorrect*. A picture of a leatherback turtle labeled "bath towel." *Incorrect*.

But the failures are not in vain. Mistakes trigger corrective signals, rippling across the network's tens of millions of constituent parts, each assessed for its contribution to the result and pushed, proportionately, to behave differently next time. It's the simplest form of learning—to do less of whatever failed, and more of whatever didn't—blown up to a mammoth scale. Scrutiny is applied to every detail of every error: every patch of light and shadow, every pattern and texture, every soft gradation and hard edge.

It doesn't amount to much in the early stages, and the next time AlexNet sees a photo like the one it misclassified, it will likely be wrong again. But it will be *less* wrong. And so it goes until it gets something right, even if only by sheer luck. This time, the signal is intended to reinforce, not diminish; to accentuate whatever appeared to be pointing in the right direction. The training continues. *Incorrect. Incorrect. Incorrect. Correct. Incorrect. Incorrect. Correct. Correct. Incorrect.*

The vastness of ImageNet—even the subset of a thousand categories chosen for the competition—ensures it will be a long process. It spans objects as varied as digital clocks, picket fences, disk brakes, stopwatches, Italian greyhounds, microwaves, and currants, each well-stocked with a thousand variations thereof. But AlexNet is vast as well. Its 650,000 individual neurons are networked together by way of 630 million connections in total, with 60 million tiny, nearly imperceptible weights influencing the strength of those connections, making some stronger and others weaker, as signals flow from one end of the network to the other.

Taken as a whole, they provide a canvas large enough to paint the world. The weights change from one round to the next, some growing stronger, some weaker, and some merely vacillating, making for a pliable fabric that responds to its training with organic grace. Bearing the weight of these gargantuan quantities are two Nvidia GPUs, highly specialized silicon running in parallel, conducting round after round at maximum speed.

The training continues nonstop, from morning till night, until every pixel of every image has been studied. Hours become days, and days stretch into a week. The GPU pushes. ImageNet challenges. AlexNet adapts. All across the network, larger and more extravagant structures emerge as tens of millions of weights are tempered again and again and again. A blacksmith's hammer against glowing steel. One increment at a time, until near-invisible perturbations become mountains and valleys, reaching out into a multithousand-dimensional hyperspace. A ghostly average of the world's innumerable details, the imprints left by a thousand different pictures of a thousand different things. A thousand Dalmatians accumulate here, a thousand laundry hampers there, a thousand marimbas somewhere else.

Like something out of geology, these imprints coalesce into a single terrain that reaches from one end of AlexNet to the other. Pencil sharpeners, mosques, starfish, hockey pucks—all embedded somewhere in the landscape. The algorithm hasn't merely "seen" these things; it's *become* them. The photos we spent years chasing across the internet have shaped an entire manifold of machine awareness, primitive but potent. A single unified representation of it all.

After 1.4 million rounds, the last trickle of images are less a trial than a coronation. The network's focus strides across the pixels, lighting up as familiar patterns register, routed to the next layer, where they're combined with others to form greater and greater constellations of awareness. The responses are no longer random, and most are no longer wrong. A coyote. *Correct.* A table lamp. *Correct.* A convertible. *Correct.* It's an apparently magical combination of hardware, software, and data, and it's come closer than anything our field has ever built to capturing the spirit of the evolution that shaped the minds of mammals like us.

Now in its final form, the diversity that it took a world of crowd-sourced volunteers to curate has forged a topology so varied, so robust, that a kind of holy grail has been attained. This neural network, the largest our field has ever seen, trained by more data than any in history, can *generalize.*

It would take months to truly appreciate what we saw in that room, but even in the moment, it was clear we were in the presence of something extraordinary. After so many years of hoping ImageNet would spur the creation of something new, I realized what it had all been for: the long-awaited recognition of something timeless. A biologically in-spired algorithm, staring us in the face for decades. It had just needed the proper challenge.

The afternoon also provided an occasion to reflect on the last decade of work in our field. My lab had bet everything on a yearslong pursuit of data at an unprecedented scale, while Hinton's had staked their reputations on a commitment to a family of algorithms the field had all but abandoned. Both were gambles, and both could have been wrong. But on that day, as we saw the incredible capabilities of neural networks brought to life with the training power of ImageNet, I realized that although both were vindicated, it was only because they were undertaken at the same time. Unbeknownst to all involved, we'd been relying on each other at every step.

I spent more time traveling to and from Florence than I did on the ground. But the flight home felt different from the one that had brought me there. It was no less cramped, and the haze of exhaustion was even heavier, but my mind wasn't racing anymore—at least not in the same way. I'd seen the work for myself. There had been no mistake, no oversight, no clerical mishap. Neural networks had come back from the dead, bigger, more complex, and more powerful than ever. And ImageNet had taught them everything they needed to know, placing them within striking distance of human-level capabilities in a single attempt.

Half a billion years after the emergence of biological vision led to the Cambrian explosion beneath the waves of an ancient ocean, it was hard not to wonder if we were on the verge of a similar inflection point. Would the advent of machine vision trigger a new avalanche of evolution, this time in a digital form?

In place of the previous flight's manic thoughts and burning questions was something unexpected. It wasn't quite serenity, but rather a dawning sense of awareness. Reflection. I was content to sit in silence this time, from takeoff till landing, with a single thought reverberating in my head: history had just been made, and only a handful of people in the world knew it.

9

WHAT LIES BEYOND EVERYTHING?

"Well, *this* is a little creepy."

The student wasn't wrong. As the lights flickered to life and the shadows receded, we took in the strange, geometric tableau that surrounded us: a grid of disused cathode ray tube monitors arrayed on the floor, as if trapped in some liminal state between storage and recycling, locked for years in the dark. It was hard to imagine that this dusty, forgotten space was ever anything more than the glorified antique closet it now appeared to be. But it was. With garbage bags and a dolly in hand, on an unassuming afternoon in the early months of 2013, we were standing in the former hub of the world-renowned SAIL—the Stanford AI Lab.

Over the course of decades, the field that had once boldly called itself "artificial intelligence" had fractured into a multitude of narrower disciplines, many of which downplayed their cognitive roots in favor of more mechanistic terms like "pattern recognition" and "natural language processing." Along the way, the need for a central lab faded. Important work was still being carried out under its auspices, to be sure, including seminal achievements in self-driving cars and computational biology, as well as an explosion of new ideas about probability and statistics in the modeling of real-world phenomena. But the connection between the SAIL name and the research it supported felt more like a formality than the shared mission of its heyday.

Suddenly, however, the AI winter was waning. Trends once relevant only to my closest peers were becoming hot topics as flexible algorithms like neural networks roared back to life, truly large-scale data sets emerged, and AlexNet demonstrated how powerful the two could be in practice. Our field appeared to be unifying, albeit under the banner of a slightly different moniker—and an increasingly popular buzz phrase—"machine learning."

The changes were subtle at first, like the realization that my colleagues and I were receiving more requests for media interviews than usual. The most substantial sign of change, however, came as more and more of us were gripped by a fixation on the tech industry, with a number of them departing academia altogether for Silicon Valley careers. What began as a trickle was accelerating, and two resignations in particular changed my life overnight.

The first was the miracle Silvio and I had been waiting for: a chance, at last, to unite our family. As grueling as our five years of long-distance marriage had been, it was suddenly clear we'd spent them well; while I was chasing ImageNet, he'd established himself as a leading researcher in the development of 3D perception algorithms, a subject our department found intriguing. When Sebastian Thrun left Stanford to help kick-start Google's burgeoning self-driving efforts, Silvio's reputation made him a front-runner for the position.

Although for obvious reasons I was excluded from the hiring conversation, Silvio's merits were as apparent to my colleagues as they'd always been to me, and he was overwhelmingly approved as the newest member of our faculty. With a single decision, a half decade of weekly cross-country flights, to say nothing of our attempts at parenting a toddler across state lines, finally came to an end. Homelife would be more crowded than ever, admittedly, as the ongoing question of my mother's health meant my parents would likely be permanent residents of the house I now shared with my husband, but it was a small price to pay.

Next, Andrew Ng, who'd long balanced his role as an educator with leadership positions across Silicon Valley, stepped down as the director of SAIL. A number of senior colleagues supported me as his replacement, making me the lab's seventh director, and the first woman to hold the title. So, with a call to an electronics recycling specialist and the offer of free lunch to lure my fellow professors to a new schedule of meetings, I set about reestablishing SAIL—not just as a channel for funding, but also as the social, interpersonal, and even cultural center of our community.

My own lab, a smaller outfit I'd been running since relocating from Princeton, known as the Stanford Vision and Learning Lab, occupied the southeast corner of the Gates Computer Science Building's second floor, near the far edge of the university where the outskirts of campus blend into the hills of Palo Alto. It was a place I loved to wander whether or not I had anything on the calendar. Every room seemed to house a new clutch of students, at least one of whom was always free for a few minutes of chatting about their research or some stray idea.

Of special importance to me was the graduation of my first crop of PhD candidates, including the preternaturally patient Jia. The creative fire that gripped him in the aftermath of ImageNet continued to burn, and only seemed to intensify with the promise of his own doctorate now months away. His attitude was emblematic of the lab as a whole: refreshed, focused, and eager to explore.

It also meant he was stretching himself thinner and thinner across an impressive but taxing workload. As the breadth and nuance of his own scholarship expanded, it became clear that it was time for a successor as the contest's lead organizer. Olga, now a year into her time with our lab, happily took the reins, maintaining its many operational details while establishing herself as an uncommonly capable spokesperson for what was, by nature, as much a technical challenge as a community event.

Meanwhile, a new generation of students had arrived, their fidgety eagerness contrasting endearingly with the veterans' poise. Thanks to ImageNet's success, our lab had become a magnet for a particular kind of young thinker. As the first generation of students to come of academic age in this era of newly revitalized AI, they enjoyed a rare privilege. They were old enough to recognize history in the making, but young enough to catch it at the dawn of their careers.

Each of them followed the news, online, on television, and in the buzz they'd overhear as they walked the halls or talked to their professors. It all pointed to a future that seemed to be arriving decades ahead of schedule, and one that offered them more than any previous generation could have expected. For the first time, the highest ambition of a computer vision student wasn't one of a handful of coveted faculty positions scattered across the country, but a path into the technology industry, whether a job with a start-up or one of the giants.

It was an uncommonly exciting prospect in a world like ours, and maybe even a lucrative one. But our actions suggested a simpler motivation, even among the rookies: that we'd never been more eager to explore, the unknown stretching far over the horizon. We were possessed by an especially ambitious brand of creativity, the kind that makes for manic days and sleepless nights. So, while the industries of the world surely had their own plans for ImageNet and the many applications they'd no doubt wring out of it, we knew that was their path, not ours. The North Star was still out there. We weren't yet done with the science.

Giggles erupted across the lab as Jia clicked his way through the slides. The topic of the presentation didn't seem particularly funny at first glance—a novel approach to addressing failures in image classification—but, in an attempt to study the kind of input that confuses an algorithm, a collection of Photoshopped monstrosities had been assembled, ranging from the whimsical to the unsettling. Each earned some combination of chuckles and winces: a kangaroo with zebra stripes and a ram's horns, a kitten emerging from the waves with shark teeth, and a hippo with the skin of a watermelon. But it was the image now on the screen that really sent the crowd over the edge: a duck's body with the head of a full-sized crocodile, standing peacefully in a park without the slightest apparent strain on its tiny legs, like a monster from Greek mythology repurposed for a children's book. Jia pressed on, unmoved, as if laughter were a frequency he couldn't hear.

"I call it a 'duckodile,'" he explained, his tone so matter-of-fact I almost wondered if he believed it was an actual species. "Jon calls it a 'cruck.' What's most important, however, is what our model called it." With another click, a single-word description appeared over the duck-reptile hybrid: *"Animal."*

Although the label drew another round of guffaws from the crowd, it was, in Jia's typical style, a moment of understated brilliance. The presentation was based on his latest published work, "Hedging Your Bets: Optimizing Accuracy-Specificity Trade-Offs in Large Scale Visual Recognition," which he'd coauthored with Jon Krause, an up-and-coming PhD student. In it, they'd confronted a growing challenge for even state-of-the-art image classifiers: making intelligent decisions in the face of ambiguity. Indeed, while the "duckodile" defied accurate classification, it was a mark of sophistication that their model reacted not by venturing a surely incorrect guess, but by retreating to a higher, safer level of its ontology—simply concluding that, strange details aside, it did appear to be *some* kind of animal.

The work was a reminder that as heavily as our research focused on vision, language was an inescapable part of the picture. ImageNet wouldn't have been possible without WordNet, after all—it provided the framework that gave each category not just its label, but its place within a tree of connected ideas. And it's hard to imagine WordNet without the work of psychologist Eleanor Rosch.

Rosch contributed significantly to our modern understanding of categorization and the role it plays in thought, with a globetrotting portfolio of experiments that examined the ways that human beings conceptualize the world, whether grad students at UC Berkeley or the Highland tribes of Papua New Guinea. Although the study of categories dates back to Aristotle, Rosch's experimental approach, which blended crisp logic with empirical data, had set the field ablaze in the 1970s.

In a seminal 1975 paper, she formulated a more precise vocabulary for understanding hierarchy, the way so many concepts can be situated on a spectrum that runs from general to specific. Take one of Jia's animal categories, for example, like "duck." Ducks exist at a particular level of detail, requiring more information to understand than shallower categories like *"Anatidae"* (the biological family that includes ducks, geese, and swans), "animal," "living thing," and, ultimately, "thing"—what Rosch termed "superordinates"—but less information than deeper "subordinate" categories like "mallard," "mandarin duck," and "ringed teal." When taken as a whole, such hierarchies, ImageNet's included, look like trees. Moving toward the root means less specificity and differentiation, while moving toward the leaves— the furthest ends of each branch—means more.

Jia and Jon brought this principle to computer vision. If a classifier has good reason to believe it may be looking at a duck *or* a crocodile, but not enough information to decide between the two, it's only sensible to move up a level to a broader superordinate, trading some of the specificity of the deeper level for the safety of the shallower.

With the spectacle of catsharks, hippomelons, and kangarams out of the way, they next demonstrated how effectively their technique performed in more plausible scenarios. A close-up shot of a corgi, mislabeled by traditional classifiers as "golden retriever," was now more safely hedged as "dog"; a taxi with strange cladding and confusingly mismatched paint that had been mislabeled as "tank" was now hedged as "vehicle," and so on.

I couldn't help but note that, yet again, the power of big data was on full display. For all its subtlety, this work simply wouldn't be possible without a gargantuan stockpile of photographs like ImageNet. It didn't just provide the raw data needed to explore a universe of hierarchical concepts in the first place, but—and this was probably even more important—its scale and ontological organization allowed these conceptual relationships to be *discovered*. No one had to tell the model how to move from a higher level of detail to a lower one; there was no need to curate a new list of connections or paths to follow. ImageNet was so comprehensive that everything the model needed was already there. It just took some new tactics to harness it.

Jia and Jon's "hedging" technique was an application of the kind of thinking I found most inspiring. While elegant and intuitive—even simplistic, once understood—it required genuine insight to develop. Artful yet precise, it was a sterling example of the many ways computer vision was evolving.

The next presentation addressed a more expansive, recondite question: what awaits us if we push in the opposite direction, and venture *deeper* into the branches? What will our algorithms make of a subtler, more complex world than the one they were built to understand?

Jon stood up next to answer. A mild-mannered Ohioan who seemed most at home in a T-shirt and cargo shorts, he shared Jia's quiet demeanor but expressed it in a quirkier way; he quickly became known for his fascination with red pandas, for instance, and kept a printout of the animal permanently posted above his workstation monitor. But he was no pushover, and like the best researchers in my lab, was firmly opinionated when he felt the need to make himself heard.

With a click, a split-screen image appeared. On one side was a photograph of a car, and on the other its equivalent computer-assisted design, or CAD, wireframe, the schematic created by its designers. The latter image was then superimposed over the former, with digital red lines tracing the contours of the real-life vehicle's grilles, windows, and body panels, highlighting the features a classifier would have to recognize in order to identify the precise model.

"Cars?" someone asked.

"Oh, just wait," Jon replied with a knowing grin.

He wasn't kidding. It was our first glimpse into a topic that was far bigger than any of us realized.

I always felt that the true contribution of ImageNet was its dual nature. Its mammoth scale was powerful because of the ontological hierarchy that organized it, while its ontology was powerful because it was so large and comprehensive, spanning such a diverse range of categories. Neither virtue would have been sufficient alone. But, like size itself, a term like "category" is relative. As the hedging technique demonstrated, valid categorical answers can be found at multiple levels of depth, depending on the question being asked. The deeper the level, the closer the concepts creep toward one another, separated by fewer and fewer details. *Thing. Living Thing. Plant. Tree. Maple. Acer pseudoplatanus.*

But ImageNet was not entirely the paragon of vastness and detail it seemed to be. Although some categories were exceptionally fine-grained—trees a particularly good example—others remained a collection of comfortably distinct ideas that were still coarse in their scope, separated from one another by wide gaps of conceptual differentiation. They ensured that in many domains, the work of our classifiers never got too difficult.

Cars were one of many examples of a topic that all but obliterated those gaps, and Jia and Jon's afternoon crash course impressed on us how labyrinthine it could be. For instance, we might find it obvious that a photograph depicts a Toyota (though, to be sure, most of us were abysmally unprepared to talk cars). Whether it was a Toyota Yaris also seemed knowable after a bit of study. But was it a *2008* Toyota Yaris or a *2009* Toyota Yaris? Suddenly the question was a lot harder. Was it a 2008 Toyota Yaris in *blazing* blue pearl or a 2008 Toyota Yaris in *bayou* blue pearl? Both choices were offered that year, and both were . . . blue. Was it a *base-model* 2008 Toyota Yaris in blazing blue pearl or a 2008 Toyota Yaris *liftback sport* in blazing blue pearl? Amazingly, the questions didn't even stop there. All this to understand a single variant of a single model from a single manufacturer. And that's just cars.

Someone in the audience pointed out a few recent computer vision papers on bird species, of which ImageNet had included a seemingly robust collection of fifty-nine. Although a project at Cornell University dwarfed that number with a data set of photographs covering hundreds, it's estimated there are more than ten thousand species across the world, leaving even the state-of-the-art orders of magnitude behind reality. I grinned, reminded of the breathless tone taking hold in the tech press, with article after article heralding the age of machine learning and declaring image classification a suddenly "solved problem." *The sycamore maples, whooping cranes, and Toyotas of the world say otherwise*, I thought.

These were our first object lessons in what became known as "fine-grained classification," a research topic that examined the ever-narrowing detail required to identify objects of increasingly similar classes. While it might seem like a mere extension of our previous work, from distinguishing obvious differences to parsing the less obvious, it suggested something more jarring and instructive: that even at our most grandiose, we were still thinking small.

Among science's greatest virtues, however, is its ability to recast a lesson in humility as a moment of possibility. We'd spent years collecting images—*billions* in all—enlisting a global workforce to help us make sense of them, but all it took was a flip through the Kelley Blue Book to realize that we'd barely scratched the surface. We were still much closer to the root of the tree than its leaves. Years of effort and a global competition between some of the brightest minds on earth, all for a baby step toward true visual intelligence.

And yet, when I looked around the room, I didn't see intimidation or despair on my students' faces. I saw the gears behind their eyes beginning to turn. I had no doubt we were each, to a person, thinking the same thing: *The journey isn't over yet. We have so much more to explore.*

Biederman's number was, indeed, vast, but it was also a necessary fiction—a conveniently truncated definition of "everything" that was tractable enough to wrap our minds and algorithms around, if only barely. Now, we stood on the precipice of a new vastness. We were about to find out what lies *beyond* everything.

An ornate wooden spice rack had caught my eye. I picked it up to get a closer look. Noticing my interest, my father walked over to join me.

"Oooh," he said. "It's beautiful, but . . ." He peered closer. "Ah, yes—it looks handmade, don't you think? A carpenter must live here." He spoke in a slightly hushed tone, as if he didn't want his Mandarin to be overheard.

Maybe, I said to myself, before glancing at the other table. "Anything interesting over there?" I asked.

"Yes, lots. Some gloves I liked. And there's a very nice-looking tool set. I noticed even better ones in the garage, but I don't think they're for sale. You know, I really do think the owner's a woodworker of some kind."

As is so often the case in life, the demands of a career, a marriage, and motherhood had seemed to explode overnight. But I still made time, on occasion, at least, to tag along with my father when he was pursuing his favorite activity. They were rare moments of stillness and nostalgia in a life that felt perpetually accelerated, and they helped preserve the bond that had seen us through from our earliest days in a strange new country. I was especially charmed by the care and thought with which he'd turn the items for sale on card tables in a driveway into vignettes about strangers' lives. Whether he was right or wrong, the attempt always felt sincere, and in its own way, reasoned.

Over the years, it had become a habit of mine as well.

Another Tesla. Less than a year after the release of the Model S in mid-2012, the car had become a Palo Alto fashion statement I saw everywhere. *Probably another tech guy. Venture capital, maybe.* The next vehicle I passed wasn't as fancy, but still said something. It was some kind of a hatchback, painted beige but faded from what looked like years of outdoor parking. *Looks like something one of my students would drive.*

I'd been invited to dinner at a newly opened hot pot restaurant and used Google Maps to find it, including a few photos of the storefront from Street View to make sure I'd recognize it from the car. Along the way, my usually ambient interest in visual minutiae—a habit that never quite turns off, but recedes to a kind of white noise most of the time—felt more active than usual. If half of me was navigating to dinner, the other half was obsessed with what I was seeing on the way.

For all the things cars might say about people, from individuals to communities, there are limits to the scale at which they can be evaluated. It's the kind of information that surveys have historically attempted to collect, but paying professionals to create city-sized maps of car ownership is costly and time-consuming, and can't be practically deployed beyond modest-sized regions. But what if these limitations could be overcome? What if, somehow, such an analysis could be performed at any scale we wished? And what if it weren't just cars, but everything? *Anything?* What new insights—societal, cultural, even political—might be revealed by simply looking more closely at the world that surrounds us every day? It was a question that seemed impossible to answer without an entirely new form of perception. Then it hit me: Google Street View. Car models. Fine-grained classification. *What if we're already building it?*

Like any dominant organism, AlexNet's offspring—a new generations of neural networks making impressive leaps, year after year—all but monopolized their environment, proving so effective, so elegant, and so far-reaching in their applicability that virtually every other technique fell by the wayside almost overnight. Darlings of the academic community that had enthralled researchers only a year or two earlier—algorithms like support vector machines and Bayesian networks—all but vanished from conference lectures, published articles, and even conversation around the lab. All anyone wanted to talk about was the latest developments in neural networks.

We knew this because so many of those new models were submitted to the ImageNet Challenge. Little more than five years since the data set's debut at CVPR in 2009, the contest had grown into a foundational event in the field of computer vision, providing the shared benchmark for progress we'd always hoped it could. Although our lab had a policy of not submitting our own models to avoid any apparent conflicts of interest, simply watching had become a regular event that rivaled Christmas. Every year brought new advances, steadily narrowing the gap between machines and human-like performance. Lower and lower fell the error rates, ever closer to our own, as humans. And then, perhaps, even lower.

And yet, even as the technology approached "human performance," the very idea felt like a contrivance, if not a mirage. Our capabilities are, of course, far richer than any single metric can capture. But our shortcomings can be just as instructive as our strengths. For instance, humans might be better than computers at explaining *why* they believe the bird on a nearby branch is a coastal blue jay, drawing on all sorts of general knowledge, visual cues, and intuitions, but we can only stretch that ability so far. Even experienced bird-watchers can rarely identify more than a couple hundred species, which leaves the vast majority of the avian universe inaccessible to any one observer.

As AI struggled to overcome the last few percentage points that divided human-level performance in general object classification from its own, it seemed tantalizingly close to outclassing us in other dimensions—and quite dramatically. We just can't hold anywhere near as much knowledge in our heads as a computer can.

That's when the dots started connecting in a new way. Thanks to Street View, we now had high-resolution imagery of nearly every neighborhood in the country. Although its primary purpose was to aid navigation, I was awed by the detail it conveyed about our world. Trees, streetlamps, mailboxes, and, of course, the cars we drive—Street View provided a chance to peer into those hidden dimensions of information that lie unseen, all around us. When I thought about our lab's work in precisely distinguishing car models, the opportunity that Street View provided felt like another burst of serendipity.

More and more, it seemed fair to ask if we were still even talking about "vision" at all. Whatever this new ability was shaping up to be—some combination of visual acuity with encyclopedic depth of knowledge about every imaginable topic—I was beginning to believe it was far more than the machine equivalent of human eyes. It was something altogether new: a deeper, more finely polished lens, capable of revealing our world from perspectives we'd never imagined.

Reviewing our growing repository of car models, painstakingly cobbled together from sources scattered across the internet, I imagined how hard it'd be to explain to my teenage self what any of this had to do with science. The details of the work were, of course, immaterial; it was just the latest testament to the lab's central values: an abiding respect for the complexity of the world and a hunger to explore it, no matter the cost. We felt like art lovers on a guided museum tour, each new exhibit challenging us while stirring the awe we felt for the boundless detail surrounding us.

We didn't waste time worrying if any of this would pay off in the way we hoped. The mere fact that we were confronting it—embracing the world for what it is, on its terms, without compromise or distillation—felt like a mission worth dedicating our lives to. Whether our window into the world was car models, bird species, or something else entirely—perhaps our next project would explore variations of paved roads or reptile scales or violin finishes—each felt like a small step closer to the moment when we'd see reality through entirely new eyes. No matter what we found, I was convinced it'd be worth the journey.

In the meantime, we had the usual battery of hurdles to overcome. Scale, of course, was an inescapable challenge. But we were ready this time. After ImageNet, we were inured to the headaches that this volume of data compilation entails. We scoured websites like Craigslist, Cars.com, Edmunds, and other online marketplaces to produce a training set of images covering virtually every unique variety of car on the road in 2014—all 2,657 of them—and channeled it into the largest and most precise classifiers we'd ever built. And we harnessed a torrent of Google Street View images, filling our servers with photographic depictions of avenues, boulevards, corners, intersections, and cul-de-sacs, crisscrossing the entire country. Another microcosm of the world was coming together in our lab, and it wouldn't be long before we could peer directly into it, laying bare the secrets it held.

Those secrets wouldn't reveal themselves without a fight, however. Because we intended to use cars as a proxy for exploring larger socioeconomic questions—correlating them with aspects of their owners' identities like income, education, and occupation—we had to face the fact that dramatic gaps in monetary value often translate to only subtle differences in outward appearance. So while we had little trouble distinguishing a Cadillac sedan from a Toyota pickup truck, early experiments suggested it was perilously easy for a "naively" trained classifier to mistake a Cadillac for, say, a Honda Accord, especially when the cars were painted in similar colors—precisely the kind of mistake we sought to avoid. Trickier still was disentangling a Cadillac ATS from a CTS, to say nothing of the innumerable variations *within* each model line. We found the concept of trim levels especially vexing, as option packages totaling thousands of dollars, and sometimes more, often entailed only minor modifications to the car's body style and badging.

"Hey, uh, everyone, before we break, I had an idea I wanted to share."

Our weekly research meeting for the Street View project was ending when a graduate student named Timnit Gebru spoke up. We were gathered in my office, a small, narrow rectangle on the third floor of the Gates Computer Science Building, a space that lived up to the academic stereotype—cramped quarters made even more so by piles of books, papers, and knickknacks spilling from the shelves and creeping toward the center of the room. Framed cozily by the clutter on all sides, our now three-strong team of students was packed onto my bright red couch.

"Okay, so—the idea is to apply our image classifiers to all these Street View images, track all the car models we can, and see what kinds of patterns they reveal, right? Well, I've been digging around, and I think we found the perfect way to do it."

Timnit was the most junior of the trio of students working on the project, but she was driven to a degree that lent her a formidable presence. Though short, like me, her confidence and gifts as an orator ensured she had no trouble commanding the room. And with Jia defending his PhD thesis and Jon juggling a number of other projects, Timnit hadn't hesitated to take the initiative.

We'd first crossed paths about a year earlier, when she attended one of my advanced seminars. She was a third-year graduate student in electric engineering, with little previous background in AI. But she made an immediate impression on me—not just because she was the only Black woman pursuing an engineering PhD, but because her willingness to ask questions demonstrated a hunger to learn that professors immediately notice. When she asked to join the lab, I said yes without hesitating, dispensing with even basic formalities like reference letters.

I could hear the conviction in her voice as she continued. "It's the U.S. Census Bureau. Every year they conduct a nationwide survey called ACS—the American Community Survey—tracking a ton of sociological information about regions all over the country."

"And you're suggesting we incorporate this into our analysis?"

"The possibilities are just *endless*. The census is an absolute treasure trove of data, all organized by neighborhood, county, state, even voting precinct. But it takes so much time and effort to collect. Can you imagine correlating all that with the objects our classifiers pick up?"

She'd more than made her case intellectually, but it was her eagerness that impressed me the most. Moments like these—when a student presents something creative, novel, and entirely unexpected, all on their own—are among the most rewarding a professor can hope to experience. And her instincts were correct. As we pored over the census data she helped us acquire, we marveled not just at its scope and variety, but at the ideas it explored. At our fingertips was a nationwide snapshot of politics, education, income, and even crime, all ready to be correlated with a fundamentally new signal about the world—computer vision. It was data of a sort that our lab had never encountered before, and it imbued the work with a gravity no one expected. This was shaping up to be much more than a data-mining project.

The kitchen was a mess, but my favorite kind of mess. With the fluency of an artisan in his workshop, Silvio darted back and forth between scattered pots and pans, making momentary use of the utensils that were balanced alongside them, and grabbing occasional handfuls of ingredients from a rainbow of bags, boxes, and jars lining the counters.

"What's all this?" I asked.

"I guess I was just in the mood to make something special for dinner tonight. It's *polpo alla luciana*. Octopus. I've also got some zucchini pasta going, some grilled peppers, burrata, and arugula, that type of thing."

"Wow, I can't wait! Let's, uh, lock the door, though."

He knew what I was getting at. Life in a three-generation, two-culture family quickly taught Silvio the art of cohabitating with my mother, who took kitchen cleanliness to an almost pathological extreme—following the maxim of cleaning while one cooks so slavishly it might be more accurate to say she cooks while she cleans. As much as she enjoyed Silvio's cooking, elaborate dinners like these were a recipe for domestic tension. I watched his performance for another minute or two before chuckling to myself.

"What?" he asked.

"You know, it's funny. I can *instantly* tell when it's a night like this. When I just know we'll have to keep Mom out of the kitchen. There's some magical arrangement of pots and pans and commotion that tells me you've got something big planned, and I pick up on it the moment I walk past. There's no conscious thought—just immediate awareness. You know what it makes me think of? Jeremy Wolfe."

Silvio's stirring slowed for a moment. "Wolfe . . . Wolfe . . . Oh, the, uh, cognitive scientist? From Harvard? The 'gist' guy, right?"

"Good memory! God, he wrote this totally obscure article in a journal in like 1998. It wasn't even research. Just an opinion piece. But it was easily one of the most influential things I read at Caltech. Easily. I still think about it."

A world-renowned researcher interested in the inner workings of visual memory, Jeremy Wolfe found our ability to quickly comprehend a scene fascinating, and dedicated much of his work to understanding it. The 1998 article, entitled "Visual Memory: What Do You Know About What You Saw?," was written in an almost colloquial tone, but its conclusions were incisive. Seeing an image, as he put it, prompted our brains to "remember the *gist* of the scene."

"Right, right. I remember thinking 'gist' was a funny word to see in an article like that." Silvio chuckled, arranging the burrata, arugula, and tomato, and glancing occasionally at the door to make sure it was still closed.

"That's part of why I loved it so much," I replied. "The ideas were so big, but the language was totally straightforward."

Silvio hated being distracted while cooking. I knew this, and he knew I knew this. But he was a sucker for science talk, too, and he'd long since learned that once I got worked up about a topic like this, he was better off letting me get it out of my system. I grinned a little, knowing he was probably reminding himself of all this as he sliced into a pepper.

"His idea," Silvio added, "was that our first glance at something is all it takes to understand it, at least on some level, right?"

"Right. That includes the basic stuff like objects, of course. We're good at scanning for 'things' very quickly. But we're *great* at noticing how they're placed and arranged. You know, angles and positions and stuff. How we interpret it."

"The relationships *between* the things."

"Yes, exactly! But what's amazing is that we do it all without thinking. It just *happens*, in a flash, like I did tonight when I saw what you were cook—"

"Fei-Fei? Are you in there?"

It was my mother. Silvio and I looked at each other, our eyes instantly wide.

"Why is the door closed?" she continued.

"Uh, uh—Silvio was, uh—there was a lot of steam, and, uh—"

"That doesn't make any sense!" he attempted to whisper while smirking.

"Stop *giggling*!" I shot back as I angled the door just enough to slide out, trying and failing to act natural as my mother stared blankly.

Wolfe's notion of the "gist" had stayed with me long after I read it, inspiring me so deeply that I dedicated much of my time at Caltech to exploring it myself. The work bore no explicit links to computer science or AI, but directly confronted the question of what, exactly, humans perceive when they glance at the real world. Although Pietro, Christof, and I considered such nuanced awareness a distant dream for computer vision, we were convinced that the journey could only begin with a better understanding of what humans do, and devised a way to explore it. Fittingly, our findings were published in the neuroscience-focused *Journal of Vision* in 2007.

In our experiment, twenty-two subjects were shown a collection of ninety photographs, each in a brief exposure ranging from five hundred milliseconds (a half second) all the way down to twenty-seven milliseconds (about half the time a single frame of motion picture film is visible). The photos were conceptually simple but detailed: everyday scenes involving multiple people, events, and activities, including indoor and outdoor locations and natural and artificial surroundings. The subjects' task was to describe what they saw—or, more accurately, what they remembered seeing—in as much detail as they could muster.

Like all experiments, it began as a gamble; half the fun was the thrill of not knowing what, if anything, we would discover. But it paid off, and I still marvel at the responses we collected. For instance, when shown a photograph of a Victorian-era residential interior for five hundred milliseconds, one subject wrote:

> *Some fancy 1800s living room with ornate single seaters and some portraits on the wall.*

In just a half second, they'd seen enough to produce a simple but essentially perfect description of the scene, including reasonable estimates of the century, the nature of the wall decorations, and the structures of the individual pieces of furniture. But even at twenty-seven milliseconds—about *one-fortieth* of a second, surely short enough to rob the subject of almost all opportunity for depth and detail—genuine awareness persisted:

> *Couldn't see much; it was mostly dark w/ some square things, maybe furniture.*

"Maybe furniture." Two words that reveal so much. How astonishing it is that even during such a brief interval, a notion so complex—not a shape, not a color, not even some natural phenomenon baked deep into our genes, but something as modern and arbitrary as *furniture*— can register.

With or without the time constraints, I found this ability captivating. Photographs may be still, but we excel at extracting the motion frozen within them, from the grand and sweeping to the nearly imperceptible, and all with impressive acumen. We naturally consider the angle of bodies, arms, and legs, and instantly sense where they came from and where they're going; speed and force, weight and balance, energy and potential. We imagine the circumstances leading to the moment the picture captures and the outcome that may result, as in the fraction of a second following a photograph of a skateboarder leaping off a curb, or the lifetime that follows an image of a young couple exchanging wedding vows.

Even intent can be inferred. We can write volumes about the tension we sense in a figure's pose, the proximity of one person to another, or something as simple as the angle of an eyebrow. It's often more than enough to conclude who we're looking at, how they relate to one another, and what they want. An impatient boss looms over an overworked employee. A sympathetic parent helps a struggling child. Close friends. Complete strangers. Affection or anger. Work or play. Safety or danger.

It was an ability I'd grown especially conscious of myself. Every evening, as soon as I came home from work and closed the door behind me, I did something very specific, usually before I even set down my bag. It wasn't quite a ritual, as it lacked a ritual's deliberate structure, but it unfolded in the same way and at the same time every day. It was a moment known well to anyone caring for an ailing family member: I'd find my mother, wherever she was in the house—in the kitchen, the living room, or maybe the backyard—and know, in a single glance, whether I should be worried about her or not; whether she'd had one of her good days, and I could exhale, or whether it was . . . something else.

That was all it took. The most important judgment call I could make, carried out with a burst of cognitive magic so fast and so automatic that it was all but opaque, even to someone in my line of work. *Mom's peeling potatoes at the sink. Dad's got an apron on, and he's pouring olive oil into a wok on the stove, with what looks like a bowl of diced chicken ready to be thrown in after. Both seem content. Neither have glanced up at me yet. No looks of confusion or concern. Thank God. I can breathe out. Tonight will be a good night. For now, at least.*

But it wasn't always like this. *Mom's on the couch. She's not quite sitting or lying, and she looks uncomfortable. Her head is in her hand; her eyebrows are bunched together. The cat is curled up next to her, but Mom's free hand sits limply on the cat's back. She's not petting her.*

Not good. Time for a home blood pressure test, a temperature and pulse check, and then maybe a call to the doctor.

It's an ability of remarkable speed and power. I rarely had any conscious memory of enumerating the individual objects surrounding me—the roomful of furniture, my mother and father, the clothes they wore, kitchen utensils, an unopened package or envelope, Silvio's espresso machine, the family cat, and so on. For all the work we spent laboring to teach machines to classify objects, it was a task that seemed to turn on more than just visual acuity. Something much deeper was happening in moments like these; I wasn't merely *seeing* my mother, but *understanding* her state: evaluating her posture, estimating her attitude, drawing life-and-death inferences from something as intangible as the wrinkles on her brow or the angle of her body as she leaned against a counter.

It's a capacity that instantly puts even our most advanced algorithms in perspective. Here we were, celebrating fractional reductions in classification error rates—about as shallow a perceptual achievement as could be imagined—while our own brains filled every moment with such fluent awareness of our world that its vibrancy had become all but invisible to us. Back in the 1970s, the researcher and mathematician Anatol Holt summed up this myopia by saying that AI was a technology that can make a perfect chess move while the room is on fire. How relevant that diagnosis still felt, even now. Modern AI behaved like a kind of game-playing savant, mastering isolated tasks that lent themselves to narrow metrics like "error rate," while failing to notice the burning embers that were falling on the board.

For all our limitations, human perception is the antithesis of this. We see the world holistically, not just identifying but *understanding* its contents—their relationships, their meanings, their pasts, and their futures. The *gist*. We aren't merely witnesses, but storytellers. It felt like it was time for algorithms to learn how to do the same.

"Here, read this." I dropped a printout of my *Journal of Vision* paper onto the desk of Andrej Karpathy, a second-year grad student and an especially promising new addition to the lab. Tall, slender, and perpetually fast-talking, Andrej was born in Slovakia and raised in Canada. He had a zeal for solving complex problems, and the technical talent to bring his ideas to life. Like many of the students in my lab, he had the grit and tenacity of an engineer, as comfortable disassembling a transistor radio as he was covering a whiteboard with equations. If Einstein, Bohr, and Wheeler were cosmic dreamers, students like Andrej were different, cut from the same cloth, perhaps, as Edison or the Wright brothers. The distinction was all but invisible to the outside world, but so pertinent in our lab that it seemed to color every conversation. They were opposing but complementary styles, each destined to challenge, engage, and mildly annoy the other. But when it came to attempting something new—especially something difficult, as was so often the case around here—the combination was powerful.

"What's this?" he asked as he picked it up and scanned the abstract.

"Our next challenge."

Meetings with Andrej became a fixture on my calendar. Even by the high standards set at our lab, the idea of an algorithm that could describe an entire scene, rather than simply label whichever object appeared to reside in its foreground, felt like the future of our work—maybe even of the entire field. But my passion made me an especially harsh critic.

"All right, well, Andrej, this *looks* excellent."

"But . . . ?" he said with a hesitant chuckle. He knew what was coming.

The display on his workstation seemed to be exactly what we'd aimed for: a photo provided as input, with a sentence describing it as the output.

"*But*"—his work was clever, extremely so, in certain respects; still, I knew we had a longer road ahead of us. This was a glimpse of the solution, not the full picture—"we're just not there yet."

He slumped in his seat.

The issue was a subtle one, but it demonstrated a phenomenon that I'd become acutely aware of in my years as a professor. As is often the case with students, Andrej was so maniacally focused on *whether* his model worked that the question of *how* it worked fell by the wayside. Admittedly, it did appear to do the job, at least upon initial inspection. But our regular check-ins had given me a detailed window into his thinking, and while his approach was literate and well-reasoned, the resulting model was, ultimately, a kind of caption-matching system.

Simply put, too much of the description displayed on the screen had come from the training data in one form or another, as if his algorithm were searching for it in some kind of elaborate database. In effect, it spared the model from the ultimate goal, as I saw it: *generating* a caption, entirely from scratch. In practical terms, I was certain it wouldn't generalize—that even though it appeared to perform well when tested, it'd be confused by images from outside its training set, leading to captions that might be incorrect, malformed, or both. But the real issue was scientific. The model was *retrieving* its output. It still wasn't truly *authoring* it.

Andrej sighed, fully appreciating how much harder I was making

things for him. But as irritated as he clearly was, I knew he could recognize that the gulf was worth crossing.

"All right, let me rethink this," he said. "I get that the caption needs
to be written word by word. That raises a lot of questions about how
we'll follow the visual features of the image *and* produce something
grammatically correct at the same time, but . . . I'll think of something."

I smiled. He did little to hide his frustration, but it was clear that
he had the right idea. The scientist in me refused to accept anything
less, and he knew it. How he'd actually *do* any of this was still anyone's
guess, but I knew the engineer in him was as relentless as I was. He'd
get there.

Language and vision are very different things. The fundamental unit
of an image is the "pixel"—a now common term that began as a con-
traction of "picture element"—an almost imperceptible dot capturing
the color at a single tiny point within a scene. It can take hundreds of
pixels, if not thousands, or more, to depict anything meaningful. The
phones in our pockets capture massively detailed images composed
of tens of millions of such points. But pixels themselves tell us essentially nothing about an image when evaluated individually. The job of
a vision algorithm, whether the gray matter in our skulls or the silicon
in our machines, is to group these pixels into ever-larger regions of a
two-dimensional image, then somehow scan for patterns within them
that correspond to the three-dimensional features of the real world:
space, volumes, surfaces, textures, and the like.

In contrast, the fundamental unit of a language like English, at
least the way it's spoken and written in everyday use, is the word. Unlike a pixel, words typically convey distinct meaning, even in isolation.
And the full range of words is, although very large, finite. Nevertheless, as words are placed next to each other, their meaning is mod-
ulated, if not transformed entirely—consider the difference between
word pairs like "rock bottom," "rock fragments," and "rock music," for

instance. The phenomenon compounds as more words are strung together to form longer sentences, to say nothing of paragraphs, pages,
and volumes. In total, the combinatorial potential of words to convey
ideas is all but endless.

While the early headlines of this new, dawning era were dominated by computer vision breakthroughs, it was every bit as productive
a time for natural language processing. An early jewel of this period
was the recurrent neural network, or RNN. A family of algorithms
tailor-made to match the linear sequences of words, RNNs were able
to quickly infer basic properties of text, in much the same way that
convolutional neural networks like AlexNet processed images. Like
CNNs, RNNs had existed for decades, but it wasn't until now that
their true power was realized.

Perhaps more tantalizing than progress in any one field, however, was
the cross-pollination that began to occur between AI's many subfields.
The growing family of neural networks gave vision, language, speech,
and other forms of perception a shared algorithmic framework, inspiring
labs like ours to blur the boundaries that separated them in the quest to
achieve more integrated, human-like capabilities.

"I think I've got an idea," Andrej said through the door to my office.
A few days had passed since our last conversation, and he looked less
put-upon this time. I could tell he had something good. "Imagine
pairing a CNN with an RNN," he said as he took a seat on the couch.
"One to *encode* visual information and pair it with words, and the other
to *generate* language. We'll train our model on pairs of images and
human-written descriptions."

Now we're getting somewhere, I thought, nodding as I mulled it over.

"Keep going," I said, curious about what else he was thinking.
"Then what?"

"Well, there are definitely some unknowns to iron out, but I'm
thinking the RNN generates each new word in the description con-
ditionally, based on the words *already* in the sentence. That way, we're

describing the contents of the image while following whatever grammatical patterns have been inferred from the training data. The result, at least in theory, should be a completely novel description, in more or less natural language."

It was hard not to be impressed. If even half of this worked, he'd have engineered his way out of the hole I'd left him in. I couldn't wait to see what came next.

Our Google Street View car project was complete, and the depth of the data we'd collected was astonishing. Over fifty million images collected from more than two hundred cities passed through our classifiers, covering more than three thousand ZIP codes and almost forty thousand voting precincts. All told, our classifiers identified more than twenty-two million vehicles—almost 10 percent of the entire United States fleet—unleashing observations of amazing statistical significance. Some were amusing confirmations of stereotypes, such as our finding about a city's ratio of sedans to pickup trucks: when the former is higher, the city is 88 percent likely to vote Democrat; when the latter is higher, it's 82 percent likely to vote Republican. But that was just the beginning.

For instance, the correlation in our results between car owners' ethnicity and their preferred brand was so robust that it nearly mirrored American Community Survey data on the racial makeup of the same neighborhoods. Similarly accurate predictions could be made about a region's average education and income levels. Again and again, our model generated color-coded maps of entire cities, tracing the fluctuations of socioeconomic and political indicators from one end to the other, all of which were uncannily similar to those collected using traditional methods by the Census Bureau. And all by simply observing the cars found on their streets.

The real discovery, though, was the potential of the process we'd demonstrated: a fast, scalable, and comparatively cheap alternative to manual surveys—an expense in the United States alone of more than $250 million a year. It was among the largest and most ambitious undertakings in our lab's history, published in the pages of the *Proceedings of the National Academy of Sciences*, or *PNAS*, with Timnit listed as lead author—a well-earned honor given her impressive effort. I was proud of the work on a technical level, but most excited by what it said about the power of AI to show us our world in entirely new ways.

I turned sideways to push open the lab's doors with my shoulder, juggling my purse, my phone, and a half-finished cup of Starbucks chai. I was in the daze typical of an overbooked morning, hurrying from one meeting to the next and scrambling to catch up with the agenda of each, when Andrej waved as I passed his office.

"Check it out," he said, nodding toward his workstation. The look on his face was noticeably more confident this time.

I hurried in, so excited to see the latest that I almost forgot where I was originally going. On the screen was a photo of a teenager and a skateboard, both in midair, against a backdrop of blue sky and distant bushes. In a tiny command-line window beneath the image, a sentence was printed out.

A person on skateboard.

I was smiling before I even realized it. Andrej let the moment linger for a second, then pressed a key. Another image appeared, this one depicting a messy construction site with two workers in orange vests pouring cement. It was followed after a second or two by another sentence.

Construction workers working on the curbside.

He hit the key again. Another image, another caption. Then another, and another, and another. The quantity and variety of the scenes made it clear that these sentences weren't just being dug up from a training corpus somewhere. The model was *writing* them.

Andrej was beaming, too. However, as with any good scientist, his pride was tempered with caveats. "Still got a few issues to work out, of course. For instance, uh . . ."

He clicked again, and a new image came up, snapped by a tourist in a rustic Spanish plaza that I later learned was the town square of Trujillo, a city noted for its wealth of Renaissance architecture. I'd just about gotten lost in the imagery when the caption appeared.

A man riding a horse down a street next to a building.

It took another beat before we both laughed at the near-perfect description and its sole, crucial omission: that the man and the horse were made of bronze. The highlight reel of gaffes continued. A pet seal sleeping on a couch was described as a cat. A baby playing with a toothbrush was identified as a young boy holding a baseball bat. And zebras grazing on a savanna were described perfectly, except that the model had completely failed to notice the stunning rainbow just behind them. Algorithmic mistakes often have a childlike clumsiness to them that can be surprisingly endearing. It was heartening to be reminded that although we still had much to learn, so did our machines. But it was Andrej's accomplishment, warts and all, that was most memorable.

"We need to write this up for publication," I said.

"Really?" he asked. "Already?"

"Yes, absolutely," I replied with an urgency that surprised even me. I didn't know why, but I was suddenly anxious. Maybe it was the influence of the still-growing media frenzy over our field, or a rush of pride as the lab's director. Whatever it was, it didn't go away.

"The sooner the better," I said.

* * *

"You mean dating . . . a machine? Like, in *Her*?"

The student's comments sent a wave of laughter across the room. *Her*, the Spike Jonze movie about a man who falls in love with his AI companion, was still fresh in the minds of most in attendance.

"Why not?" the other student replied. "If it were intelligent enough to converse at a human level—I mean *real* human conversation; you know, like the way we're talking right now—who's to say there wouldn't be potential for something like a romantic connection?"

"I don't know . . . It just sounds a little ridiculous to me."

"But there's nothing preventing it *in principle*, right? Can we at least agree on that?"

It was one of the last Fridays before the winter break, and I was attending my new favorite event: a twice-monthly closed-door gathering for SAIL students and faculty called "AI Salon," which provided a venue for topical conversations about our field. We'd explored a wide range of topics since the inaugural meeting, from cultural issues like the depiction of AI in movies and television to a philosophical debate about whether categories and symbolic structures are fundamental facts of language or, as the title of that particular talk rather pointedly suggested, a "fantasy of linguists."

Today we were discussing *Superintelligence*, a provocative tome by Oxford philosopher Nick Bostrom exploring the future of AI. The book had become an unexpected mainstream success after figures like Bill Gates and Elon Musk tweeted both their praise for it and their fears about its implications, reviving the age-old sci-fi cliché of an impending showdown between man and machine. Our conversation had been appropriately eclectic, spanning killer robots, the potential for subjective consciousness within algorithms, and, in the final moments, the idea of falling in love with a computer. But even the afternoon's most provocative detours carried a weight I wouldn't have expected in previous years. It's hard to dismiss talk of the future when it suddenly seems to be arriving so fast.

The shock waves of the 2012 ImageNet Challenge were still reverberating. It was a watershed moment for computer vision obsessives like us, but the world was discovering that the results of this once obscure contest weren't merely a turning point for the understanding of pictures—they were a turning point for understanding everything. The almost magical combination AlexNet demonstrated—large-scale data sets, high-speed GPUs, and deeply layered neural networks—was a blueprint destined for mass adoption in fields far beyond ours. Fittingly, a new name was catching on. This wasn't simply the age of machine learning, but, in a nod to the ever more lavishly layered networks being built in labs across the world, *deep learning*.

It was the birth of an entirely new paradigm, much as the early years of the twentieth century were for physics. I was reminded of the stories that captured my imagination as a teenage girl, daydreaming about life as a physicist in those heady days, trying to conjure the mystery and awe those early pioneers must have felt. It was hard not to envy them, their view of reality elevated—so radically, and so suddenly—by an awakening to the mysteries of the quantum world and the relativistic majesty of the cosmos. They were born at just the right time and in just the right places to receive some of history's most breathtaking gifts. It didn't feel like hyperbole to wonder if this modern incarnation of neural networks was our generation's equivalent.

Even then, though, there were reasons to acknowledge the future wouldn't be a purely poetic one. Among the more jarring harbingers of change was the transformation of academic conferences related to AI. They'd been modest affairs for decades, attended exclusively by professors, researchers, and students, blissfully free of media attention and endearingly cash-strapped. Corporate sponsors were rare, generally limited to academic publishers like Springer, and relegated to a few long bench desks in the corner of an exhibition hall. But in the years after AlexNet, names from the very apex of the Fortune

500 transformed the events into spectacles, each new gathering more closely resembling an industry expo on the Las Vegas Strip. Towering, logo-emblazoned booths bathed in colored lighting were commonplace within a matter of years, and companies like Google and Microsoft held extravagant parties for grad students considering career options.

A hunger gripped the field as the demand for *more* set in. More layers to make neural networks deeper and more powerful. More silicon to speed up the training process and make ever-larger networks feasible to deploy. And, of course, more data. More imagery, more video, more audio, more text, and anything else a network might be trained to understand. More of *everything*.

It was exciting to think about the capabilities this newly organized data might enable, but harrowing as well; in my own lab, we'd already seen that more was always hidden in the stuff than we'd realized. It was never *just* imagery, or audio, or text—data allowed a model to form a *representation* of the world, and bigger data meant more powerful, nuanced representations. Relationships, connections, and ideas. Truths and falsehoods. Insights and prejudices. New understandings, but also new pitfalls. The deep learning revolution had arrived, and none of us were prepared for it.

In the meantime, our lab's research agenda was showing a voraciousness of its own; no matter how much we achieved, each new publication seemed to spawn ten follow-on ideas that someone, whether a postdoc or a first-year grad student, was willing to pick up and run with. That's exactly how I liked it, even if it often felt overwhelming.

I wondered, in fact, if the true value of the North Star as a metaphor wasn't just its ability to guide but the fact that its distance remains perpetually infinite. It can be pursued until the point of exhaustion, the object of a lifetime's obsession, but never be reached. It's a symbol of the scientist's most distinctive trait: a curiosity so restless that it repels satisfaction, like opposing magnets, forever. A star in the night, a mirage in the distance, a road without end. This, I realized, was what AI was becoming for me. ImageNet was a turning point, and one certainly worth celebrating, but it wasn't the end of the journey. If anything, it was the start of an even grander one. And beyond that, I was now certain, more awaited than could fit in a career, and even a life.

With a publishable demonstration of our image captioning technique within reach, Andrej and I spent the next few weeks refining our methods and documenting our results. The outcome of our gambit had been everything I'd hoped; although the sentences were still simple and terse, they were accurate and reasonably natural in their phrasing. It truly was, in the words of Jeremy Wolfe, an algorithm that captured the "gist" of what it saw.

It was time for us to share it with the world. Ultimately that meant an academic audience, and our work had been accepted for inclusion at the 2014 Neural Information Processing Systems Conference, or NeurIPS, which was several weeks away. In the meantime, I'd been invited to lecture at an IBM seminar in Alameda, on the other side of the Bay, and I couldn't resist revealing what we'd achieved ahead of schedule.

Sharing unpublished work was an unorthodox move, but the phone call I got immediately after confirmed it was the right one. It came from John Markoff, a technology reporter for *The New York Times*, while I was still in the back seat of my Stanford-bound Uber. I'd had a soft spot for John for some time, as he was among the few people in the media to appreciate the importance of ImageNet in its early days, covering it for the *Times* a couple of years earlier. Still, an impromptu call was unusual.

"John? Uh, hi! How's it going?"

"Good, good. Hey, guess who was in the audience at IBM this morning?"

Huh. It hadn't occurred to me that a journalist might be in attendance. I sensed something strange was afoot.

"This algorithm of yours—the one that generates sentences to describe images—you said it's still unpublished, right?"

"That's right. But we'll be presenting it officially at NeurIPS in December."

"Ah, that's great to hear," John said, coyly, before getting to the point. "Look, I wanted to let you know that I have some material in my hands—under embargo, of course—about another research team. I can't tell you who it is, but they claim that they've built the first algorithm to, uh, well"—he laughed awkwardly—"generate sentences that describe images."

What?

It didn't make sense. Andrej and I had no idea anyone else was working on this problem. But John was right. Just a few days later, the *Times* ran his piece, entitled "Researchers Announce Advance in Image-Recognition Software." He wrote: "Two groups of scientists, working independently, have created artificial intelligence software capable of recognizing and describing the content of photographs and videos with far greater accuracy than ever before."

Academic rivalries are nothing new, and competition between researchers has always been part of the magic that makes our world such a fertile ground for innovation. Still, it was strange that I'd been caught so completely off guard by this. The research world is famously open, sometimes to a fault; apart from the bragging rights of discovering something first, our work isn't generally treated like intellectual property, let alone something confidential, like a trade secret. It's meant to be shared with the world, including our fiercest rivals, and it's not uncommon to have at least some sense of who's working on what, well before the results are published. Then I read deeper, and it all became clear.

For years now, my colleagues and I had been rolling our eyes at the way the press tended to exaggerate depictions of AI's advances. But for once, a newspaper article made me see just how fast the world was changing. Our rival wasn't some mysterious team of researchers at another university. It was Google.

10

DECEPTIVELY SIMPLE

I felt my phone vibrating as the music began. It was a summer afternoon in 2013, and Silvio and I were attending a friend's daughter's bat mitzvah. It was a good moment to be interrupted, as the solemnity of the ceremony had just given way to the party vibe of the reception. I gestured that I needed to take the call—an excuse Silvio surely found convenient given my reluctance to dance in public—and ducked outside.

"Hey, Dad, what's up?"

His tone answered my question before his words.

"I think your mom has a fever. She's been struggling to breathe, and she says she's feeling chest pain. Where are you? What should I do?"

I drew in a sharp breath as my heart sank. It was a moment I'd never get used to, no matter how familiar it became. *Here we go again*, I thought. *Again.*

For more than twenty years, our family had endured more close calls and late-night scares than I cared to remember, spending what felt like whole chapters of our lives in ERs, ICUs, OR waiting rooms, and other acronymic hospital spaces. The heart disease that took root in my mother's teenage years, induced by a severe rheumatic fever and left to progress unencumbered for decades, was always the central culprit, but it triggered falling dominoes in every direction, from medication side effects to a near fatal brain hemorrhage we caught by sheer luck. I had sat with my mother as we struggled to navigate the warrens of insurance, chased financial aid options, and even made a trip back to China when local treatment options ran dry. Along the way, my role evolved from teenage Mandarin translator to something like an unofficial caseworker, tracking down specialists, arranging for consultations and treatments, monitoring symptoms, and overseeing a schedule of medication and recuperation that never quite seemed to stabilize things for very long. It was, by any practical measure, a second career.

My mother's trademark tenacity remained intact through it all, even as one calamity seemed to blend into another. But each new jolt stayed with me. The shocks didn't abate so much as they ossified, forming the bedrock of a life lived in continual anticipation of the next round of bad news—any of which threatened to be the last, of course—my stomach sinking every time I saw her name on the screen of my phone. No matter where my life took me, I felt consigned to a permanent state of vulnerability.

After another two-day whirlwind, the latest ordeal was over. A heart fluctuation made worse by a fever. Maybe a flu. Scary, but not existential. I fell back into the plastic seat in the corner of the hospital room, opened up my laptop by instinct, and lost myself in a few minutes of clicks and clacks. It's hard to overstate the value of loving one's work in moments like this. But something was strange. I could feel it, like a tingling on my periphery.

Am I being watched?

I glanced over the top of the screen to see my mother had woken up. She was, indeed, watching me.

"Is everything okay?" I asked.

I could tell something was on her mind, but it wasn't her health. She took another moment to think.

"Fei-Fei, what exactly do you *do*?"

It was a strange, perfect time to laugh as loudly as I did.

"Uh, *what*?" I said, attempting to speak seriously through my giggles. "You're asking what I do? Like, for a living?"

"I know you're a scientist. Something about the brain. But in all these years, we've never really talked about what *kind* of scientist. 'Mad scientist' is how your dad describes it, but I'm sure there's more to it than that."

My mother's making jokes. The nurse said to call if I notice anything unusual.

"Yeah, a little bit," I said, still grinning as I considered her question.

Laughter aside, she was right. In all these years of treating her like a patient, I'd developed a habit of keeping my work to myself, and I wondered now if I'd been neglecting the rest of who she was. The brainy instigator was still in there, even when hospital gowns and IV bandages suggested otherwise. So I dove in, starting from the very beginning. The mysteries of the mind. The importance of object categorization in visual understanding. ImageNet. GPUs. The explosion of neural networks. A world suddenly changing. And she listened, true to form, but with the air of a mom humoring her babbling kid. Something wasn't clicking.

"I don't know," she said after a pause. "This all sounds like science fiction to me."

I shouldn't have been surprised. She had the intellect to keep up, but science for its own sake was never her style. She thought in terms of stories and characters. Passions and conflict. I decided to improvise.

"You know, they're gonna let us out of here in an hour or two, but you've got a few days of recovery ahead. You won't be able to run errands without me, or Dad, or Silvio, or someone. But what if you could get yourself around anyway?"

"You mean, like, the bus?"

"Nope. Even the round trip to the bus stop would be pushing it. I'm talking about a car that does the driving for you. Picks you up from your doorstep, drops you off, all of it."

Flashy brands like Waymo and Cruise were still years away, but autonomous vehicles had been on my mind since Sebastian Thrun, a pioneer in the field, left our department to bring his expertise to Google. My interest had only been reinforced by the growing wave of media attention. I didn't expect to see fully autonomous cars on the road anytime soon, as impressive as Sebastian's project had been—a heavily modified Volkswagen Touareg called "Stanley" that was the first car in history to successfully complete a desert race orchestrated each year by the Defense Advanced Research Projects Agency, or DARPA, entirely on its own. In the real world, however, driving was orders of magnitude more complex, and I hardly considered it a realistic near-term goal. But it gave me a chance to bring something abstruse down to earth.

"Huh," she said, her tone brightening. "That would certainly make a difference for someone like me."

Then, after another few seconds of silence, she asked a deceptively simple question.

"Fei-Fei, what *else* can AI do to help people?"

I believe I became a scientist the moment I laid eyes on Biederman's number, inspiring the journey that would define so much of my career. I'd later look back on the question my mother posed from that hospital bed, almost in passing, with similar reverence, as it was the moment I was given a chance to be a humanist as well. It was something new to chase, motivated by far more than the satisfaction of a curious spirit. I couldn't predict where the road would lead, exactly, but I'd spent too many years in rooms like this not to feel as if some hint of the answer were already staring me in the face.

Perhaps now, for the first time, I had the presence of mind to put two and two together—to combine a lifelong love of AI with the agonizing privilege of caring for someone in chronic need. What could AI do in a hospital? We'd built a lens that could see the world in ways humans can't, turning Google Street View into sociology. What might AI show us in a place like this? We'd created an algorithm that could turn images into stories, spinning pixels into language and meaning. I now wondered whether here, where we'd spent so much of our lives, I was in the presence of the stories that most needed to be told.

Dr. Arnie Milstein was a legend in his field. A professor at the Stanford medical school, a longtime industry consultant, and a former clinician himself, he was an expert's expert. By the time we met, his career had shifted to improving the way care is delivered in hospitals—the quality of processes, outcomes, and the patient experience—all while reducing costs. His gray hair, verging on white, testified to the depth of his experience, but he was unpretentious and energetic, with an easy smile and a natural friendliness.

In the months since my mother and I had discussed AI in her hospital room, thoughts of somehow uniting AI and patient care had never left my mind. I chatted with colleagues whenever I could, both within my department and far beyond it, planting conversational seeds everywhere I went. As a mutual acquaintance introduced me to Arnie, one seed eventually blossomed, and although our initial conversation revealed how different our worlds were—we both felt the other was speaking a foreign language—we sensed a kinship immediately. Neither of us had any idea what kind of collaboration awaited us, but we were both certain one was in our future. In an attempt to jump-start the process, he invited me to join him for a closed-door demonstration, high above San Francisco, of a remote hospital monitoring technology being developed by Philips.

"Thank you all so much for coming." A representative from the company walked to the center of the demo room, where a row of nurses was posted in front of workstations outfitted with large flat-screen monitors. "You're about to see a demonstration of a technology we're calling 'eICU'—a remote-monitoring solution for intensive care units. It's still in the proof-of-concept phase, but we've already begun piloting it in a number of hospitals."

I realized the screens were displaying live feeds of ICU patients in a real hospital somewhere, with multiple dimensions of their vital signs superimposed over the video, allowing the nurses to keep watch from here. In the event they noticed something dangerous or abnormal, a panel of buttons allowed them to immediately notify on-site personnel.

"No one likes to think about mistakes in health care, but they pose constant threats to hospital patients. Infections, misplaced surgical tools, drug mix-ups, dosage mistakes, even something as simple as an elderly patient falling. The list goes on and on."

Great. Sounds like I'll have plenty to think about the next time I'm in the waiting room.

"Tragically, these lapses are responsible for approximately a hundred thousand fatalities a year—most of which are entirely preventable."

Wait, what? My mind was suddenly reeling. *A hundred thousand deaths a year? All from mistakes?*

"eICU is a first step toward preventing a particularly dangerous error: patients left unattended for too long in the ICU. It allows larger, geographically distributed teams to keep a closer eye on a hospital's most vulnerable population."

It was a nice idea, but I couldn't get over the number I'd just heard. *A hundred thousand.* It kept repeating in my head.

"This is an example of what I call a 'dark corner' of health care, Fei-Fei," Arnie leaned in to whisper. "It's when a patient, whether they're in a hospital, a senior care facility, an OR, or wherever, escapes the attention of a clinician."

I thought about my mother in her hospital bed, and my nightly routine at the front door, wondering if I was about to stumble upon a sign that her condition had worsened while I was away.

"This is an attempt at solving a *very* old problem," Arnie continued. "Just about everyone in health care is overworked to the point of exhaustion. And in a way, all the technology built for them over the last few decades has made things worse, because now they're overwhelmed with *information*, too. It's a dangerous combination, and too many patients fall through the cracks."

The demo was polished and impressive, but my anxiety continued well after its conclusion.

"I can't get that number out of my head," I said as the elevator doors closed.

"The hundred thousand deaths a year?" Arnie replied. "That figure has probably done more than anything to motivate my work over the last decade or two."

A single number at the heart of an obsession. Arnie and I have even more in common than I thought.

"I have a question for you," he continued. "Imagine any hospital, or senior facility, or even a home care program. What are caregivers trying to accomplish when they make their rounds?"

I thought about the doctors and nurses who visited my mother during her hospital stays, many of whom didn't seem to have more than a minute or two to spare before rushing off to their next task.

"Face time? Bedside manner?"

"Sure, but think even simpler."

"Uh, I dunno, just checking in, I guess?"

"You got it. They're doing their best to share *some* of their attention with every patient in their care. But even at their most diligent, how long are they actually face-to-face? Inevitably, most of a patient's time is spent unmonitored."

"And that's when all these accidents are happening?" I asked.

"It's why a hundred thousand people needlessly die each year."

"Hmmm." I paused for a moment, trying to wrap my head around it all. "It sounds like the common denominator is attention. Awareness."

"*Precisely.* Awareness is what it's all about. It's the *single* most precious resource in all of health care. And it's the one thing we can't scale."

I felt like I'd been transported back to the Red Door Cafe, puzzling over the experience of vision with Pietro and Christof. I thought about Thorpe's EEG readouts, Biederman's photographic experiments, and Kanwisher's attempts at mapping the anatomy of the cortex. But I reflected on Treisman most of all, and the observation at the heart of her work: *the more chaotic the scene, the longer it takes to make sense of it.* It was a sobering thought in a world of overworked doctors breezing past handwashing stations and nurses too distracted to notice frail patients on the verge of falling. So much of my research had revolved around the nature of perception. Where it came from. What it did. What it was capable of. It wasn't until I met Arnie that I began to realize what it was worth.

"Sorry," I said, taking a moment. "I'm just a little stunned by these figures."

A few weeks after the demonstration, I met Arnie at his office to continue our discussion. We were flipping through *To Err Is Human*, an unsettling but comprehensive survey of medical errors throughout the hospital environment. At the time of its publication in 2000, the authors concluded that lapses in protocol and attention claimed more lives annually than well-known causes like car accidents, breast cancer, and AIDS.

"Yeah. It's a lot to wrap your head around."

It was a necessary exercise, though. Our conversation hadn't stopped since we'd left the eICU demo, our excitement growing as we decided to undertake a small research project. This was our first proper meeting to plan it.

"I say we start with *this*," Arnie said, planting his index finger on a passage near the bottom of the page:

According to the CDC, even today, "handwashing is the single most important means of preventing the spread of infection." Yet, repeated studies indicate that after more than 150 years of experience, lack of or improper handwashing still contributes significantly to disease transmission in health care settings.

It may sound prosaic, but handwashing remains a serious challenge in health care delivery. According to the Centers for Disease Control and Prevention, it's estimated that caregivers are required to wash their hands a hundred times a day as they make their rounds, corresponding to each transition between patients and tasks. Given the frequency and the nature of human error, occasional mistakes would be inevitable under the best of circumstances. But as shifts drag on and stress and fatigue weigh more heavily, the risk is dramatically compounded. Ultimately, some percentage of those mistakes lead to infections—"hospital-acquired infections," as they're officially known—and a truly incomprehensible amount of human suffering.

As scary as the topic was, it made for a comfortable place to begin our work. By focusing our attention on the behavior of caregivers, rather than patients, we could avoid some of the trickier complexities of medical research when people undergoing treatment are involved. And according to Arnie, it was an issue administrators at Stanford Hospital had been looking into for some time. The appetite for a novel solution was already there.

I quickly learned that Arnie was the kind of guy who got things done. Within what felt like an hour or two of our conversation, he was texting me with updates that read like achievements unto themselves: calling in favors, arranging meetings with decision makers, and securing hospital access. I'd grown to love this sort of planning in my own work, taking pride in the craft it took to lay the groundwork for a new experiment. But this was his world, not mine, and I was awed by how much happened when he snapped his fingers.

Without knowing it, Arnie was picking up where Pietro and

Christof had left off, a mentor who blurred the lines between disciplines in the hope of solving problems. My contributions would begin soon enough, as the technological side of our project came together, and I looked forward to it. For the moment, though, I was content to follow a veteran's lead. It felt good to be a student again.

But even as Arnie worked his magic, the magnitude of the challenge began to sink in. Our initial goal—an automated technique for ensuring that caregivers wash their hands consistently and thoroughly throughout hospital spaces—would demand far more than the image classification techniques that had come to symbolize our field, or even the image captioning work I'd done with Andrej. Our solution would have to recognize specific kinds of motions—not merely the presence of something, but the way it moved, and what those movements meant— and with a degree of accuracy high enough to pass clinical muster.

Thorny questions abounded. For one thing, what does the classification of "proper" handwashing entail, exactly? It's certainly more than locating a clinician in the vicinity of a handwashing station. The goal appeared to require an algorithm capable of recognizing every step in the process: approaching the sink, turning on the faucet, dispensing soap, rubbing two hands together beneath it, and sustaining the action for a sufficient period. It was, in every sense, the most advanced perceptual task I'd ever faced.

Thankfully, it wasn't without precedent, and my lab had been tackling many of the underlying capabilities such a system would require. Andrej, for instance, had worked on a research project in collaboration with Google to identify scenarios depicted in sports footage—a batter taking a swing in baseball, for example, or a basketball player dribbling—a classification task largely dependent on recognizing movements and actions. Another student of mine, Juan Carlos Niebles, had written his entire PhD dissertation on recognizing human activities in video. He was now a professor at the Universidad del Norte in his home country of Colombia, where he and his students had recently curated a data set called "ActivityNet"—the "ImageNet of activities," as the name suggests—which organized tens of thousands of short video clips, each of them annotated with the physical motions they depicted: walking, running, dancing, playing a musical instrument, and the like. In other words, while analyzing video with the precision we envisioned wasn't a fully solved problem, it wasn't outside the realm of possibility, either: the sweet spot for research.

I sent out my usual email to the department's graduate students advertising a fresh batch of assistant positions. Projects like ImageNet had conditioned me to keep my expectations modest, and this was no exception. As a small but respectable number of replies trickled in, I threw some slides together to explain our thinking and set up a first round of interviews. In the meantime, we needed a name. Arnie and I envisioned a technology meant to fill a space with smart, reliable awareness, but defined by its unobtrusiveness. Unlike human auditors, our technology would blend into the background discreetly, keeping a silent watch and speaking up only when it sensed danger. We called it "ambient intelligence."

"So, that's the plan. Ambient intelligence for health care delivery," I concluded. "Any questions?"

My audience of one, seated on the red couch in my office, was an especially bright double major who divided his time between computer science and statistics. He was starting his second year as a PhD candidate and, conveniently for us, was looking for a more permanent place to finish the remainder of his research. But the mood wasn't as relaxed as I'd have liked. All three of our previous interviewees had decided not to join our team, making him our fourth attempt. I did my best to conceal the fact that our morale was getting low.

"I mean, it sounds super interesting," he replied, his tone sincere enough. I chose to ignore the fact that he was the fourth candidate in a row to call us "super interesting."

"What I'm wondering, though, is whether I'll still get to publish in the usual venues. You know, NeurIPS and CVPR and stuff."

"Absolutely," I said with a smile. "We're exploring a *lot* of unsolved problems."

It was true. As unorthodox as the hospital setting was, the computer vision under the hood would be absolutely state-of-the-art. We were advancing the frontier of identifying human activities, rather than static objects—already a delicate, experimental technique—and our algorithms would face the extra pressure of recognizing unusually subtle movements with high demands for accuracy. At the same time, we were taking object recognition to the next level, as our classifiers would have to contend with dense layers of movement, clutter, and ambiguity. It would be exceptionally hard work, offering plenty of opportunities to build a reputation.

"Frankly, though, we're looking to make a real, clinical impact here. That means partnering with clinical collaborators and submitting to clinical journals, too—not just computer science."

The student took a moment to consider it. "Okay, but, like, what's the timeline for journals like that?"

Given how much an academic career depends on publication, especially in the early years, it was a good question. He saw the glacial pace of medical journals as an anchor, weighing him down when he needed to sprint, and he wasn't wrong to worry. He'd be lucky if he published half as frequently as his peers. I winced inwardly as I answered.

"Honestly, I haven't done it myself. But my partner, Dr. Milstein, says they tend to take a year or two."

Wide eyes. Another pause.

"Wow. That's . . . a lot longer than I expected. I mean, computer science papers normally take like a few months."

He was stating the obvious, but he was right. There wasn't much I could add.

"Uh, Professor Li, one last question," he began as he folded his arms. "I know how long you spent building ImageNet, and how important it was for computer vision. Will we have access to a similar data set for this, uh, ambient intelligence idea?"

I sighed, probably too loudly.

The answer was no. Yet another "no" among so many others. No data sets. No known literature to base our ideas on. No labs working on similar problems to collaborate with. Although issued politely, his answer was no as well.

As the months wore on, our struggle to recruit even a single collaborator began to keep me up at night. I was on the precipice of what promised to be the most meaningful chapter of my career—a chance to truly do good with AI, exactly as my mother's question suggested— but we wouldn't get anywhere without help. I thought about the lonely early days of ImageNet. They felt tame by comparison.

Today, however, I'd have the luxury of distraction. Perhaps noticing I needed a push to keep my head in the game, Arnie had sent me on a field trip.

"Are you sure this is gonna be okay?" I asked as I adjusted my mask. I'd spent so much of my life surrounded by people in scrubs, but it was the first time I'd worn them myself.

"Absolutely. We do it all the time. Nurses, med school students, graduates doing their residency, you name it. Don't worry. You'll blend right in."

Arnie had arranged for me to shadow Dr. Terry Platchek, a pediatrician at Lucile Packard Children's Hospital, so I could observe the realities of maintaining hand hygiene throughout a hospital shift. But I wanted to see everything: the patients, the nurses, all of it. The full gamut of their experience. I knew their world was chaos, and I wanted to see it the way they do.

I had no idea what I was in for.

Christmas season had come to the general ward, and I couldn't believe how many children were there. Each had a story, and each was heartbreaking. Some encounters were good news, some were bad, and most were just another step in a long, often numbing journey. Some parents asked who I was and why I was there. Most didn't even seem to think twice, so used to a revolving door of faces as they attempted to understand what their loved one was going through.

I was supposed to be keeping track of something mechanical and easily quantified, but I couldn't take my eyes off what I quickly understood to be the real demonstration: the human act of delivering care. A good doctor is a fount of information, a source of strength, and sometimes the bedrock for patients and their families in moments of distress. Years of caring for my mother had made me confident I knew the health care space intimately, but my time with Dr. Platchek completely upended that assumption. I was sure that no technology, no matter how advanced, could replace what I saw that day.

Nevertheless, I learned that in certain, decisive moments, new tools were sorely needed. I met a veteran nurse who had recently had a patient fall—the first of her career—and was surprised by how deeply it affected her. It was a statistical inevitability that *someone* would get hurt on her watch at some point—she'd been a nurse for decades, after all—but when the moment finally came, her lifetime of distinguished performance didn't make a difference. She seemed as emotionally devastated as she would have been had it happened on her first day. If AI could help avoid this—two people profoundly wounded—it seemed more than worth the effort.

As physically demanding as the day was, my emotional exhaustion overshadowed whatever fatigue my body felt at the end of the shift. It was as if I'd watched every moment I'd faced with my mother, but playing on a loop, hour after hour. Dazed, I shook hands with my host and exchanged pleasantries as I prepared to leave. But something occurred to me on the way out.

"Terry, I'm curious about something. What made you so willing to let me into your world? I mean, let's be honest—I'm a bit of an outsider."

He thought for a moment before responding.

"You know, there's a lot of talk in the news lately about AI, and frankly, I don't like most of it."

I smiled, perhaps cynically. I knew where this was going.

"Sure, it'd be great to automate more of my day. Whatever. I get it," he continued. "But I'm a little tired of tech executives talking about putting people like me out of a job. You and Arnie are the only ones who actually seem to want to *help* me, rather than replace me."

I considered my response for a moment. "I know we've talked a bit about my mother, and how my experience with her health over the years has influenced me," I said. "But there's another side to that story. In all the time I've spent in rooms like this, there's been one silver lining."

"What's that?"

"There's something special about . . . I dunno, I guess you'd call it the *act* of delivering care, whether it's a nurse helping my mother sit up or a specialist outlining a treatment strategy. It's just so *human*— maybe the most human thing we're capable of, you know? It's not just that I can't imagine AI ever replacing that—I wouldn't even *want* it to. I appreciate the role technology is playing in keeping us all alive these days, but it's not an exaggeration to say that the real reason my mother and I have made it through it all is *people*. People like you."

The sun had set during our shift, and I emerged from the hospital to the brisk air of an evening well underway. The relative quiet was all the license my thoughts needed to unravel, the day's memories replaying with a dull tingle. But as harrowing as it'd been, Arnie was right. This was exactly what I needed. It was an education that no degree in computer science could offer: the bustle of the ward, the pleading looks of uncertainty, the desperation for comfort in any form. Sore feet and worn tennis shoes. Cold pizza in the break room. Hour after grinding hour.

Arnie knew that for all my years of experience at my mother's side, I still had no idea what it was like to be a clinician. So he'd invited me to see it for myself.

A strange thought occurred to me as I made my way home: I was glad we hadn't recruited any students yet. I'd have inundated them with a computer scientist's reading list, conditioning them to think in terms of data, neural networks, and the latest architectural advances. That was important, of course—there was no dodging the science on a project like this. But I now knew that wasn't the right place to start. If AI was going to help people, our thinking had to begin with the people themselves.

A decision was made, instantly. From that day forward, no prospective member of our team would write a single line of code until they'd had the experience I just had. Shadowing would be every new recruit's initiation. And it would be nonnegotiable.

Through some combination of changing luck and the energizing effect of my experience in the hospital, progress picked up enough to keep the vision alive. It took nearly two years, and a lot more patience than I was used to having, but Arnie and I assembled a team just big enough to begin our work in earnest. And while it was clear that ambient intelligence would remain a niche among researchers for some time—demand for AI expertise was simply too strong, and competing opportunities too lavish—the caliber of our recruits suggested we were onto something. It was, without a doubt, the most intellectually diverse team I'd ever been a part of.

Among our first recruits were a first-year computer science grad student, a PhD candidate in electrical engineering, and a postdoc studying the perception of human activities and social navigation in robots. Arnie then matched my hires with a cadre of young doctors he picked himself: a hospital pediatrician, a geriatrician, and an intensive care specialist. Crucially, we agreed from the start that neither half of the team was in charge; Arnie and his colleagues needed our experience to build the technology, but we needed theirs to build it right: to ensure its presence wasn't just efficacious but respectful and humane.

Arnie saved his most impressive feat for last: persuading real organizations to let us demonstrate our technology on their premises. We'd begin with an attempt at catching lapses in hand hygiene throughout two different hospitals—one in Palo Alto and another in Utah—before they had a chance to affect patients. Next was a Bay Area senior care home, where our goal was to aid caregivers by tracking residents' physical activities throughout the day. Finally, there was Stanford Hospital's own ICU, where we deployed a system that warned caregivers when recovering patients were immobile for suspiciously long stretches of time.

One challenge remained, however, and even Arnie's bag of tricks wasn't deep enough to dig out a solution: data. If nothing else, the years leading up to this project had impressed upon me the absolute, unequivocal necessity of data to effectively train models like ours—real, organic data in large quantities and offering the greatest possible variety.

But in the world of health care, the kind of data we needed was, almost by nature, scarce. Patients and clinicians were rarely recorded to begin with, for obvious reasons ranging from legal liabilities to basic privacy, and clear depictions of the events we wished to detect—many of which were outliers to begin with, like falls—were even rarer. That made our job even more complicated than I originally thought; before we could train the models, we'd have to collect the necessary data ourselves.

Still, momentum continued to build. New experiments. New hypotheses. Rolling up our sleeves with new hardware and new software. It was, as I'd expected, the most scientifically demanding project my lab had ever attempted. But it was the *mission* that truly captured our hearts. Meaning suffused everything we did, and it made the career I'd known for the whole of my adult life seem like an entirely new world. The private life I'd worked so hard to separate from my journey as a scientist had burst through the dam, washing over everything in its path. It was long overdue.

"Call the nurse," my mother pleaded, her words barely audible between faint, guttural groans. "The IV . . . It's itchy again. Where they stuck the needle in." We were back in the hospital, this time for the latest in the series of heart imaging procedures that now stretched across years, each slightly more intense than the last. I buzzed for help.

Our caregiver for the evening was Mandy, a traveling nurse from central California. She was young, upbeat, and still working toward her certification and a more permanent position. I knew I liked her from the moment she entered the room.

"I'm sorry," I began. "I know it's like the third time we've called in just a few hours."

"Not at all," she insisted, with a smile that seemed to belong to a different face than her fatigued eyes did. She had the kind of warmth that isn't easily faked. "Oh, you poor thing!" she said, turning her attention to my mother and practically radiating goodwill. "It looks like we'll have to flush that IV again. I know it hasn't been a fun night."

It was a sight I'd seen a thousand times, but it hit me differently. Maybe it was the hint of innocence I picked up in Mandy's demeanor, or the fact that our research had made us all armchair experts on the daily lives of nurses. But there was a lump in my throat I'd never felt in all the years I'd spent in rooms like this. Sympathy, awe, gratitude, and a blur of other feelings I couldn't put a label on. Mandy's presence—the simple, life-changing act of *caring*—caught me off guard. Tears were forming in my eyes.

I was usually focused squarely on my mother at moments like this, but the work we were doing had permanently changed my thoughts. *The average nurse walks four to five miles per shift.* I knew where this woman had been before coming to our room and how many other faces she'd seen. *They're expected to complete more than 180 unique tasks.* I knew she was probably exhausted. *Shifts are increasing, despite the well-documented pitfalls of caregiver fatigue.* And yet she was unstinting with her kindness. *Today, the average shift lasts twelve hours.* She did it all while smiling.

If my research could indeed help anyone, then nurses like Mandy were at the top of my list. I couldn't imagine more worthy beneficiaries.

"Do you work here?" Susan asked. The next morning had arrived, and with it, a new nurse to cover the early shift.

I looked down at my Stanford medical school badge, which I often wore in the course of my work with Arnie. I realized I'd forgotten to take it off.

"Oh, this?" I chuckled. "No, I'm actually involved in a research project."

"Huh. What kind of research?" she asked.

"I'm from the computer science department, and my students and I are collaborating on a project that uses artificial intelligence to track hand hygiene."

Her smile faded a bit, looking more polite than friendly. "So, uh . . . there's a camera watching us?"

"No, no, no! Of course not!" It wasn't the first time this question had been asked, but I still felt a rush of embarrassment every time. "It's more of a sensor than a camera. There's no footage being recorded. But it provides a kind of image for our algorithm to analyze. It's learning to look at different handwashing patterns. We're still getting started, mostly trying to figure out if the algorithms are even up to the task. But no one's watching you, I promise!"

I did my best to keep it light. Everything I was saying was true, of course, but I couldn't blame her for assuming the worst.

"All right, I guess that sounds okay," she said, exhaling. "You know," she continued, lowering her voice, "your non-cameras should definitely keep an eye on the doctors." Susan was every bit as kind as Mandy, but she had an edge to her. A wry smile spread across her face. "They're the worst. But the administrators only yell at us nurses."

"Bossware."

More politely known as "employee monitoring," a new kind of software was popping up from warehouses to offices, scrutinizing their targets to a degree many considered invasive and even dehumanizing. Although marketed as a way to boost productivity and safeguard conduct in professional settings, it achieved near-instant disdain among workers and was soon a recurring topic in the tech press. Now, before we even had a chance to prove ourselves, our work faced the prospect of being swallowed up by its dystopian connotations. The association felt unfair at first—our technology was intended for patient safety, not performance reviews—but the concern was understandable, and all too obvious in hindsight. This was my first encounter with an aspect of AI that would soon haunt the public imagination: its capacity for surveillance.

Looking back, it's easy to forget how sudden the change was. It was 2015, and the privacy implications of AI were still coming into focus for most of us; it'd only been a few years, after all, since the accuracy of image classification even approached a useful threshold to begin with. Now, in what felt like the blink of an eye, researchers like us were flirting with capabilities of such power that the technical challenges were giving way to *ethical* ones. And our journey through the world of health care brought it all home to our lab.

"No one wants bossware," one of the students said.

The team had returned from Lucile Packard Children's Hospital, where they'd hoped to put the finishing touches on a plan to move forward with a pilot study, but the visit had been an unexpected bust.

To a person, nurses from across the units we'd asked to participate had rejected our plans to install a batch of prototype sensors. It was a serious setback, but after my conversation with Susan, I couldn't pretend I was surprised.

It was a reminder that even an explicitly multidisciplinary team can have blind spots. As knowledgeable as our clinicians were, they were researchers more than practicing caregivers—a distinction that made all the difference in a situation like this. Simply put, we'd amassed a deep well of health care expertise, but none of us were nurses. Arnie and I convened an emergency meeting to discuss our options.

"I can see only one path forward," one of the doctors suggested. "The nurses need to meet your researchers. They need to talk. And I mean *really* talk."

"Yes, absolutely. And include as many as you can," said another. "*Listen*. Understand their perspective."

A third chimed in. "What about a town hall? I could help organize it."

Thank God for every last one of you, I thought. I couldn't imagine doing this without Arnie and his colleagues.

"Our IRB language needs to be watertight," Arnie asserted, sternly. "Our partners need reassurances that *no one's* privacy will be compromised. Not *once*. Is everyone clear on this?"

The IRB, or Institutional Review Board, is the governing body that oversees clinical research like ours. Navigating their expectations to ensure a study is approved requires finesse and a kind of diplomatic savvy, not to mention deep clinical experience. I'd grown accustomed to it myself, beginning with the psychophysics research I conducted at Caltech with Christof, but it was an entirely new concept to most of my computer science students. This was true medical research, with real human beings involved—and a new world of professional norms to consider.

What none of us were prepared for, though, was the possibility that our research would reach beyond the boundaries of the IRB altogether. As the students told us more about the visit to the hospital, we were heartened to learn the nurses weren't concerned with our study in particular; many of them had gotten to know us and trust our motivations, and were comfortable with our work. It was where the work might *lead* that worried them: how the technology might evolve, who else might start using it, and how its reach might expand. Their misgivings were perceptive, and underscored the fact that our challenge was assessing the future of AI, not just its present—ideas even the IRB wasn't designed to consider.

Ensuring our devices were beyond reproach meant that nothing could be transmitted to remote data centers or, to invoke a term that was just beginning to enjoy mainstream acceptance, "the cloud." It was a buzzword that could garner media attention and venture capital funding in almost any other context, but it was anathema to us. Instead, we had to pursue another emerging trend: "edge computing," in which all necessary computational resources are packed into the device. It was the paradigm we needed for our research, but it was an entire field unto itself, and none of us understood it as well as we'd have liked.

Challenging as it was, we knew the complexity was inevitable. The days of bulk-downloading from the internet felt positively carefree by comparison, as we now faced the prospect of collecting perhaps the most sensitive data imaginable: moments of genuine human vulnerability, captured with enough fidelity to train machines to spot them reliably. And we'd have to do it all while making certain—*absolutely* certain—that our subjects were kept safe and anonymous from the very first step in the process, living up to the high standards of IRB guidelines, the common decency I knew we all brought to the work, and legal frameworks like HIPAA—the Health Insurance Portability and Accountability Act.

So the team kept growing. What had begun as an already diverse mix of engineers, researchers, and experts in health care policy would soon include practicing clinicians, a bioethicist, and a JD PhD from the Stanford Law School. And our technology partners grew more diverse as well, with experts in sensors, cybersecurity, and, of course, edge computing. It was an ambitious vision, but through a combination of funding from my own lab and Arnie's Clinical Excellence Research Center, a Stanford-based organization for advancing the quality and affordability of care, we pulled it off.

The frontier remained wide open, and we'd answered only a small fraction of the questions our research was raising. But we were making progress. Most important, I recognized for the first time that to see AI as a science unto itself was to miss its greatest potential. Our research was demonstrating that, when integrated with other fields, and pushed by other forms of expertise, AI's possibilities might be limitless.

"Mom, *please*."

My mother's latest surgery had come to a merciful end, but the road to recovery this time would be especially long. Critical to getting there was a regimen of lung exercises, performed by breathing multiple times a day into a handheld device known as an incentive spirometer. Lung infections are common after the procedure she'd just endured—and potentially deadly—and the spirometer is a simple, effective means of prevention.

For a woman who'd braved multiple heart failures, a brain hemorrhage, and now open-heart surgery, it should have been a simple task. But she refused. She pretended to breathe into the device when it was presented to her by her doctor, but she would set it aside as soon as he left. And she repeated the charade when her nurses checked in. I saw it all, of course, but no matter how much I pleaded, I couldn't get her to do it.

It just didn't make sense. For days, my anxiety grew. It seemed no sequence of words, no matter how carefully reasoned or how emotionally freighted, could convince her. She nodded when the nurses warned her, and feigned compliance when her doctors scolded her.

But her theatrics didn't change reality: liquid was accumulating in her left lung, and she would have to undergo another painful procedure to drain it.

Finally, after still more weeks in the ICU, where she was now recovering from a second, entirely unnecessary operation, the ordeal came to an end, and we brought her home. Exhausted, we retreated to the backyard to enjoy our first quiet afternoon in what felt like ages. My father had been neglecting his gardening while she was away; relieved to have her back again, he resumed his routine.

"Mom, I need to ask you something."

I hated to spoil the serenity, but I just couldn't let it go.

"Remember that little gadget the doctors wanted you to use? The spirometer?"

It was amazing how much she could convey while remaining perfectly still. She clearly didn't want to talk about it.

"Mom, I'm just trying to understand. Please, help me out here."

She let another few moments slip by before answering. "I don't really remember," she eventually said, still not looking at me. "I was on some pretty heavy medication. It's all very fuzzy."

I knew that wasn't true, but I couldn't force her to explain herself. I let the question linger, and simply enjoyed the moment with her. It was sunny, and the gardenias were in bloom.

Finally, she broke the silence.

"You know, Fei-Fei," she said softly, "being a patient . . . it's just *horrible*." She was facing me now. "It's not just the pain. It's the loss of control. It was like my body, even my mind, didn't belong to me in that room. There were all these strangers—doctors and nurses, I know, but they're strangers to me—and that expectation to follow their every order . . . It just became intolerable."

I continued to listen.

"Even *you* had orders for me!"

We both chuckled, lightening the mood by the tiniest increment.

"I know you were trying to help," she added. "I know you all were. I realize these things were important for my health. But there just came a point where I couldn't keep up with the demands."

Then, after another moment of reflection, she put her finger on it. "My dignity was gone. *Gone.* In a moment like that . . ." She seemed to trail off. I was about to encourage her to go on when she finished the thought. ". . . even your health . . . just doesn't matter."

I'd learned a lot since this project began. Lessons that unfolded slowly and often painfully. I'd come to see my mother's struggle with her health in a different light and developed a new kind of empathy for the caregivers we'd relied on for so many years. I'd been horrified by the scope of human vulnerability in hospitals and inspired by the chance to do something about it. But the deepest lesson I'd learned was the primacy of human dignity—a variable no data set can account for and no algorithm can optimize. That old, familiar messiness, reaching out to me from behind the weathered lines and weary eyes of the person I knew best and cared for the most.

More than two years had passed since my mother had set my career on an entirely new path by simply asking what AI could do to help people. Seeing my field through her eyes instantly expanded my motivation beyond the curiosity that had propelled me for all these years, potent as it was. For the first time, I saw it as a tool for doing good, and maybe even lessening the hardships families like mine faced every day. I experienced my first run-in with the ethics of AI: a nascent idea for so many of us, but one that was quickly becoming inescapably real. And, after a career spent within the confines of familiar territory, I found myself in a new world altogether—one so foreign that I'd have been helpless without a partner. My work with Arnie taught me two essential lessons: that the greatest triumphs of AI wouldn't merely be scientific, but humanistic as well, and that achieving them would be impossible without help.

11

NO ONE'S TO CONTROL

Hey, uh, it's 'Fei-Fei,' right?"

The man gestured politely as I turned toward the sound of his voice.

"I'm Dave," he said, reaching out to shake my hand. "I heard you the other day on some podcast. I forget which one. You know, my firm has been talking about AI, like, *nonstop*," he continued. "We've closed *four* A rounds in the last few months alone, all in this space."

I smiled, but wasn't entirely sure how else to react. It was 2014, and the jargon of venture capital could make me feel like an outsider in my own field.

"Hey, have you met Jeff?" He turned to wave at another man across the room, decked out in what looked like the exact same jeans and fleece pullover.

"Jeff, c'mere for a sec! I want you to meet someone! Jeff's the VP of product development over at—"

"All right, everyone, if I could have your attention we can get started," a new voice mercifully interrupted from the other side of the room. "I want to thank everyone for coming tonight. Preschool is a big step, and we've got some great stuff planned for your kids this year."

"We'll talk more later!" the man whispered, squeezing himself into a miniature wooden chair next to the hamster cage.

Whatever we academics thought AI was, or might become, one thing was now undeniable: it was no longer ours to control. For more than a decade, it'd been a private obsession—a layer of thoughts that super-imposed itself quietly over my view of the world. By the mid-2010s, however, it was deafeningly public. Billboards along Highway 101 heralded the hiring sprees of AI start-ups. There were cover stories about it in the magazines in my dentist's waiting room. I'd hear it in fragments of conversation on my car radio as I changed stations. And, evidently, it was a hot topic at preschool parent meetings.

The world was becoming a surreal place. My colleagues and I had spent our careers exploring the *science* of AI, but we were suddenly confronted by something like—I didn't have precisely the right word for it—the *phenomenon* of AI. For all the mysteries posed by the technology, its suddenly growing interactions with industries and governments, journalists and commentators, and even the public at large were every bit as complex. After decades spent *in vitro*, AI was now *in vivo*. It was restless, hungry, and eager to explore. And although I hesitate to liken it too explicitly to a living organism (our field's history is replete with attempts at anthropomorphization that are more misleading than insightful), it had undeniably evolved into something new.

Less than a year earlier, the news that Google was nipping at the heels of my work with Andrej was shocking. Now it felt quaint. It'd simply become a brute fact that university labs, once the alpha and omega of AI research, were not the only institutions advancing the frontier. We shared a crowded landscape with tech giants like Google, Microsoft, and Facebook, start-ups all over the world, a voracious network of venture capitalists, and even software developers in the open-source community, whether they were sharing code on platforms like GitHub or discussing the latest developments on forums like Reddit.

They had plenty to talk about.

In 2015, Jia and Olga published a retrospective on the impact of the competition thus far, including the results of research conducted by Andrej estimating the *human* error rate when labeling a thousand images at around 5.1 percent. Although he'd been motivated by simple curiosity, Andrej's findings supercharged the event; suddenly, the algorithms were no longer competing only with each other but with *humans* as well. When GoogLeNet, Google's neural network classifier, achieved an all-time-low error rate of just 6.67 percent in 2014, we humans came unnervingly close to losing our place at the top of the leaderboard.

But although AlexNet and GoogLeNet were true leaps forward for computer vision, our understanding of their full potential was far from complete. We were certain, for instance, that network depth was among the defining secrets to their performance, and the affordability of GPUs meant we finally had the horsepower to make them bigger than ever before. The simple act of adding more layers, however, wasn't a panacea—deeper networks demonstrated higher and higher accuracy scores at first, but soon reached a point of diminishing returns. As our ambitions pushed us to build bigger and bigger, we inadvertently turned neural networks into labyrinths, their excessive layering corrupting the signal along the journey from one end of the network to the other, halting the training process in its tracks and rendering the system useless.

It was clear that the grand heights we sought wouldn't come easy, no matter how much silicon we threw at the problem. And it meant that the power of data sets like ImageNet, even now, wasn't being fully harnessed. Our networks simply couldn't absorb them in their entirety. The status quo was in need of evolution—not just in scale, but in innovation—exactly the kind of thing I'd hoped the ImageNet Challenge would inspire.

Fittingly, that innovation came later in 2015, when the Deep

Residual Network, a submission led by a young Microsoft researcher named Kaiming He, changed the game yet again. Nicknamed "ResNet" for short, it was enormous—a staggering 152 layers—but employed an architectural twist whereby some of those layers could be bypassed during the training phase, allowing different images to direct their influence toward smaller subregions of the network.

Although the fully trained system would eventually put all its depth to use, no single training example was obliged to span its entirety. The result offered the best of both worlds: the increase in layer count required to boost performance and absorb more data—more of ImageNet than anyone had managed to leverage thus far—but the simplicity necessary for signals to flow freely without degradation. It was a textbook example of the ingenuity that drove our field in its best moments.

ResNet's design was only half the story, however. It was far more effective than even its authors had anticipated, yielding performance so startling it generated headlines in mainstream press outlets like *The New York Times*. It was no surprise the world was taking notice: ResNet's error rate of 4.5 percent soundly beat Andrej's estimate of human accuracy. Simply put, the challenge of visual categorization appeared to have been met, as machines breezed past their creators on a task that had seemed almost impossible just a few years before. It was a breathtaking milestone, but before long, we realized it would be just the first of many.

Hey are you following this AlphaGo thing
Any idea who's gonna win
Should I be placing bets lol

I was only days out of the hospital after the birth of my second child when the texts began flooding in. If anything might have insulated me from the world for at least a week or two, it should have been this. *No such luck*, my buzzing phone giddily reminded me.

By early 2016, media attention was ramping up around a London-based start-up called DeepMind, which was preparing for a match between Go grandmaster Lee Sedol and, of course, a machine. The company had been a mostly obscure tech story until then (and even my awareness of it was only cursory), but now seemed on its way to becoming a household name. The year before, Google had gone on an AI start-up acquisition spree, with DeepMind the most expensive of its purchases by a wide margin at more than half a billion dollars. But even more memorable than its price tag was its mission. "They claim to be working on *AGI*," I recall one colleague telling me with the world-weary laugh of an academic.

I sympathized. "AGI" was an abbreviation for "artificial *general* intelligence," a form of AI so sophisticated and flexible that, rather than simply performing narrow tasks like image classification or translating text between languages, it can replicate *all* human cognitive capabilities, from the analytical to the creative. I couldn't pinpoint when the term entered the lexicon, but I'd certainly never heard it used in a computer science department. After all, such "general" intelligence had been the whole point of AI since its inception; the fact that we still had such a long way to go didn't mean we'd set our sights any lower. To the ears of researchers like us, the new term sounded a bit superfluous. But it was catchy, and it made the ultimate ambitions of our field clear to outsiders. And it positioned DeepMind as an unusually bold player in an already competitive ecosystem.

I was bombarded with questions from students, friends, and even loose acquaintances, all of them wondering if I had any predictions to share. I didn't, really, but I couldn't resist asking the other AI professor in the house about it when he popped in with a fresh bottle of formula.

"Eh, I could probably go either way," Silvio said. "Deep Blue did it with chess twenty years ago." He appeared to do a bit of mental arithmetic. "Well, nineteen, to be precise."

Nerds are nerds.

"Anyway," he continued. "I know Go is a lot harder than chess, but it's still a board game. No matter how complex, it's straightforward. Mathematically speaking, at least."

Realizing he was slipping into the professorial tone we both tried, and often failed, to check at the door, he smirked as he carefully placed the bottle in the warmer. We almost said what came next at the same time. "As opposed to *this!*"

He was right. For all the fancy talk about modeling a combinatorially incomprehensible game of strategy, something as simple as preparing a bottle of baby formula and setting it down in the warmer was still a roboticist's holy grail—and far from a solved problem outside of tightly controlled laboratory conditions.

It was true that a computer had officially surpassed a human chess grandmaster in the now infamous 1997 match between Garry Kasparov and IBM's Deep Blue supercomputer. But Go isn't simply a more complex game than chess. In truth, its rules give rise to a space of possibilities so expansive that the board's nineteen-by-nineteen grid of cells can be arranged in 10-to-the-360th-power configurations—a number so gargantuan that it doesn't just exceed the number of particles in the universe, but does so by many, many orders of magnitude. Humans play the game effectively by developing intuitions over a lifetime of practice, reducing a functionally infinite menu of options at each turn into something manageable. But even cutting-edge AI lacked the cognitive depth to replicate that ability.

Still, there was reason for a kind of casual optimism. While the amount of computation needed to search for an optimal move in Go is indeed enormous, there's still something fundamentally tidy about the game. It follows a finite set of rules, and the winner—whichever side's stones claim the largest areas of territory on the board—is clearly and objectively determined. By the standards of moon shots, Go was among the more straightforward. But it was, to be fair, still a moon shot.

"Even if it wins, though," Silvio added, "it'll be a while before it makes better lasagna than humans."

With a single reply, he'd put modern AI in perspective and made me hungry at the same time.

AlphaGo did, in fact, win, and the world went nuts. Global media attention spilled forth—especially in Asia, where the event inspired an absolute frenzy. For me, the biggest indicator was a personal one.

"飞飞，我的老同学们问我你知道AI下围棋是怎么回事吗？"—*"Fei-Fei, my friends are asking me: do you know what's going on with AI playing Go?"* said the next of what felt like endless WeChat messages my dad had taken to forwarding from friends abroad. "他们听说我女儿是AI教授，都在问我呢！"—*"They heard my daughter is an AI professor, so they're all asking me about this!"* Headlines were one thing, but when my parents' network of Chinese grandmothers and grandfathers was part of the conversation, it was a sign the world was truly changing.

It was a time of turning points, but even the most dramatic breakthroughs were familiar to us, insofar as they were expressions of the technology to which we'd dedicated our lives. Stories like ResNet and AlphaGo inspired conversation and debate, and motivated us to reach even further in our own research. Even I couldn't resist borrowing Silicon Valley's favorite term, as I realized that this new era of AI was more than simply a phenomenon: it was, as they say, a "disruption."

The little red couch in my office, where so many of the projects that defined our lab's reputation had been conceived, was becoming the place where I'd regularly plead with younger researchers to keep some room in their studies for the foundational texts upon which our science was built. I'd noticed, first to my annoyance and then to my concern, how consistently they were being neglected as the ever-accelerating advances of the moment drew everyone's attention to more topical sources of information.

"Guys, I'm *begging* you—please don't just download the latest preprints off arXiv every day. Read Russell and Norvig's book. Read Minsky and McCarthy and Winograd. Read Hartley and Zisserman.

Read Palmer. Read them *because* of their age, not in spite of it. This is timeless stuff. It's important."

arXiv (pronounced "archive") is an online repository of academic articles in fields like physics and engineering that have yet to be published, but are made available to the curious in an early, unedited form known as a "preprint." It had been a fixture of university culture for decades, but in recent years had become an essential resource for staying current in a field that was progressing so rapidly that everything seemed to change from one week to the next, and sometimes overnight. If waiting months for the peer review process to run its course was asking too much, was it any surprise that textbooks written years ago, if not entire generations ago, were falling by the wayside?

It was just the start of the distractions competing for my students' mindshare. More overtly, the hunt was on as tech giants scrambled to develop in-house AI teams, promising starting salaries in the six figures, and sometimes more, alongside generous equity packages. One machine learning pioneer after another had departed Stanford, and even postdocs were on the menu by the middle of the decade. In one especially audacious episode, Uber poached a record *forty* roboticists from Carnegie Mellon University—all but decimating the department in the process—in the hopes of launching a self-driving car of its own. It was a hard enough thing for my colleagues and me to witness. But for my students, young, eager, and still developing their own sense of identity, it seemed to fundamentally warp their sense of what an education was for. Ultimately, the trend reached its peak—for me, anyway—with an especially personal surprise.

"You're *really* turning them down? Andrej, it's one of the best schools in the world!"

"I know. But I can't pass this up. There's something really special about it."

Andrej had completed his PhD and was heading into what must have been the most fertile job market in the history of AI, even for an aspiring professor. But despite a faculty offer from Princeton straight out of the gate—a career fast track any one of our peers would have killed for—he was choosing to leave academia altogether to join a private research lab that no one had ever heard of.

OpenAI was the brainchild of Silicon Valley tycoons Sam Altman, Elon Musk, and LinkedIn CEO Reid Hoffman, built with an astonishing initial investment of a *billion* dollars. It was a testament to how seriously Silicon Valley took the sudden rise of AI, and how eager its luminaries were to establish a foothold within it. Andrej would be joining its core team of engineers.

Shortly after OpenAI's launch, I ran into a few of its founding members at a local get-together, one of whom raised a glass and delivered a toast that straddled the line between a welcome and a warning: "Everyone doing research in AI should seriously question their role in academia going forward." The sentiment, delivered without even a hint of mirth, was icy in its clarity: the future of AI would be written by those with corporate resources. I was tempted to scoff, the way my years in academia had trained me to. But I didn't. To be honest, I wasn't sure I even disagreed.

Where all of this would lead was anyone's guess. Our field had been through more ups and downs than most; the term "AI winter" is a testament to its storied history of great expectations and false starts. But this felt different. As the analysis of more and more pundits took shape, a term was gaining acceptance from tech to finance and beyond: "the Fourth Industrial Revolution." Even accounting for the usual hyperbole behind such buzz phrases, it rang true enough, and decision makers were taking it to heart. Whether driven by genuine enthusiasm, pressure from the outside, or some combination of the two, Silicon Valley's executive class was making faster, bolder, and, in some cases, more reckless moves than ever. We were all about to find out what that philosophy would yield.

"Ape," for god's sake.

It was a label generated automatically by Yahoo's Flickr image-hosting service in May 2015 for a portrait of William, a fifty-six-year-old Black man captured in monochrome. The reaction was swift, well-deserved anger, and it was only the first in a string of blunders for the new technology. Flickr's troubled rollout also tagged a photo of the gate at the Dachau concentration camp "jungle gym," and applied "ape" yet again to a white woman with colored powder on her face. And it wasn't just Yahoo; by June, Google faced a similar controversy when its Google Photos service mislabeled a pair of Black teens as "gorillas." In a matter of weeks, the cut-and-dried success story of image classification had grown far more complicated.

It was hard not to feel a twinge of culpability, even for those of us not working for the companies involved. That the mishaps weren't malicious was cold comfort, as the issue they revealed was, if anything, even more disquieting: the consequences of insufficiently diverse data sets, ImageNet included, exacerbated by poorly tested algorithms and questionable decision-making. When the internet presents a predominantly white, Western, and often male picture of everyday life, we're left with technology that struggles to make sense of everyone else.

It was the inevitable outcome of what journalist and commentator Jack Clark called AI's "Sea of Dudes" problem: that the tech industry's lack of representation was leading to unintentionally biased algorithms that perform poorly on nonwhite, nonmale users. Published in *Bloomberg* in 2016, Clark's piece was an early contribution to a growing dialogue concerned that AI's potential to do good things—support the disabled, track deforestation, and safeguard human life in any number of new ways—was accompanied by an equal potential to do bad.

I recalled the years we spent struggling to assemble ImageNet, and how, even at our most creative and improvisational, we'd been largely ignorant about issues like these. Ten years before, the explosion of content organized by the Googles and Wikipedias of the world seemed to offer a window into human life as it truly is, as opposed to the provincial glimpses found in legacy media like TV networks and newspapers. And in a way, of course, they did. But as vivid as it seemed, and as exuberant as our expectations were, the view was still far from complete.

This was an issue long overdue for confrontation, but the dialogue wasn't enough to comfort my inner engineer. Although lopsided data sets were clearly a big part of the problem, there were countless other factors worth our consideration. What about the models? Were there undiscovered weaknesses hiding in the architecture of the algorithms weaned on all that data? What about the learning techniques that facilitated the training process? The questions outnumbered the answers, and the ratio only seemed to be growing more skewed.

The questions weighed on Olga's mind as well. As two of the relatively few women in an overwhelmingly male field, we'd done our share of commiserating over the years, comparing discouragingly similar notes on the experience of being female in AI. By the middle of the decade, however, she'd had enough, and resolved to either do something about it or leave academia. She opted for the former, and we decided to do it together.

Recognizing that problems of representation tend to start years before they're consciously felt, we opened SAIL to a handpicked class of ninth- and tenth-grade girls. The two-week AI crash course that followed, although intense, demonstrated to everyone in attendance that it takes surprisingly little to convince the historically excluded that they belong, too. The idea proved so popular that it snowballed into a national nonprofit, spreading to campuses across North America and expanding its mission. Soon, we were offering similar courses to other marginalized groups, including students of color and the economically disadvantaged.

In just a few years, the initiative was officially branded AI4ALL, and it even attracted some capital, with a transformative round of funding coming from Melinda French Gates's Pivotal Ventures and Nvidia founder Jensen Huang. It was a small step on a journey that would probably take generations to complete, but it was a start. And it was welcome reassurance, however modest, as we watched the industry chase the future of this technology with far more abandon than introspection.

Still, seeing companies like Yahoo and Google learn an excruciating lesson in real time, while the world watched and judged, reminded us that it wasn't enough to simply invest in the next generation and hope for the best. Olga, who'd been offered a professorship at Princeton and took it, set about expanding her new lab's research agenda from the mechanics of machine perception to the larger issue of fairness in computing, including a special emphasis on "debiasing": a formal, mathematically rigorous attempt to quantify and neutralize the bias lurking in our data. With people like Olga bringing such socially conscious ideas to the table, my hope for the future began to grow again.

I believed in the value of this technology with all my heart, from its potential to shed new light on the mysteries of intelligence to the real good I saw in my work with Arnie in hospitals. But the price of even a moment's overconfidence was rising fast. Worse, that price would be paid by others, likely the most vulnerable among us. AI was out of the lab and largely out of our control; while the whirlwind of new ideas, new faces, and new institutions was invigorating, there were just as many new concerns. Even the promise of commercial investment in the field, a seeming godsend for shoestring researchers like us, was flooding everything with such force that it felt more like a dare, ominous and fraught, than a lucky break.

Words continued to fail. "Phenomenon" was too passive. "Disruption" too brash. "Revolution" too self-congratulatory. Modern AI was revealing itself to be a *puzzle*, and one whose pieces bore sharp edges. Nevertheless, as disturbing as it was to realize, this growing sense of danger was also the kind of thing scientists are wired to appreciate. It stoked a different form of curiosity in me, uncomfortable but compelling. I just needed a way to see it up close.

* * *

"So far the results have been encouraging. In our tests, neural architecture search has designed classifiers trained on ImageNet that outperform their human-made counterparts—all on its own."

The year was 2018, and I was seated at the far end of a long conference table at Google Brain, one of the company's most celebrated AI research orgs, in the heart of its headquarters—the *Googleplex*—in Mountain View, California. The topic was an especially exciting development that had been inspiring buzz across the campus for months: "neural architecture search," an attempt to automate the optimization of a neural network's architecture.

A wide range of parameters define how such models behave, governing trade-offs between speed and accuracy, memory and efficiency, and other concerns. Fine-tuning one or two of these parameters in isolation is easy enough, but finding a way to balance the push and pull between all of them is a task that often taxes human capabilities, and even experts struggle to dial everything in just right. The convenience that automation would provide was an obviously worthy goal, and beyond that, it could make AI more accessible for its growing community of nontechnical users, who could use it to build models of their own without expert guidance. Besides, there was just something poetic about machine learning models designing machine learning models—and quickly getting better at it than us.

But all that power came with a price. Training even a single model was still cost-prohibitive for all but the best-funded labs and companies—and neural architecture search entailed training *thousands*. It was an impressive innovation, but a profoundly expensive one in computational terms. This issue was among the main points of discussion in the meeting.

"What kind of hardware is this running on?" a researcher asked.

"At any given point in the process, we're testing a hundred different configurations, each training eight models with slightly different characteristics. That's a combined total of eight hundred models being trained at once, each of which is allocated its own GPU."

"So we're looking at about—"

"Eight hundred, yes."

Eight hundred GPUs. It was a dizzying increase, considering that AlexNet had required just two to change the world in 2012. And the numbers only grew more imposing from there. Recalling from my own lab's budget that Nvidia's most capable GPUs cost something like $1,000 (which explained why we had barely more than a dozen of them ourselves), the bare minimum expense to contribute to this kind of research now sat at nearly $1 million. Of course, that didn't account for the time and personnel it takes to network so many high-performance processors together in the first place, and to keep everything running within an acceptable temperature range as all that silicon simmers around the clock. It doesn't include the location, either. In terms of both physical space and its astronomical power consumption, such a network wasn't exactly fit for the average garage or bedroom. Even university labs like mine would struggle to build something of such magnitude. I sat back in my chair and looked around the room, wondering if anyone else found this as distressing as I did.

By 2016, I was due for a twenty-one-month sabbatical from my professorship, and my inbox was being inundated with courtship messages from companies like Nvidia, Uber, and Google. I retained a well-honed instinct to dismiss them out of hand, but more and more, I caught myself lingering for a moment first. *This might make more sense than before*, I thought with a sigh. *I mean, just a little.*

I had to admit that the idea of a job in private industry didn't feel as alien as it once did. More colleagues than I could count had made the transition themselves, and even my students were taking breaks from their degrees for high-paid sojourns at tech firms all over the world—and not always coming back. Now, with so much changing so fast, I had to wonder if my aversion to doing the same had outlived its utility. I wanted to see what modern AI looked like outside the borders of Stanford and the pages of science journals. This, perhaps, was the chance to do exactly that, at least for a little while.

After considering my options, I chose to take the position of chief scientist of AI at Google Cloud. Although Google was a long-established powerhouse, its newly formed cloud computing division was only a year or so old, and it struck me as a chance to help build something from the ground up. I also happened to know the company's newly appointed CEO, Diane Greene—one of the few women to conquer Silicon Valley as cofounder of virtualization giant VMware—and looked forward to working alongside her in an industry with such a skewed gender balance.

This wasn't like the suspiciously gilded Wall Street gig I was offered as an undergrad, or the fast-track McKinsey position I agonized over at Caltech. I could no longer pretend a job in the private sector was some cynical bribe to abandon the lab. These days, it was an invitation to run an even bigger one. Capabilities beyond anything I'd ever imagined. High-performance computing at any scale I wanted. Teams of PhD researchers orders of magnitude bigger than any I could assemble at Stanford. And most fascinating of all, access to data in quantities I'd never dreamt of. Sure, my work would be driven by the company's product road map, at least indirectly, but those products have always been downstream of the fundamental research that makes them possible anyway.

Best of all, Google Cloud meant I wouldn't see just a single example of applied AI, but thousands. As cloud services found footholds in just about every industry imaginable, providers like Google became fixtures in all of them. This was a chance to see where AI was being used— and the data that powered it—in manufacturing, agriculture, insurance, transportation and logistics, retail, financial services, and even government. It was a level of scale and variety beyond anything a university could offer, all at once.

It took some time to hammer out the details, especially since I wasn't planning to leave Stanford entirely, even during the sabbatical. I'd continue to spend one day a week on campus, allowing me to stay in the loop with the lab and meet with students. Logistics, clearly, would be a challenge. But I'd made my decision.

Nothing I'd seen in all my years at universities prepared me for what was waiting for me behind the scenes at Google Cloud. The tech industry didn't just live up to its reputation of wealth, power, and ambition, but vastly exceeded it. Everything I saw was bigger, faster, sleeker, and more sophisticated than what I was used to.

The abundance of food alone was staggering. The break rooms were stocked with more snacks, beverages, and professional-grade espresso hardware than anything I'd ever seen at Stanford or Princeton, and virtually every Google building had such a room on every floor. And all this before I even made my way into the cafeterias.

Next came the technology. After so many years spent fuming over the temperamental projectors and failure-prone videoconferencing products of the 2000s, meetings at Google were like something out of science fiction. Cutting-edge telepresence was built into every room, from executive boardrooms designed to seat fifty to closet-sized booths for one, and everything was activated with a single tap on a touch screen.

Then there was the talent—the sheer, awe-inspiring depth of it. I couldn't help but blush remembering the two grueling years it took to attract *three* collaborators to help build ambient intelligence for hospitals. Here, a fifteen-person team, ready to work, was waiting for me on my first day. And that was just the start—within only eighteen months, we'd grow to *twenty times* that size. PhDs with sterling credentials seemed to be everywhere, and reinforced the feeling that anything was possible. Whatever the future of AI might be, Google Cloud was my window into a world that was racing toward it as fast as it could.

My Fridays at Stanford only underscored the comparison, as word of my new position spread and requests for internships became a daily occurrence. This was understandable to a point, as my students (and the occasional professor) were simply doing their best to network. What worried me, though, was that every conversation I had on the matter, without a single exception, ended with the same plea: that the research they found most interesting wouldn't be possible outside of a privately run lab. Even at a place like Stanford, the budgets just weren't big enough. Often, in fact, they weren't even close. Corporate research wasn't just the more lucrative option; it was, increasingly, the only option.

Finally, there was the data—the commodity on which Google's entire brand was based. ImageNet was my first glimpse of the potential of data at a large enough scale, and almost all of my research since had built on that idea. Decades of car models with Jon, reams of photos paired with descriptions with Andrej, an entire country of Street View images and Census Bureau records with Timnit—the volumes of data kept growing, and the capabilities of AI grew alongside them. Now, I was surrounded—and not just by an indescribable abundance, but in categories I hadn't even imagined before: data from agriculture businesses seeking to better understand plants and soil, data from media industry customers eager to organize their content libraries, data from manufacturers working to reduce product defects, and so much more.

Back and forth I went, as the months stretched on, balancing a life between the two institutions best positioned to contribute to the future of AI. Both were brimming with talent, creativity, and vision. Both had deep roots in the history of science and technology. Hell, they were even accessible from the same freeway, spaced just a few exits apart on 101. But only one seemed to have the resources to adapt as the barriers to entry rose like a mountain towering over the horizon, its peak well above the clouds.

My mind kept returning to those eight hundred GPUs, gnawing their way through a computational burden a professor and her students couldn't even imagine overcoming. So many transistors. So much heat. So much money. A word like "puzzle" didn't capture the dread I was beginning to feel.

AI was becoming a privilege. An exceptionally exclusive one.

Since the days of ImageNet it had been clear that scale was important, but the notion had taken on nearly religious significance in recent years. The media was saturated with stock photos of server facilities the size of city blocks and endless talk about "big data," reinforcing the idea of scale as a kind of magical catalyst, the ghost in the machine that separated the old era of AI from a breathless, fantastical future. And although the analysis could get a bit reductive, it wasn't wrong. No one could deny that neural networks were, indeed, thriving in this era of abundance: staggering quantities of data, massively layered architectures, and acres of interconnected silicon really had made a historic difference.

What did it mean for the science? What did it say about our efforts as thinkers if the secret to our work could be reduced to something so nakedly quantitative? To what felt, in the end, like brute force? If ideas that appeared to fail given too few layers, or too few training examples, or too few GPUs suddenly sprung to life when the numbers were simply increased sufficiently, what lessons were we to draw about the inner workings of our algorithms? More and more, we found ourselves *observing* AI, empirically, as if it were emerging on its own. As if AI were something to be identified first and understood later, rather than engineered from first principles.

The nature of our relationship with AI was transforming, and that was an intriguing prospect as a scientist. But from my new perch at Google Cloud, with its bird's-eye view of a world increasingly reliant on technology at every level, sitting back and marveling at the wonder of it all was a luxury we couldn't afford. *Everything* this new generation of

AI was able to do—whether good or bad, expected or otherwise—was complicated by the lack of transparency intrinsic to its design. Mystery was woven into the very structure of the neural network—some colossal manifold of tiny, delicately weighted decision-making units, meaningless when taken in isolation, staggeringly powerful when organized at the largest scales, and thus virtually immune to human understanding. Although we could talk about them in a kind of theoretical, detached sense—what they could do, the data they would need to get there, and the general range of their performance characteristics once trained—what *exactly* they did on the inside, from one invocation to the next, was utterly opaque.

An especially troubling consequence of this fact was an emerging threat known as "adversarial attacks," in which input is prepared for the sole purpose of confusing a machine learning algorithm to counterintuitive and even destructive ends. For instance, a photo that appears to depict something unambiguous—say, a giraffe against a blue sky—could be modified with subtle fluctuations in the colors of individual pixels that, although imperceptible to humans, would trigger a cascade of failures within the neural network. When engineered just right, the result could degrade a correct classification like "giraffe" into something wildly incorrect like "bookshelf" or "pocket watch" while the original image appears to be unchanged. But while the spectacle of advanced technology stumbling over wildlife photos might be something to giggle at, an adversarial attack designed to fool a self-driving car into misclassifying a stop sign—let alone a child in a crosswalk—hardly seemed funny.

Granted, it was possible that more engineering might help. A new, encouraging avenue of research known as "explainable AI," or simply "explainability," sought to reduce neural networks' almost magical deliberations into a form humans could scrutinize and understand. But it was in its infancy, and there was no assurance it would ever reach the heights its proponents hoped for. In the meantime, the very models it was intended to illuminate were proliferating around the world.

Even fully explainable AI would be only a first step; shoehorning safety and transparency into the equation after the fact, no matter how sophisticated, wouldn't be enough. The next generation of AI had to be developed with a fundamentally different attitude from the start. Enthusiasm was a good first step, but true progress in addressing such complex, unglamorous challenges demanded a kind of reverence that Silicon Valley just didn't seem to have.

Academics had long been aware of the negative potential of AI when it came to issues like these—the lack of transparency, the susceptibility to bias and adversarial influence, and the like—but given the limited scale of our research, the risks had always been theoretical. Even ambient intelligence, the most consequential work my lab had ever done, would have ample opportunities to confront these pitfalls, as our excitement was always tempered by clinical regulations. But now that companies with market capitalizations approaching a trillion dollars were in the driver's seat, the pace had accelerated radically. Ready or not, these were problems that needed to be addressed at the speed of business.

As scary as each of these issues was in isolation, they pointed toward a future that would be characterized by less oversight, more inequality, and, in the wrong hands, possibly even a kind of looming, digital authoritarianism. It was an awkward thought to process while walking the halls of one of the world's largest companies, especially when I considered my colleagues' sincerity and good intentions. These were institutional issues, not personal ones, and the lack of obvious, mustache-twirling villains only made the challenge more confounding.

I thought back to my work with Arnie, and how difficult it had been to deploy small, hand-built prototypes in just a few hospitals. Innovation unfolded gradually in the hypercautious world of health care, and while that was an occasionally frustrating fact, it was also a comforting one. I wondered if it was an example worth following more widely.

Silicon Valley had never been accused of a lack of hubris, but the era of AI was elevating corporate bluster to new heights, even as our understanding of its pitfalls seemed to grow. CEOs on stages around the world delivered keynote speeches that ranged from the visionary to the clumsy to the downright insulting, promising cars that would soon drive themselves, virtuoso tumor detection algorithms, and end-to-end automation in factories. As for the fates of the people these advances would displace—taxi drivers, long-haul truckers, assembly-line workers, and even radiologists—corporate sentiment seemed to settle somewhere between half-hearted talk of "reskilling" to thinly veiled indifference.

But no matter how thoroughly the words of CEOs and self-proclaimed futurists might alienate the public, the growing deployments of the technology would give people even greater reasons to fear AI. It was an era of milestones, and the darkest imaginable kind was approaching. For the first time in the history of our field, blood would be shed.

Elaine Herzberg was killed when a self-driving car prototype being tested by Uber's Advanced Technologies Group ran her down as she pushed her bicycle across a road in Tempe, Arizona. Less than three years after Uber had orchestrated a faculty exodus from Carnegie Mellon's robotics department, the company's self-driving ambitions had become an object of public scorn. If AI's now frequent brushes with prejudice had sickened my colleagues and me, the sensation we were now feeling defied description. While it was easy to blame Uber—an already notorious brand for reasons that had little to do with technology—it was all too clear that this would be far from the last such story.

Indeed, additional lessons were soon on the way. A series of 2016 ProPublica investigations documented the widespread use of biased AI in helping lenders process loan applications and even in assisting judges in making decisions about parole. Similar reporting discovered questionable uses of the technology to screen job applicants before they'd been interviewed by humans, often with unintentionally (but unsurprisingly) discriminatory effects. Elaine Herzberg's death rightfully triggered the dissolution of Uber's self-driving initiative and put a damper on the entire field, but such swift corrections wouldn't be possible for these subtler, more institutional forms of harm. These were nearly silent problems, operating at a far larger scale, and with considerably less oversight. It wasn't realistic to expect the same level of public outrage. But awareness was growing, and the media was realizing that when it came to coverage of AI, questions like bias, fairness, and privacy shouldn't be ignored.

As I began to recognize this new landscape—unaccountable algorithms, entire communities denied fair treatment, and a human life cut short—I concluded that simple labels no longer fit. Even phrases like "out of control" felt euphemistic. AI wasn't a phenomenon, or a disruption, or a puzzle, or a privilege. We were in the presence of a force of nature. Something so big, so powerful, and so capricious that it could destroy as easily as it could inspire. It would take a lot more than corporate bromides to make it worthy of our trust.

It was a complex situation routinely exacerbated by the fact that AI wasn't even the tech world's only threat to the public good. Unfolding in parallel were events like the Cambridge Analytica scandal, widespread concerns of misinformation during the 2016 United States presidential election, and rising reports of the ill effects of social media and news feed filter bubbles. Still, the common denominator was consistent enough. The world was waking up to the idea that data wasn't just valuable, but influential—even deterministic—to a degree that had never been seen before.

By 2018 there was no longer any doubting the stakes. Scrutiny was intensifying for social media apps like Facebook and Instagram as the hyperpersonalized content they served—honed to an unsettling, tailored edge by AI for maximum "engagement"—emerged as a potential cause of teenage depression and anxiety. Amazon was lambasted in the press for its warehouse practices, which leveraged a range of surveillance tools, including monitoring wristbands, to track worker productivity from one moment to the next. Microsoft faced criticism of its own from privacy advocates and civil liberties groups as it attempted to market its AI-powered facial recognition technology. I found myself at the center of controversy as well, when a Google Cloud contract with the Department of Defense, known internally as Project Maven, sparked widespread debate within the company. Tensions spilled out into the press within months, reigniting generations-old questions about the role of our technology in military affairs. The techlash had arrived, and there'd be no separating AI from it now.

"We'll be waiting, right here," I said.

It was 5:30 in the morning. I watched as the nurse wheeled my mother into the operating room for another open-heart procedure—the most invasive yet. I spoke the rest of my well-wishing under my breath, in the silent tradition of Chinese families.

Love you, Mom.

Not quite sure what to do with myself, I stood up after a few listless minutes and paced the halls until I found a quiet bench, far from any noise and movement, then slumped back down. Its metal surface was colder than I expected, causing me to shiver. It was just me, a head full of thoughts I wasn't ready to face, and the empty space to my left where my mother might have been sitting on any other day. Prickly and judgmental, perhaps, but always there, and always on my side.

A moment passed, and I realized the space wasn't empty after all. My father had found me. He looked like he had something to say, but didn't quite know how to get the words out.

"Fei-Fei . . ." he began. His tone was uncharacteristically grave. Adult, even. But it wasn't strength or authority I was sensing. It was vulnerability.

"Everyone loved my father when I was a boy," he eventually continued. "Especially me. Have I ever told you about him? We weren't rich, but we were comfortable, especially for a town as small as ours. It was a very fortunate upbringing. I felt . . . special."

I didn't know what to make of what I was hearing. It was so rare for him to talk about his past—the absent grandfather, the boyhood he'd never seemed to grow out of, our family beyond me and my mother. But he continued, delving further and further into a story I'd never heard.

My father didn't grow up with his mother, due to some severe but vague psychological condition he spoke of in circumspect terms. In spite of this, or more likely because of it, his father—my grandfather—spoiled him with abandon. My grandfather wasn't particularly wealthy or powerful, but he occupied an administrative position in a town so small that even the hint of status was enough to confer a modest perk or two. It was a happy time for my father, insulated from the complexities of the era and full of the adventures I'd imagined someone with his disposition must have grown up with.

I laughed out loud when he told me about his favorite childhood pet: a *bear*—a real, actual bear—that he raised himself before it grew to such a dangerous size that it had to be donated to a zoo. I shouldn't have been surprised, of course; most boys with even a nominal shred of privilege might dream of parlaying it into their education or career prospects, but my father wasn't most boys. Of *course* he'd use it to walk a bear around town on a leash. The knot in my stomach loosened. He hadn't been much of a parent by conventional standards, but there was still something impressive about moments like these. He really could bring warmth to any occasion.

But the story took a turn as my grandfather was afflicted with an abrupt spell of ill health. It began mysteriously, as such things often did at the time, and it was made worse by their isolation. It was just the two of them, in a town of such limited means that adequate medical attention was all but impossible. My father was helpless to intervene, even as my grandfather's symptoms—fatigue, confusion, and a fast-dwindling appetite that left him gaunt—grew worse and worse.

In the absence of proper care, my grandfather simply unraveled, reduced in mere months to an invalid. My father could only watch from his bedside, helpless to stop him—the center of his entire world—from disappearing before his eyes. When death finally came, it felt senseless and undignified. A doctor, arriving all too late, tried to explain the way extreme malnourishment had exacerbated a gastrointestinal condition, ultimately pushing his body further than it could handle. But explanations mattered little to a boy so suddenly alone. There was no sense to be made of any of it.

It was 1961. My father was fourteen years old.

Miraculously, a colleague of my grandfather's volunteered to step in, taking over as my father's legal guardian in the absence of any living relatives. He kept him in school, ensured that his basic needs were met, and saw to it that he reached graduation. The man's generosity allowed my father to survive a period that would have otherwise eaten him alive. But he was never the same.

When my grandfather died, some part of my father died with him. What remained was a fraction of a boy, the sole surviving proof that the world he loved, and lost, ever existed. So he resolved to stay as he was. Even as he became an adult, earned a degree, and eventually became a husband and father, he continued to live that boy's life as he remembered it.

One thing did grow, however. Behind the sweet smiles, the goofy wordplay, and his eternal rejection of responsibility, a secret pain refused to heal, still seething after all those years. And it formed the basis of his sole conviction: that the capricious, cruel world that took his father would never take him. It would never take my mother. And it would never take me.

That's when it clicked. My father wasn't simply revealing my family's history, or the private reasons he shared my mother's desire for escape. These were the words of a man who was desperate to prepare his daughter, somehow, for the loss of her mother. He was exhuming his oldest, deepest grief, buried beneath decades of a new life, so we could face a new grief together. He was protecting me. For so many years I'd thought his adolescence had never ended, when the truth was that it had—far too soon. He'd always seemed like a child frozen in time, but I saw something new in that moment. Beneath it all, a father's heart was beating.

The end of my second decade in AI was approaching, along with the end of my second year at Google, and I'd never felt so ill at ease. The chaos in my field was enveloping everything, including me. But I was also becoming cognizant of a pattern that seemed to define my life. No matter how difficult things got, something would remind me of what it means to be a human in the midst of it all. Every time, I was grateful.

Conversations about professional ethics are tricky in just about any setting, but the high-wire act felt especially tense one day in the fall of 2018 as I stood in a packed conference room and attempted to answer questions from the team of engineers and product managers who now reported to me. After so much turmoil—both within our industry and beyond it, from culture to politics—a moment of reflection felt overdue.

"You know," I began, long pauses separating my words, "I've loved physics for almost as far back as I can remember. But there's no separating the beauty of the science from something like, say, the Manhattan Project. That's just reality. AI has boogeymen of its own, whether it's killer robots, or widespread surveillance, or even just automating all eight billion of us out of our jobs. These are scary things, and they're worth worrying about. But they're also the extremes, and they're probably not going to happen tomorrow."

I subjected the room to another long pause, mulling over my next words.

"And that, I guess, is where things *really* get tricky. Because there's so much else to consider in the meantime. A lot of good things and a lot of bad things, some of which actually *might* happen tomorrow. So, I hope you can appreciate the opportunity we're facing. We're playing a role in whatever comes next. We *have* to take that seriously. That's what makes an ethical framework so important. Something to help us evaluate every step we take, before we take it."

The room was quiet for a moment.

"Um, can I ask a question?" The voice belonged to a newly hired research scientist seated in a far corner of the room. She was brilliant and highly technical, having recently graduated from one of the world's most elite schools. But she sounded timid. "This idea of an 'ethical framework' . . ."

"Yes?"

". . . what does that *mean*, exactly?"

It was a more fundamental question than I was expecting, and probably the one we all needed to be asking.

Join the team helping local singles find love with big data, analytics, and artificial intelligence! Now hiring!

I squinted at another billboard on 101 from the back seat. I began to wonder if the real threat of AI was that it was becoming impossible to advertise anything *other* than AI. A few months had passed since my conversation about the ethics of our work with my team, and it'd been on my mind frequently ever since. My colleague's voice interrupted the thought.

"Hey, take a look," he said as he handed me a few printed pages. "Just some talking points from the PR team that we might want to use."

I smiled as I glanced down, but it wasn't the words that lifted my spirits as our car crawled through another morning of southbound traffic. We were on our way to Mountain View to participate in an annual tradition I was about to experience for the second time, when Google brings its hundreds of summer interns—a sprawling cohort from offices all around the world—to the Googleplex to meet the leadership and learn more about the many paths their careers might take. For the company, it was a recruiting event. For me, it was a break from corporate life that evoked the best moments of being an educator. A room full of bright, young, and surely consequential thinkers. And I'd get to talk to them.

I was usually happy to follow the script. In contrast to my experience as a freewheeling professor, being a Google spokesperson meant answering to so many executives, PR consultants, and even lawyers that the idea of going rogue could be downright scary. My statements were usually some reconfiguration of the same boilerplate about AI and business, delivered politely and without incident to this reporter or that, or to an audience of analysts. I'd gotten to the point that I could practically recite the words from memory.

But these were strange times, and something inside me hungered for change. My thoughts returned to the meeting with my team. That final question repeated over and over: *what does "ethical framework" mean, exactly?* To the extent that I myself had any idea what such a thing might constitute—and it wasn't clear I did, the more I thought about it—much of what I knew about the ethics of technology was a happy accident of an unconventional career. Institutional Review Board proposals with Christof at Caltech. Years of work with people like Arnie in hospitals, deepened through accompanying doctors on their rounds and listening to the concerns of nurses. A parent at home whom I never stopped worrying about. Life as a teenage immigrant.

The stark truth was that fields like health care had norms, precedents, and an ethical foundation that was built over the course of centuries, if not millennia, informed by the inescapable reality of life and death. AI, by comparison, was so young that its own code of ethics was all but nonexistent. Our field's journey toward self-understanding was still only getting started. So it wasn't just Google that lacked an ethical framework, nor individuals like that young engineer who'd asked the question. It was all of us.

I feigned interest in the PR team's work, scanning the passages highlighted in neon, but I'd already made up my mind: for better or worse, this talk would be unrehearsed. I was about to address seven hundred of tomorrow's most influential tech workers, and I resolved to speak entirely from the heart. Besides, with my sabbatical coming to an end, I was feeling more than a little introspective.

Although often disorienting in the extreme, I couldn't feel more grateful for my time at Google Cloud. I was handed an opportunity that scientists rarely get: to meet people being affected by the impact of my field's research at the largest scale, and to see it, even momentarily, from their perspective. For two years I spoke regularly with executives, product designers, and developers of all kinds, at start-ups and Fortune 500 corporations alike, in industries like financial services, agriculture, health care, energy, entertainment, and transportation. It taught me lessons more humbling, and more clarifying, than I ever could have imagined, and it was my most direct reminder yet that AI is no longer an intellectual curiosity but a societal turning point on the verge of transforming life for entire populations. Ultimately, I knew no institution would be able to survive without reckoning with this technology on some level. The signs were unmistakable. I'd ruminate on what I saw day after day, week after week, month after month, trying to better understand the inflection point we were facing, and what it'd take to navigate it responsibly. I was proud, and optimistic, and still enthusiastic. But the weight of that responsibility had never felt heavier.

Wherever I was going next, my path would begin with the words I spoke when I stood on the stage before those interns. I'd depart from the corporate messaging I'd been steeped in for almost two years and offer a kind of confession instead. I planned to acknowledge, in words I'd yet to formulate, that a difficult future lay before us, and that whether we were students or professors, interns or CEOs, we were all in the dark. There was bad news to confront, difficult truths to grapple with, and the very real possibility of doing harm. But there was good news, too: it wasn't too late to face this together.

I felt the old, familiar butterflies in my stomach as I mounted the stage. I took solace, though, in the sight of the audience that I loved most: students.

"Good afternoon!" I said into the microphone. "It's great to be here."

They were the last scripted words I'd speak that day.

I heard the monotone defiance in my mother's voice, just like always—even now, only two weeks after the open-heart operation that felt like our family's closest brush yet with the unthinkable. Whether she was healthy or sick, young or old, it was simply her natural state.

"We've been having this conversation for twenty years now, Fei-Fei."

I looked back at the screen, the email still visible. In a message dated June 7, 2018, the deputy staff director of the U.S. Congress's House Committee on Science, Space, and Technology appeared to be inviting me to testify. It was an intimidating offer for someone who'd never done such a thing, and with the hearing set for the twenty-sixth, it was less than three weeks away. When I reflected on the events that had led to the present moment—the techlash, biased AI, and so much else—it seemed like a categorically bad idea to accept. And knowing how much my mother needed me, whether she'd admit it or not, made it even worse. Frankly, I just wanted her to make the decision for me, to insist that it was an irresponsible time for me to leave. But true to form, she was in no mood to offer shortcuts.

"Fei-Fei, do you remember when we landed at JFK? Our first moment in this country? What it was like when Dad didn't show up to meet us?"

"Yes, of course."

"Those hours we spent at baggage claim, helpless? Terrified? And now, two decades later, you get an invitation like this? To go to this country's capital? To testify about the subject you love most?"

"Yeah, but what if it's not that simple? What if they think I'm part of some scandal? What if—"

"Then you'll stand up for yourself! You'll tell them you've spent twenty years contributing to this country, that your family gave everything to be a part of it, and that you refuse to be treated like an outsider!"

Had this all come from anyone else, I'd have scoffed. Standing up to a congressional committee with a tone like that is the kind of thing most of us are better at imagining than actually doing. But knowing my mother, it's exactly what she would have said if someone dared to question her character. I wondered if I could just send her to testify in my place.

"Think about how desperately people around the world *long* for this kind of thing. An open hearing. Public dialogue between leaders and citizens. Why do you think your father and I brought you to this country?"

With the strike of a gavel, the hearing began. There was no turning back now.

"The Committee on Science, Space, and Technology will come to order," Virginia representative Barbara Comstock, the committee's chair, said casually into her microphone. "Good morning, and welcome to today's hearing, entitled 'Artificial Intelligence—With Great Power Comes Great Responsibility.'"

I understood the Spider-Man reference, at least. That had to count for something. Even so, neurotic worries of all kinds danced through my mind. A thousand pairs of eyes seemed to drill into the back of my head as I second-guessed every detail of the journey that had brought me here. My life as an immigrant. My role in the development of an increasingly divisive technology. The techlash. All of it.

But the more I listened, the more it dawned on me that my paranoia about this moment had been misplaced. One after another, the representatives' statements revealed a thoughtful, searching posture that took me by surprise. Their voices reflected their curiosity, sincerity, and willingness to grapple with real ideas, as complex as they might be. Gradually, I realized that I wasn't here to be grilled. I even got a chance to weave in my mother's condition and the role it played in inspiring my own research at the intersection of AI and health care. What I had feared would devolve into a confrontation was turning out to be a conversation about something simpler, yet more profound: what will Americans' lives look like in the coming decades?

It was in direct response to the mention of my mother that Representative Comstock looked away from her prepared remarks and spoke to me directly, sharing her thoughts on the challenges the U.S. will face as our population ages.

When she yielded the floor, Texas representative Randy Weber asked about my mother's health as well. I happily reassured him that her condition was stable enough for me to be here, and that she was watching from her hospital bed. "Hi, Mom!" Representative Comstock interjected playfully, as Representative Weber shared his own well-wishes in a folksy drawl. The exchange was unexpectedly sweet, and it pushed aside any remaining fears I had.

I channeled my good feelings into a précis of what I felt AI could, and should, be. I recounted the experiences that had inspired AI4ALL, and how much I'd learned from the program since its inception. I talked about ambient intelligence and how dear the topic was to my heart. And I talked about the future, and how much I believed AI could do to close gaps of opportunity around the world.

It was about as amiable a conversation as I'd ever had on the topic. We even veered into nerdier territory, thanks to the influence of Illinois representative Bill Foster, a physics PhD who worked at the Department of Energy's Fermi National Accelerator Laboratory before entering politics. His inquisitive nature energized me and emphasized yet again how new AI is as a field of study, centuries younger than more established pursuits like chemistry, biology, and physics. Even modern AI is closer to the pre-Newtonian age of Galileo and Tycho Brahe, when phenomena were being observed, cataloged, and predicted, but a unified model had yet to be formalized. We were living in an exciting, nascent moment, I said, still awaiting the dawn of our "classical" era.

"I thank the witnesses for their testimony and the members for their questions. The record will remain open for two weeks," Representative Weber recited. "The hearing is adjourned." With another strike of the gavel, it was over.

Okay, I thought, blinking a few times as my awareness of what had just happened seemed to catch up with me. *I can breathe again.*

As I walked back to my hotel, the mood of the capital's streets felt entirely different. My adrenaline levels were starting to taper off, and my thoughts settled into a more recognizable cadence. I felt more like myself. But I was still rudderless, unsure of what the next North Star worth following would be.

I turned my phone back on and called Silvio, ignoring the near-constant buzz of notifications. "Hey! How's she doing? Any updates?" I asked.

"Your mom's doing fine. I just called the nurse to double-check. How are *you*?"

"I survived, as far as I can tell. What did you think?"

"I think it went well," he said, having probably just watched more C-SPAN than at any other time in his life. "Not a lot of nerves that I could see."

Thank God. It wasn't just me.

"But you know what? I guess I got the wrong idea from movies, because it really wasn't all that *exciting*, either," he added with a chuckle.

I laughed louder than I'd have expected.

With the hearing finally behind me, I found myself imagining all the ways it might have gone differently. It could have been a lot longer, for one thing. And it could have involved a lot more witnesses, with a wider range of expertise. The agenda could have spanned more topics as well, and the results could have been made available in more forms. But even terms like "longer" and "more" felt small, somehow. There was just so *much* to explore.

Besides, we were still in the middle of what felt like a global storm. Each day seemed to bring new headlines about the threat of automation to workers worldwide. The concerns of journalists and human rights activists were only growing as AI's use in surveillance matured, modernizing age-old threats to privacy and the dignity of individuals. And despite the initial outcry, algorithmic bias still loomed over the technology as a whole, along with the problems of representation so often associated with it.

I'd used many different words to describe this new incarnation of what I once had viewed purely as a science. "Phenomenon." "Disruption." "Puzzle." "Privilege." "Force of nature." But as I retraced my steps across the capital, one new word took precedence. AI was now a *responsibility*. For all of us.

This, I felt certain, was a challenge worth facing. Deep learning was evolving so fast it felt like an entirely new field with each passing year, its applications growing in depth and variety so rapidly that even full-time grad students and postdocs—to say nothing of professors—had trouble keeping up with the literature. There was no end to the possibilities, nor to the challenges that remained. Even in such a dark time, AI had a power to inspire like nothing else. Truly addressing all of this—problems of global urgency, opportunities of historical scale, and open questions that might take generations to unravel—would demand much more than a corporate strategy or an academic curriculum could deliver.

What makes the companies of Silicon Valley so powerful? It's not simply their billions of dollars, or their billions of users, or even the incomprehensible computational might and stores of data that dwarf the resources of academic labs. They're powerful because thousands of uniquely talented minds are working together under their roof. But they can only *harness* those minds—they don't *shape* them. I'd seen the consequences of that over and over: brilliant technologists who could build just about anything, but who stared blankly when the question of the ethics of their work was broached.

The time had come to reevaluate the way AI is taught at every level. The practitioners of the coming years will need much more than technological expertise; they'll have to understand philosophy, and ethics, and even law. They'll need to see all the things Arnie made sure the ambient intelligence team saw, and they'll need to integrate it into a multitude of subjects. Research will have to evolve, too. And after the day I'd had, I knew we needed a new approach to policy as well— starting by offering an education on the topic to elected officials like the ones I'd just met.

It was a lot to imagine, but the vision was tied together by something important: the university. AI began there, long before anyone was making money with it. It's where the spark of some utterly unexpected research breakthrough is still most likely to be felt. Perceptrons, neural networks, ImageNet, and so much since had come out of universities. Everything I wanted to build already had a foothold there. We just needed to put it to use.

This, collectively, is the next North Star: reimagining AI from the ground up as a human-centered practice. I don't see it as a change in the journey's direction so much as a broadening of its scope. AI must become as committed to humanity as it's always been to science. It should remain collaborative and deferential in the best academic tradition, but unafraid to confront the real world. Starlight, after all, is manifold. Its white glow, once unraveled, reveals every color that can be seen.

12

THE NEXT NORTH STAR

I t felt good to be back.

Despite its neutral colors and soft lighting, the Nvidia Auditorium was brimming with energy. The lecture hall was packed so far beyond capacity that eager attendees were seated on the floor, the stairs, and against the back wall, laptops balanced on knees and cradled between crossed legs. Hundreds more were watching remotely, adding up to something like six hundred in total. It was the spring of 2019 and enrollment in CS231n: Convolutional Neural Networks for Visual Recognition had exploded since its introduction three years earlier. The class had quickly become my favorite to teach.

As I stood at the lectern, I remembered the awe I felt as a freshman at Princeton, hurrying to find a seat for the first time in that crowded hall. I recalled the jolt of anticipation as the chatter faded and the professor appeared, instantly subduing the class with what felt like a superhuman presence. I realize now how thoroughly human our ilk really is—accomplished, perhaps, but vulnerable as well, and fallible in ways I couldn't have imagined as a student. Still, the classroom remains an uncommonly special place for me, and moments like this are simply electric.

For many in attendance, today would be their first exposure to the ideas I'd loved for so long, and I'd been given the privilege of present-ing them. My experience learning from Bob came flooding back to me—Mr. Sabella, as I knew him back then—reminding me how deep an imprint a teacher can leave on a young person's life. We're entrusted with sharing a special kind of joy. The thrill of knowledge, the rush of new possibilities. The feeling can't last, of course, as it's eventually complicated by careers, publications, job interviews, and maybe even venture capital and revenue projections. But in moments like this, the mind is all that matters. Maybe some people in this room were about to discover, for themselves, something to chase.

Still, I had to acknowledge how much had changed since I last sat among those seats, and how much I'd seen in the intervening years. The conference rooms of Google. Data centers the size of warehouses. Hospitals. A panicked walk across Washington, D.C. AI was still my favorite science, but it was no longer *only* science. No matter what these students were destined to become—researchers, product design-ers, C-suite executives, policymakers, or something I couldn't even imagine—they would inherit an enormous responsibility.

"The common denominator to all of this," I said out loud, "whether it's addressing the bias in our data or safeguarding patients in hospitals, is how our technology treats people. Their dignity, in particular. That's the word I keep coming back to. How can AI, above all else, respect human dignity? So much follows from that."

It wasn't my most rehearsed moment, and it might have felt like a bit of a left turn to some of those listening. But it came from the heart, and I knew it wouldn't be the last time I spoke about these issues.

"'Human-centered AI,'" I said, finally vocalizing a term I'd been mulling over for months. "That's what I've been calling this idea. It's a phrase that I hope will aptly describe the rest of my career. And I hope it'll mean something to all of you in the years ahead."

As is typical on the first day of a course, a line formed to ask follow-up questions. But this one snaked all the way from the lectern at the front of the room to the back wall.

"Hi, Professor Li," a student asked as he reached the front of the line. "I'm really excited about deep learning. I've been reading everything I can."

"I'm excited about it, too! You've chosen a great field."

"So, you made ImageNet, right?"

"I had a lot of help, but yeah," I said with a smile. Name recognition is never a good reason to get into science, but positive feedback is always appreciated.

"Yeah, I was just curious if like . . . you've had, I don't know, any other ideas since then?"

Ouch. So much for the ego boost.

This, of course, is the charm of undergrads. They tend to be clumsy conversationalists, but they have a knack for cutting to the chase. I was tempted to share a couple of ideas my lab was working on, but changed course at the last moment.

"Actually, I think I do. It's still in the early stages, but I'm optimistic about it. In fact, I mentioned it just a minute ago."

"Oh, you mean, um . . . human-centric AI?"

"Human-*centered*," I replied with a laugh. "At least, I think. Still working on the name, too."

"Hmm . . ." The student scratched his head. "That sounds interesting, but it wasn't what I expected to hear in a class like this. I guess it makes me wonder . . . what does ethics and society have to do with writing code and stuff?"

The Gates Computer Science Building feels both grand and humble to me. With its high ceiling and marble floors, its lobby echoes like a museum, and its vaulted, theater-sized classrooms pay fitting homage to the power of ideas. But I've come to know best the cramped hallways of its upper floors, where my lab is located, along with SAIL. Now, the building is home to something new, in a refurbished wing on the ground floor: the headquarters of the Stanford Institute for Human-Centered Artificial Intelligence, or Stanford HAI.

I'm heartened by the symbolism of such an explicitly humanistic organization in the heart of one of the nation's oldest computer science departments. But Stanford HAI's ambition—to become a hub for cross-disciplinary collaboration—is more than poetic, and it's already becoming real. On any given day, I'm bound to run into someone like Dan Ho from the Stanford Law School; Rob Reich, a professor of political science; Michele Elam, a professor of the humanities; or Surya Ganguli, a string theory physicist turned computational neuroscientist. Each readily agreed to become a part of HAI, working directly with students and researchers in AI, exploring the intersections between our fields and sharing the expertise they've gained over the course of their careers and lives. We've even attracted partners from beyond the campus entirely, including Erik Brynjolfsson, the renowned MIT economist, who moved across the country to help HAI better understand AI's impacts on jobs, wealth, and the concentration of power in the modern world. It sometimes feels as if the whole discipline is being born anew, in a more vibrant form than I could have imagined even a few years ago.

One partnership in particular has done more than any other to transform my thinking about what's possible. When I first met John Etchemendy a decade earlier, he was the university provost, and I was an East Coast transplant obsessively focused on the still-unfinished ImageNet. We became neighbors and friends in the years since, and my regard for the sheer depth of his intellect as a scholar has only grown. But over many years as an administrator, John developed an expertise on the inner workings of higher education as well—the good, the bad, and the downright Kafkaesque—and knew exactly what it'd take to bring HAI's unlikely vision to life. Not merely to *talk* about human-centered AI, or to debate its merits, but to build it, brick by brick. So when he agreed to partner with me as a codirector of Stanford HAI, I knew we actually had a shot at making it work.

Among my favorite achievements of our partnership is the National Research Cloud, or NRC, a shared AI development platform supported entirely by public funding and resources, rather than by the private sector. Its goal is to keep AI research within reach for scholars, start-ups, NGOs, and governments around the world, ensuring that our field isn't forever monopolized by the tech giants, or even universities like ours.

Two years before, the NRC was nothing more than an idea. And without Stanford HAI, that's likely all it ever would have been. But in the hands of a more diverse team, including experts in law and public policy, it became a mission. John, in particular, called in a career's worth of favors, recruiting universities across the country to form a coalition as impressive as any I'd ever seen in academia, and kicked off a flurry of ideas, suggestions, cross-country flights, and debate that soon became a fully realized legislative blueprint on its way to Capitol Hill. We still have a long way to go to make AI a truly inclusive pursuit, but achievements like the NRC are significant steps in the right direction.

In September 2020, almost a decade after our first conversation, Arnie and I published a comprehensive review of our research entitled "Illuminating the Dark Spaces of Healthcare with Ambient Intelligence." It presented our complete vision for intelligent sensors that extend doctors' and nurses' awareness, allowing them to track the chaos of health care environments with a scale and consistency never possible before.

The article describes the roles that ambient intelligence could play in improving elder care, aiding in chronic disease management, identifying the symptoms of mental illness, tracking surgical tool use throughout an operation, promoting clinician hygiene throughout a shift, and much more. And it didn't appear in a journal focused on computer science, AI, or information processing; it was published in *Nature*, perhaps the preeminent journal in all of science. It was a reminder that the best work is often done in the shared spaces of science as a whole—global collaborations that dance over boundaries without hesitation—rather than within the bubbles of our own fields.

I was proud of the work, but a long road lay ahead. Just a couple of months after the *Nature* review, in December, *The Lancet* published a kind of rebuttal entitled "Ethical Issues in Using Ambient Intelligence in Health-Care Settings." It was a candid and thoroughly reasoned piece that pulled no punches, and offered a fair but rigorous examination of the implications of our work. In the words of the authors, the potential of ambient intelligence to elevate the delivery of care was paired with "a spectrum of ethical concerns," many revolving around the large-scale collection of data, new privacy pitfalls, and, more philosophically, the nature of informed consent in an environment of such immersive, decentralized monitoring technology. Although it's never easy reading a critique of one's own work, the piece was exactly the kind of ethical discourse AI needs, and I agreed with much of it.

Ambient intelligence will likely always be a pillar of my lab's research, and it never takes more than a glance at my parents to remind me why I consider it such important work. It's why, even now, I dedicate some percentage of each day to keeping up with the latest experiments, trials, and regulatory developments. But when I reflect on the breathless pace of our field over the last few years—breakthroughs in object recognition, generating human-like descriptions of photos and even video—a common thread becomes harder and harder to ignore: for all the sophistication of these techniques, they essentially boil down to passive observation. In some form or another, each is an instance of an algorithm telling us what it sees. Our models have learned to observe, sometimes in great detail and with striking accuracy, but little more. *Surely*, I find myself thinking so often these days, *something must lie beyond this.*

* * *

"Hey, do you remember what you asked me a couple of years ago on your first day of class? I'm curious if it stayed with you."

The coffee break had ended, and a student and I were heading back to the lab, lidded paper cups in hand.

"I do, actually," he recalled, smiling. "I asked you what ethics have to do with this stuff."

"Well?" I returned the smile. "Do you think you've found an answer?"

He sighed, looking up at the sky, its colors now fading as the afternoon gave way to early evening.

"Honestly? Not really. And I've definitely thought about it. How could I not? It's all over the news these days. I even took Professor Reich's class."

He was referring to Computers, Ethics and Public Policy, a course created by computer scientist Mehran Sahami, policy scholar Jeremy Weinstein, and Rob Reich, the political scientist and ethicist who still serves as one of HAI's founding contributors. I nodded.

"I know this stuff is important on paper, I guess." He took a sip of his coffee. "But I don't know. Look, Fei-Fei, my robot still can't take a slice of bread out of a toaster. The work is frustrating enough on its own, you know? And it feels like everyone's just publishing nonstop. I'm already living in fear of the next conference and its publication deadlines! How much brainpower am I really supposed to be spending on the ethics of something that still feels so primitive?"

It was a fair question. Despite the incredible progress of AI over the last decade, so much of this stuff is still in its infancy. Robotics in particular is a notoriously difficult technology that continues to make incremental progress, even in an era of widespread deep learning. In moments like this one, human-centered AI could be a tough sell.

"You know," I began, "it wasn't *that* long ago that I was a student. At the time, just telling cats from dogs was still pretty much science fiction. Then deep learning changed it all, overnight, and our algorithms were being used in ways we'd thought were still decades off. Just think how much we're talking about facial recognition now. Journalists, politicians, activists . . . they've all got questions—suddenly—and they're good ones! Is this all leading toward more surveillance? More biased algorithms? Maybe even AI weapons? And it all crept up on us so fast."

We reached the lab. I swiped my badge over the card reader, and we pushed through the double doors.

"My point," I concluded, "is that things can change a lot quicker than you think."

I knew I hadn't convinced him. Not entirely. But for all his misgivings, he cared enough to keep listening. It was a start.

Skepticism is common among new recruits. But inside the lab, the signs of a human-centered ethos could be seen wherever I looked. A whiteboard from the previous evening still bore notes from a project to train neural networks on sensitive information while preserving the privacy of its owners, while a similar effort was working to obfuscate human faces in image data sets without compromising the effectiveness of the resulting model.

We'd even turned a critical eye to our own legacy, embracing research quantifying the bias ImageNet absorbed from those millions of photos we originally scraped from the internet with respect to race, gender, and sexuality. The findings have guided the replacement of large numbers of images with alternatives that present a more balanced picture of human identity, and the removal of category labels with offensive connotations.

Perhaps most inspiring, at least to me, was the fact that our work had never been more grounded in the real world. One junior researcher's misadventures with toast aside, the decade's renaissance in machine perception had transformed robotics so fundamentally that it was now hard to separate it from AI itself. As if to illustrate the point, two sleek mechanical arms, lovingly named Charlie and Ada, were posed patiently on a metal bench as they awaited their next exercise. These days, they're as integral to what our lab does as any algorithm.

Still, even the flashiest hardware is a means to an end, which is why the guiding principle of our work remains the well-being of people, not merely the efficiency of processes. That's the thinking behind our collaboration with the Digital Economy Lab, an even newer research group organized under Stanford HAI, using survey results from the U.S. Bureau of Labor to better understand how people value the work they do—where they welcome the convenience of automation, and where they find its incursions threatening, or even dehumanizing. It's a distinction I first became aware of working with Arnie on ambient intelligence—that AI should always strive to enhance human capabilities, not compete with them. Now it's a fundamental value of our lab.

What exactly that value means is a question for each individual researcher to answer, but heartening examples abound. For instance, one of our lab's biggest endeavors entails the painstaking 3D modeling of everyday spaces like homes, offices, and hospitals, each in numerous varieties, floor plans, and styles. It's an attempt at immersing our algorithms in the kinds of environments where people live and work, and where intelligent machines might make the most difference, especially for those living with illness and disability. A related project uses VR headsets and motion-tracked gloves that allow researchers to demonstrate tangible, meaningful tasks, from folding clothes to preparing food, digitally encoding their movements to create benchmarks for evaluating robotic performance. Still another explores a new approach to machine learning in which digital agents are designed with a kind of innate curiosity, and placed in virtual environments that encourage them to play—an essential part of the way children attain such an intuitive connection with their surroundings.

Each of these stories represents another change in how we think about data, and what we expect of it. Where we once sought to give our algorithms a kind of encyclopedic awareness—all categories and things—we now aim for something richer. A more intimate understanding of the spaces and moments and even meaning in which those things are embedded. An expansion of not just quantity, but detail and nuance. New approaches to data that go beyond simple curation and cataloging to the simulation of entire environments and the actions that unfold within them. It's why, as the humanism behind our work grows, it corresponds with an explosion of technical complexity as well. Forming such a holistic view of real life—a more authentic *representation* of the world than ever before—will demand a depth and fidelity that I don't believe even our most sophisticated techniques are currently capable of. And so, once again, the excitement lies in the challenge. Once again, we'll have to evolve.

The exact form of that evolution remains a mystery, of course, but intriguing hints are already taking shape. Among the more consequential developments in recent years has been a growing range of alternatives to the human bottleneck in training a model—the exploding costs, time, and even ethical concerns entailed by organizing enough manual labor to prepare data sets in the larger and larger volumes progress demands. But advances in the way models process that data, in terms of their size, their ability to operate in parallel, and their capacity for identifying useful patterns on their own—their "attention," as it's called in the literature—are making it possible to train with data sets *so* large that, in some cases, they constitute significant fractions of the internet itself. In the case of text, for example, that often means the entirety of Wikipedia, libraries of books and academic periodicals, and even the post histories of online forums like Reddit. The result, when every word, space, and punctuation mark has been analyzed, is a statistical model of human language so vast, and yet so dense, that it can extrapolate even a short prompt—a germ of an idea as small as a single sentence, be it a question, a statement, or a line of dialogue—into reams of shockingly lifelike prose. The resulting models, now commonly known as "large language models," or LLMs, demonstrate a linguistic competence so fluent, so uncannily human, that it's easy to forget one isn't reading the words of a flesh-and-blood author.

Now, after so many years of computer vision breakthroughs, LLMs are driving a renaissance in natural language processing, and quite possibly heralding AI's next great age. Under the hood, a new type of machine learning model known as a "transformer"—easily the biggest evolutionary leap in the neural network's design since AlexNet in 2012—makes LLMs possible by embodying all of the necessary qualities: mammoth scale, the ability to accelerate training time by processing the data in large, parallel swaths, and an attention mechanism of incredible sophistication. It's a milestone by any measure, if not an inflection point; almost immediately after its publication, the transformer was demonstrating capabilities so impressive they shocked even the experts behind its creation, and the advances haven't slowed down since.

My first exposure to text produced by a large language model was a surreal experience, and it brought to mind my work with Andrej. I recalled how exciting it was to see AI compose a single complete sentence in those days—even a clumsily phrased one—to describe what it saw. Just a few years later, algorithms have become such fluent wordsmiths that they can answer questions, write stories, and even explain jokes. What's more, the emerging class of "multimodal" networks, trained on not just text, but photographs, audio, recorded voice, and even video, are learning to *generate* this media as well. It's a development that, in practice, often feels as if it's arrived a generation or two ahead of schedule; in a span of only around ten years, algorithms have evolved from struggling to recognize the contents of photographs, to doing so at superhuman levels, to now, amazingly, creating entirely new images on their own, every bit as photographic, but entirely synthetic, and with an often unsettling level of realism and detail. Already, it seems, the era of deep learning is giving way to a new revolution, as the era of generative AI dawns.

But at the heart of this technology—one that routinely seems like absolute magic, even to me—is yet another lesson in the power of data at large scales. And to be sure, "scale" is the operative word. For comparison, AlexNet debuted with a network of sixty million parameters—just enough to make reasonable sense of the ImageNet data set, at least in part—while transformers big enough to be trained on a world of text, photos, video, and more are growing well into *hundreds of billions* of parameters. It makes for endless engineering challenges, admittedly, but surprisingly elegant science. It's as if these possibilities were waiting for us all along, since the days of LeCun's ZIP code reader, or Fukushima's neocognitron, or even Rosenblatt's perceptron. Since the days of ImageNet. All of this was in there, somewhere. We just had to make a simple idea big enough.

More and more, however, such explanations feel like mere semantics. Large language models, even the multimodal ones, may not be "thinking" in the truest, grandest sense of the term—and, lest we get too carried away, their propensity for absurd conceptual blunders and willingness to confabulate plausible-sounding nonsense makes this fact easy to remember. Still, as they generate ever more sophisticated text, images, voice, and video—to the point that a growing chorus of commentators are sounding the alarm about our ability to separate truth from fantasy, as individuals, as institutions, and even as societies—it isn't always clear how much the difference matters. It's an especially sobering thought when one realizes that this—*all of this*—is barely version 1.0.

On and on it goes. Algorithms expressing themselves at an effectively human level of sophistication. Robots gradually learning to navigate real environments. Vision models being trained not merely on photographs, but through real-time immersion in fully 3D worlds. AI that generates as fluently as it recognizes. And, rising up all around us, ethical implications that seem to reach deeper into human affairs with every passing moment. But this is what science has always been. A journey that only grows longer and more complex as it unfolds. Endlessly branching paths. An ever-expanding horizon. New discoveries, new crises, new debates. A story forever in its first act.

The decision to dedicate my life to this once obscure field took me further than I ever imagined. By some accident of history, I was part of the generation that saw it transition from academic arcana to the stuff of headlines. It allowed me to travel the world, share tables with global leaders, and, in recent years, speak from some of the largest platforms that exist. Blinding lights, neon colors, audiences seated in rows that seem to extend infinitely toward the horizon. These are rare privileges, and each has been an unexpected honor.

But the lab remains the place I love most: the hum of fluorescent tubes, the stiff chairs, the stale coffee, the endless clicking and typing, the squeaking of markers on whiteboards. So much has happened since AlexNet in 2012, since Jia and I began ImageNet in 2006, since Pietro dropped that printout of Simon Thorpe's EEG study on my desk. *Trust me. You're gonna want to read this.* Yet even now, the North Star shines down on a road that stretches out before me. The journey still beckons. There's still so much to chase.

I'm often reminded of my first meeting with Pietro and Christof, and how I saw them as giants. It's hard to think anyone might see me quite like that—my physical stature alone probably disqualifies me—but to the extent that I do have some air of authority, they taught me how to put it to good use: as an invitation, not a barrier. As a message to every student willing to work hard enough to find themselves in this place: *if you're truly passionate about this stuff—no matter who you are, or where you came from— you belong here. Let's build the future together.*

The afternoon was bright, even as the sun hung lower and lower over the trees, and the air was warm enough to keep us in the shade of the gazebo. My mother sat quietly, content, her grandkids shrieking and laughing as they kicked a soccer ball back and forth across the lawn. My father did his best to keep up, laughing along with them, every bit as youthful in his temperament. He was finally in his element as a grandfather—a role that asked nothing of him but the playfulness he'd spent a lifetime perfecting.

I looked down at my vibrating phone to see a text from Stanford HAI's policy director.

National research cloud just passed the senate
Part of a bigger bill
On its way to the president's desk

Another text came in just a minute later, this one from Jean Sabella. A video was attached. Clicking the PLAY button, I watched as two eager pairs of hands tore apart matching wrapping paper, shouting excitedly as a pair of Star Wars Lego sets were revealed.

"What do we say, guys?" I heard Jean ask from off camera.

"Thank you, Auntie Fei-Fei and Uncle Silvio!" two voices replied in gleeful unison.

Two generations later, Bob's nerdy imagination lived on, unmistakably, through his grandchildren. Their unabashed joy, however, told me that the introversion that had defined so much of him had run its course. I could imagine the smile this would have brought to his face.

Closing the video, I returned to the group chat it came from, a now yearslong thread of personal updates from Jean, her son Mark, and me. Milestones. Birthdays. Recovery from knee replacement surgery. New jobs. New pets. Happy news, sad news, and everything else that fills the years of a life.

What began with a shaky request for help in a Parsippany High math class had flourished into a connection that changed my life as an immigrant, and that now spans two coasts and three generations. Bob was a teacher, a confidant, and a friend, and my lifeline when I could barely express myself. The Sabellas' dinner table—adorned with a plate of homemade brownies, always—still stands as my greatest lesson in compassion. And the Sabellas themselves are an unequivocal extension of my own family. I can't imagine life without them, any more than life without my mother and father. It's why the loss of

Bob still hurts, more than a decade later. But the conversations never stopped. His memory still listens, and I still pour my heart out to it.

No single connection has taught me more about this country. The lessons may have begun in high school—the aspirational narrations of our history classes stood in dramatic contrast to the bleak, even violent reality of an immigrant—but they were never what truly reached me. Even after decades steeped in the same tensions as everyone else—partisanship, cultural fault lines, election cycles, and all the rest—my deepest understanding of this country didn't come from the news, or some polemicist's op-ed, or even a textbook. It came from the privilege of knowing the Sabellas, who so exemplified the humanity that I value most about this place. It's a spirit that, to me, anyway, still feels distinctly American.

I turned as I heard the rubbery squeal of the sliding glass door opening. Silvio was headed toward us, his hands empty.

"Where's lunch?" I asked, half teasingly, half hungrily. Mostly hungrily.

"The defense went long," he said with a sigh and an unapologetic smile, knowing I'd appreciate his exhaustion as much as his joy.

He'd spent the last couple of hours dissecting his latest PhD candidate's thesis, challenging her claims, listening to her explanations, and, ultimately, awarding her the degree. It wasn't hard to imagine the proceedings going well beyond the scheduled time; Silvio was gripped by a familiar passion, and neither of us had much of an off switch when it came to this stuff.

I glanced at my phone again, lingering for a moment on the many familiar names still populating my text messages. One recent conversation included Olga and Jia, both now teaching at Princeton, and both of whom remain at the cutting edge of computer vision research. Olga, in particular, is a stalwart advocate for fairness and transparency in AI, having brought AI4ALL to her new campus. There was a message from Pietro, still teaching at Caltech, pointing me toward the work of one of his PhD students, who was using computer vision to support global conservation and sustainability efforts. And another from Arnie, now a research partner and friend of more than a decade, sharing the latest on ambient intelligence.

Whether I would ever feel like a particular kind of person—Chinese, American, maybe even an honorary Italian—I had long since shed the fear that I didn't belong. The people I've met along the way and the kindness they've shown me saw to that. The path of an immigrant hasn't been an easy one, but I'm perpetually grateful for where it's taken me.

Even the gauntlet of my mother's health, a story enduring across so many years, has revealed itself to be much more complex than a simple question of fortune versus misfortune. After all, how long can the inevitable be delayed before it doesn't feel so inevitable anymore? As taxing as the journey has been, after nearly three decades, I've had to acknowledge that by the standards of unlucky families, ours was a lucky one. These thirty years have been hard, but they haven't been thirty years of grief, or loss, or mourning. We'd spent all of them together, and I can't help but feel grateful for that as well.

I catch myself reflecting a lot these days. My mother's and father's formative years come to mind often, hers locked away in a culture that was eating itself alive, and his lost in a tragedy that he never fully escaped. I remember that glimpse of her trembling hands as we boarded the plane that took us from the lives we knew, and the dread that filled our stomachs as we waited at the baggage claim of JFK, alone, stranded, night falling without my father's arrival. I recall the dull heat and the humming, mechanical ambience of the dry-cleaning shop. I think about the first time I laid eyes on Princeton.

Looking back on my career, I believe that the experience of moving across the world left a mark on me that I'm only now beginning to understand, one that continues to influence my research and thinking. It brings to mind the tensions that propelled my mother, the daughter of a politically disenfranchised Kuomintang family, to gamble so much and journey so far—now, astonishingly, living out her twilight years in a Palo Alto backyard. The life of a scientist, like the life of an immigrant—the life of an adventurer—is one in which "home" is never a clear concept. The best work always happens on the borders, where ideas are forever trapped between coming and going, explored by strangers in strange lands, insiders and outsiders at the same time. But that's what makes us so powerful. It keeps our perspectives unique, and frees us to challenge the status quo.

The future of AI remains deeply uncertain, and we have as many reasons for optimism as we do for concern. But it's all a product of something deeper and far more consequential than mere technology: the question of what motivates us, in our hearts and our minds, as we create. I believe the answer to that question—more, perhaps, than any other—will shape our future. So much depends on *who* answers it. As this field slowly grows more diverse, more inclusive, and more open to expertise from other disciplines, I grow more confident in our chances of answering it right.

In the real world, there's one North Star—Polaris, the brightest in the Ursa Minor constellation. But in the mind, such navigational guides are limitless. Each new pursuit—each new obsession—hangs in the dark over its horizon, another gleaming trace of iridescence, beckoning. That's why my greatest joy comes from knowing that this journey will never be complete. Neither will I. There will always be something new to chase. To a scientist, the imagination is a sky full of North Stars.

ACKNOWLEDGMENTS

This book is about the worlds I see, both physical and intellectual. While many overlap, and some are still unfolding, I want to thank the people who have helped, supported, and loved me in all these different dimensions of life so far.

The newest world of all to me is the world of writing and publishing a book. Because a global pandemic set in just as we finalized our publishing agreement, it took more than three years to complete the manuscript. But during that time, my writing partner, Alex Michael, and I became a team of two collaborators with one creative spirit. We called ourselves Team GAN—an inside joke familiar to AI nerds, describing a neural network that generates a picture by continually proposing, analyzing, and refining the result. While we wrote like partners, friends, and colleagues, what truly bonded us was the similarity of our stories as people—we were both writing this book while our mothers were in ailing health and declining at worrying rates. Fittingly, the book's defining theme of how technologies like AI can help people, especially in medicine and health care, reflects the experiences we endured as it was written. I'm sad to say that despite her eagerness to read the finished product, Alex's mother passed away as the manuscript was being finalized after a yearslong fight with cancer. Still, it's clear to me that we were writing for both of our mothers. Alex, this book would not have existed without you. No words can ever be enough to express my gratitude, and it's been a true honor to have shared this book-writing journey with you. I know you've forbidden me from teasing you about writing a sequel (ever). But you're forever the best writing partner in my world, so if there is ever another book, we'll be Team GAN again.

As newcomers to the world of publishing, we were incredibly lucky to work with our literary agent, Christy Fletcher, who, along with Sarah Fuentes, never stopped supporting and rooting for us, even as the years went by. We're equally thankful for Flatiron Books, where Will Schwalbe and Samantha Zukergood guided us with great care and respect and helped us turn a passion project into something real. And of course, many versions of the manuscript were read over the years as well by Aaron Brindle, Jia Deng, John Etchemendy, Surya Ganguli, Diane Greene, Jordan Jacobs, Roberta Katz, Millie Lin, Rob Reich, Janet Tan, Paula Tesch, Terry Winograd, and Morgan Mitchell. We're eternally grateful for their insights, reactions, and ideas.

The world that defines my career is the world of science and technology. I want to begin by thanking those giants who will never know that their work has not only changed human civilization but the life of a girl growing up in an inland city of China and then a tiny suburban town of New Jersey. Newton, Darwin, Curie, Schrödinger, Einstein, and so many others. You don't need my acknowledgment, but I must thank you for shining such inspiring beacons as I entered the magical world of science.

More directly, many others have shaped me as a scientist. My PhD advisors, Pietro Perona and Christof Koch, deserve special mention for transforming me from a physics undergraduate with zero knowledge of AI into a budding researcher and computer scientist. Along the way, I've become indebted to many more mentors and collaborators, including Diane Beck, Bill Dally, Diane Greene, John Hennessy, Geoff Hinton, Daphne Koller, Kai Li, Jitendra Malik, Arnold Milstein, Andrew Ng, and Sebastian Thrun, to name just a few. In the past few years, my world of AI has expanded to one of human-centered AI, both in the form of a Stanford University institute and the North Star of my lab's research. I'm grateful for the close collaborators and colleagues I have had the privilege to work with, including John Etchemendy, James Landay, Chris Manning, and all of the faculty and staff at Stanford HAI.

This book was deeply influenced by my graduate students, including Jia Deng, Timnit Gebru, Albert Haque, Andrej Karpathy, Jon Krause, Juan Carlos Niebles, Olga Russakovsky, and Serena Yeung. But additionally, I must thank every one of the students and advisees who have trusted me: undergraduate students, master's and PhD students, and postdoctoral advisees across California Institute of Technology, University of Illinois, Princeton University, and Stanford University. Your work continues to define the science I do.

The world that I owe my life to is the world of love and support. I come from a small family: just me, my parents, and a pair of maternal grandparents. But what we lack in numbers we make up for in bravery and unwavering love. Even after three decades of immigration, I am still grappling with the incredible courage that brought my non-English-speaking parents (Ying and Shun) to the U.S. in the hopes that I'd have the freedom to pursue my boldest dreams.

But I would have never made it if I wasn't supported by strangers who, although they didn't look or talk like me, became my mentors, friends, and family. Among them, the Sabellas, especially Bob Sabella, my math teacher at Parsippany High School in New Jersey, are prominently presented in this book, and with good reason. Still, no words can fully capture their kindness and generosity. They taught me lessons in humanity, compassion, and understanding I've never forgotten, and so much of who I am today reflects them. In addition to the Sabellas, I am forever indebted to all the friends, teachers, neighbors, and colleagues who have shaped my journey with their generosity, integrity, wisdom, and love.

As a mother, an only child caring for two ailing immigrant parents, and a woman of color in a field still dominated by men, the only reason I am where I am today is because of my best friend, my fellow AI scientist, my soulmate, and the love of my life, Silvio Savarese. As far as I'm concerned, AI hasn't truly arrived until it can match Silvio's excellence as a scientist, a culinary genius, a musician, a loving father, and a perfect life partner.

I've seen many worlds as a daughter, a scientist, an immigrant, and a humanist. But the most important world is the one that I will never live in, the world that will be built upon everything I'm doing now, the world I pour all my love and hope into, and the world I'm most grateful for, because it gives so much meaning to everything I do— the world my children, and my children's children, will inherit. At the dawn of the age of AI, I thank them for the privilege of being their mother, the most humbling experience I've ever faced, and one that I suspect will forever remain uniquely human.

ABOUT THE AUTHOR

DR. FEI-FEI LI is a computer science professor at Stanford University and the founding director of Stanford's Institute for Human-Centered Artificial Intelligence, as well as a founder and chairperson of the board of the nonprofit AI4ALL. She is an elected member of the National Academy of Engineering, the National Academy of Medicine, and the American Academy of Arts and Sciences.

**MOMENT
OF LIFT
BOOKS**

Moment of Lift Books, created by Melinda French Gates
in partnership with Flatiron Books,
is an imprint dedicated to publishing original nonfiction
by visionaries working to unlock a more equal world
for women and girls.

To learn more about Moment of Lift Books,
visit momentoflift.com.